THE GREAT TRAIN ROBBER

MY AUTOBIOGRAPHY

RONNIE BIGGS

with Christopher Pickard

jb

First published in the UK by John Blake Publishing
an imprint of Bonnier Books UK
4th Floor, Victoria House
Bloomsbury Square,
London, WC1B 4DA
England

Owned by Bonnier Books
Sveavägen 56, Stockholm, Sweden

www.facebook.com/johnblakebooks
twitter.com/jblakebooks

First published in paperback in 2023

ISBN: 978 1 78946 597 6

British Library Cataloguing-in-Publication Data:

A catalogue record for this book is available from the British Library.

Design by www.envydesign.co.uk

Printed and bound in Great Britain by Clays Ltd, Elcograf S.p.A.

1 3 5 7 9 10 8 6 4 2

John Blake Publishing is an imprint of Bonnier Books UK
www.bonnierbooks.co.uk

CONTENTS

LET ME INTRODUCE TO YOU, THE ONE AND ONLY RONNIE BIGGS

Ronald Arthur Biggs's story began in the London borough of Lambeth with his birth on 8 August 1929 to Henry Jack Biggs and Lillian Edna Clayton of Dalyell Road, Stockwell, SW9. The youngest of a family of five he had a sister, Iris, and three brothers, Jack, Victor and Terrance. His family was working class, but he never considered them to be poor. He wasn't left wanting for anything.

The family moved to 30 Kimberley Road in 1936, and Biggs went to school in Lingham Street, just south of what is now Stockwell Tube station.

In 1940, as war raged across Europe and the bombs fell on London, Biggs was separated from his family and evacuated to the relative safety of Combeinteignhead in south Devon and later to Delabole in north Cornwall. He returned to London at the end of 1942 and was sent to Santley Street School in Brixton. In May

1943 his mother died from a duodenal ulcer. She was just 53 and Biggs just 13.

Around this time Biggs, now studying at the Brixton School of Building, discovered that if he was good at one thing, it was taking objects of whatever size or value without having to pay for them. This led in February 1945 to his first appearance in court for stealing a pen refill and eraser from a shop display in Littlewoods. He was 15.

That same year, in the June and November, he made two further court appearances for petty pilfering, but appeared to be back on the right track when he volunteered for the Royal Air Force in 1947. It was during his short time in the RAF – although he had volunteered for eight years as a regular and four years in the reserves – that Biggs learned how to cook: his father, who had been a professional cook at one time, had already instilled in him an interest which he was never to forget.

The RAF proved to have its temptations for a man with Biggs's talents, although his first run-in with his superiors was for going AWOL and not for any of his more light-fingered activities.

But his luck ran out and after breaking into a chemist shop he found himself up before the London Sessions in February 1949, an appearance, his first as an adult, which resulted in a six-month prison sentence and a dishonourable discharge from the RAF. He was 19 and apparently destined for a life of crime.

Released from Lewes Prison for Young Prisoners in June 1949 he was up before the North London magistrates the following month for taking a car without the owner's permission. He was sent to Wormwood Scrubs and then on to Lewes, where his path crossed for the first time with Bruce Reynolds, the man who would be the driving force behind the Great Train Robbery and the reason Biggs was there.

Biggs was now firmly off the tracks, and a life of crime, court appearances and imprisonment, including in Dartmoor and Norwich, was to follow over the next 14 years.

*

As years go, 1963 was a remarkable one and one that is seen as a watershed in modern history as people tried to throw off the shackles of wartime mentality and start to enjoy and embrace the swinging sixties.

The year is often remembered as the year when John F. Kennedy was assassinated, but it was also the year when Martin Luther King had a dream. It was a year when the US, USSR and Great Britain signed a nuclear test ban treaty; the Soviet Union put the first woman into space; the Pan Am building in New York opened its doors for the first time, while on the west coast, Alcatraz closed its doors to prisoners for the last time.

Jim Clark won the Formula One World Championship in 1963 but his great rival, Graham Hill, won the Monaco Grand Prix. Manchester United beat Leicester City in the FA Cup Final, Everton won the league and at Wembley Stadium, the main soccer international pitted England against the 1962 world champions, Brazil. A one-all draw, it was the first time that the then 33-year-old Biggs had come across the Brazilians.

It was 1963 that saw the start of Beatlemania as well as being the year their great rivals to be, the Rolling Stones, released their first single.

But more sinister things were going on behind the scenes, things that were directly to affect the fate of Biggs when it came to his next day in court.

The British authorities, in the shape of the Conservative Party, that had held office since Churchill's return to Downing Street in 1951, were losing their grip on power and the trappings that go with it.

A disastrous by-election in the safe seat of Orpington resulted in then prime minister, Harold Macmillan, sacking seven Cabinet ministers in July 1962 in what became known as the Night of the Long Knives.

In 1963, rumours circulated that John Profumo, Macmillan's Secretary of State for War, was having an affair with a 19-year-old nightclub hostess, Christine Keeler. To make matters worse, Keeler was also seeing the Soviet naval attaché, Eugene Ivanov.

The government might have got away with Profumo's indiscretion if some of Keeler's other lovers had been a little more discreet. Unfortunately, one tried to shoot his way into the house of Dr Stephen Ward, a society osteopath who had introduced Profumo to Keeler and who had invited Keeler and her friend, Mandy Rice-Davies, to share his house.

The shooting put Keeler back on the front pages and resulted in an anonymous call to George Wigg, the Labour Shadow Spokesman on Defence. Wigg used parliamentary privilege to raise the matter in the Commons. Profumo was not in the House but issued a statement that denied his involvement or any 'impropriety' with Keeler, although admitting that he had been introduced to her and Ivanov by Ward at Cliveden, then the home of Lord Astor.

Sensing that he was about to be made the fall guy for the Profumo affair, Ward wrote to Wigg, MI5 and the Home Secretary, outlining the true course of events.

On holiday in Venice, Profumo admitted that the rumours were true and that he had lied to the Commons. The house of cards came tumbling down and in the June, less than two months before the Great Train Robbery, Profumo resigned, leaving an already unpopular government with more egg on its face.

*

Sixty years later it can be seen that the Great Train Robbery, which took place on 8 August 1963, was one of the final straws that broke the government's back. After the Profumo debacle it brought into question the very fabric of law and order in Britain, and made a mockery of the government and its institutions. It became clear there was one rule for those in power and another for everyone else. Sound familiar?

Much to the delight of the general public, a cheeky gang had audaciously made off with millions of pounds of the banks' and government's own money – and from one of its own trains. The government had to face the fact that a gang of train robbers were shown more respect and affection by the British public than they were.

We will never know what went on in the corridors of power during this period, but pressure was put on Scotland Yard to solve the robbery quickly, and to bring to justice the people that appeared to have mocked the establishment. Even, as it turned out, if they were innocent.

Thanks to the discovery of Leatherslade Farm, where the gang had hidden before and after the robbery, and a few tip-offs, it was not long before the Yard tracked down many of the gang. But it was still long enough for Macmillan to have resigned on the grounds of ill health so that Sir Alec Douglas-Home could take his place as prime minister and give the Conservatives a chance of hanging on to power.

Four members of the Great Train Robbery gang known to the police, including its leader, Bruce Reynolds, were still at large when a trial of those captured only added to the government's embarrassment. The trial culminated on 15 April 1964 with the sentencing of members of the gang, including Biggs, to terms of 30 years' imprisonment, a far longer sentence than was given at the time to a murderer or a spy. While the powers that be may have thought that this would act as a salutary lesson to society, it backfired and made even bigger heroes of the gang. It also sent a message to the criminal fraternity that they should arm themselves as the use of a firearm would not add one single day to their sentence.

Charlie Wilson's escape from Winson Green Prison on 12 August 1964 was yet another nail in the government's coffin, and on 15 October 1964, Labour won the general election and Harold Wilson became prime minister.

Events of the last 60 years have made us all the more cynical and suspicious and we may never know the true extent of the government's involvement in the Great Train Robbery trial. Certainly the gang didn't know – they were not political animals.

But a person, or persons, unknown that were part of the establishment at the time of the robbery were so outraged and humiliated by Biggs's flight to freedom that they and others gave their okay and support to have him kidnapped in Rio de Janeiro nearly 20 years later.

Whoever they are or were, they, and Margaret Thatcher's government at the time of the kidnapping in 1981, remained remarkably tight-lipped when Biggs was snatched from Brazil. And although it is known who was involved in the act, nobody has ever been charged or even reprimanded for it.

*

If ill health had not intervened, Biggs would have seen out his days in Rio de Janeiro. In November 1997, the last legal avenue for the British government to follow in the hope of getting

Biggs back to the UK had been blocked: the Brazilian Supreme Court ruling that the statute of limitations had run out on the train robbery as a crime.

In failing health, and with little prospect of ever earning a living again, Biggs chose to return to the UK in 2001, and you could not say the government had not been warned. In 1994, Biggs had said: 'If I'm to become a dribbling nuisance, one of Her Majesty's hostelries might be just the place to spend my twilight years.'

The smart move might have been for the British government to tell Biggs that he was not welcome in Britain and to stay where he was. But Biggs knew that there were still people in Britain who would not rest until he was back behind bars. Not for one moment did he think that he would not be welcomed back to Britain, and with open arms and cell doors.

Biggs was under no illusions, and he knew the consequences would be a lengthy prison spell, although even he could not foresee that most of that would be spent in Belmarsh, one of the UK's highest security prisons. It was argued that he was left there because of his ill health, but at the time there were many sicker people in the prison system that didn't get such star treatment. More likely it was a final vindictive act by people who have had too much time to think and ponder about Ronald Arthur Biggs.

Biggs's release from prison in 2009 was equally farcical and is surrounded by more unanswered questions. By the June of that year, Biggs had ticked all the right boxes as far as his eligibility for parole was concerned. He had been a model prisoner (except for a certain escape in 1965), and had served the required time to be eligible for parole.

The Parole Board decided Biggs was fit to be released, and that was its recommendation to the Justice Department. That should have been the end of the story, until the Justice Secretary,

Jack Straw, stepped in to block his release just two days before the agreed date.

As abruptly as his release had been blocked, there was a U-turn four weeks later when Biggs found himself released on compassionate grounds. He was a very ill man, but it was still totally unexpected by the people closest to him who had less than 24 hours' warning.

And yes, Biggs was a very, very ill man. His son, Mike, had twice been called to Norfolk & Norwich University Hospital, as they feared the end was nigh, yet each time Biggs fought back from the brink. Biggs was a fighter – if he wasn't, he would not have survived as long as he did.

*

As you read Biggs's own story, never forget that there can be a thin line between hero and villain; it all depends on which side of the fence you are sitting at the time. Biggs was neither saint nor sinner, but a very potent mix of both, which meant that life with or around him, as you will read, was never dull.

You will discover it would be a life of loss, discovery, betrayal, redemption, crimes, arrests, escape, kidnapping, fame, infamy, poverty, fortune and death. It is also a tale of sex, drugs, punk and rock 'n' roll; scandal and seduction; as well as sun, sea, sand, samba and a sprinkling of bossa nova.

But never forget that Biggs is not a folk hero because of what he did in the early hours of the morning of 8 August 1963, but rather for the manner in which he – the everyman – kept himself one step ahead of the government and media posse which chased him around the world following his daring escape from Wandsworth Prison in July 1965.

Those who knew Biggs well, as I did, knew a considerate, kind and generous man. A family man, a loving father and grandfather, a man who accepted with good grace and humour the rough with the smooth, even his ill health.

Despite what you may have read, Biggs never looked for a pardon, just a little forgiveness and understanding. Something that the last 60 years have shown only comes from the authorities when there is a financial or political interest at stake.

Read on, but as you do, remember that however remarkable the story of Ronald Biggs appears, what you are reading is fact and not fiction. It is also the truth, the whole truth and nothing but the truth as far as Biggs could remember. But as is clear, although there are people who claim that they want the truth, there are others who can't handle it and must hang on to the myths and lies that suit their version of events and of Biggs the man.

In case you had any doubts, Ronnie Biggs very much existed: he is not a myth or a lie. This is his story, and in his own words.

Christopher Pickard
Rio de Janeiro, Brazil / London, UK

Chapter 1

CONFESSIONS: NO ONE IS INNOCENT

Let me put the record straight. I was a Great Train Robber. 'The' Great Train Robber who, for unrelated reasons, ended up being the most famous protagonist from the gang of 16 that was trackside on the morning of 8 August 1963.

I was not the 'brain' behind the Great Train Robbery. That honour and credit goes to my dear friend Bruce Reynolds, whom we sadly lost at the start of 2013, appropriately the 50th anniversary of the robbery. Neither was I the 'tea boy'. Although I was the best cook at our hideout in Leatherslade Farm.

If I became famous it is only in part for what I did on 8 August 1963 at the robbery, but more because I went over the wall of the Hate Factory in July 1965 and kept on running and running (with a bit of ducking and diving), until I returned to Britain under my own steam (and a little help from my friends) nearly 40 years later in May 2001.

Since 1963, many stories have been told about me, the robbery and the robbers. Stories have included everything from a German SS connection to a Mr Big linked to the government of the day.

I have read that I shot the driver and was often accused of having coshed him, despite not even being on the train at the time. The truth about the robbery and my life, as you will now discover, was very often stranger than fiction.

The actual robbery was the labour of two London gangs who came together for the 'Big One'. I was a member of neither gang. I was on the embankment in Buckinghamshire that night because of my friendship with one man, Bruce. That, plus the work I was doing at the time on the house of a train driver. I believe in fate, and fate played a huge part in getting me involved in what is still considered the world's most famous robbery.

I first met Bruce in Wormwood Scrubs prison in July 1949. From the start it was clear that he was a cut above the other cons. We became good friends and discovered a mutual interest in music, literature and breaking the law. Our paths crossed many times – in and out of prison – but we never got up to any villainy together prior to the train robbery or after.

When I called Bruce in June 1963 to try and borrow £500 (about £10,000 in 2023), the last thing I had on my mind was returning to a life of crime, and certainly not to rob a train. The only trains I focused on were the ones that ran between Redhill and London, which never seemed to run on time.

After the call to Bruce, the rest is history. Yes, I could have stepped away, but I wanted the buzz and excitement of being involved, and that was something I was not getting from building work. The money would also come in handy, especially as my wife, Charmian, had just given birth to our second son.

As it turned out, a £5 each-way bet placed on a couple of nags on the eve of the robbery saw me win exactly the same amount of money I had asked to borrow from Bruce. Again I could have backed out, but I was not going to let Bruce down. He had his reasons for inviting me on the job, and it wasn't just about our friendship. Bruce was far too professional for that.

One of my tasks at the robbery was to look after our back-up train driver, 'Peter', and that meant I ended up in the privileged position of watching the robbery unfold. Once we had moved the train from Sears Crossing to Bridego Bridge – and Peter could have done it, given time – he and I sat in one of the Land Rovers. From our position we had a clear and unobstructed view of the bridge and the final assault on the train.

Even then I knew that I was a spectator to a historic moment, although I did not appreciate quite just how historic and famous it was going to be.

For the want of a few quid 60 years ago, I had plunged headlong into an enterprise that was to lead me into almost 40 years 'on the run' and ten years locked up behind bars. It would make me one of the world's most wanted, famous and infamous individuals.

Although I have said that I have no regrets about being a train robber, I do have regrets about the crime itself. It is regrettable that the train driver, Jack Mills, was injured.

Mills, however, wasn't the only victim that he is often made out to be. The people who paid the heaviest price for the Great Train Robbery are the families. And that is the families of all the people involved in the Great Train Robbery. The robbers' families, the families of the Old Bill, the families of the railmen and Post Office workers (and there were more than 70 of them on the train that August night), and even the families of the people that have helped us over the years. All paid a price, one way or another, for our collective involvement in the robbery. A very heavy price, in the case of my family. For that, I do have regrets, but for all of that, it has still been a life well worth living.

So God bless all of you, family, friend or foe. Whatever you do think of me, I respect your views. That is one of the great joys and benefits of freedom. Enjoy yours and keep it safe, because freedom, physical or mental, is far more precious than you can ever imagine.

Read on, but before you judge me, keep in mind that at the end of the day, no one is innocent. Not even you. We all have something to hide or regret.

My name is Ronnie Biggs, but you already knew that! This is my story.

CHAPTER 2

THE GREAT TRAIN ROBBERY

A Glasgow-to-London mail train was stopped and robbed in Buckinghamshire early today. It happened at Cheddington, near Tring, at about 3 am. The driver and fireman were attacked and injured; and two coaches of the train were detached. They contained mail of all kinds, including registered post. A police spokesman said a short time ago that it's believed a large number of men took part and that they got away with a considerable amount. Neither the driver nor fireman was badly hurt. Every senior officer of the Buckinghamshire police force has gone to the scene of the robbery.

Transcript of the first BBC news broadcast at 8 am on
Thursday 8 August 1963

It was just after 3 am on the morning of Thursday 8 August 1963 when the walkie-talkie came to life. 'This is it!!!' a voice cried out. It was Bruce Reynolds: the train had passed through Leighton Buzzard and was now less than a mile away. After a wait of nearly one and a half hours by the side of the main line between Glasgow and London, the moment had come – a moment that would come to be known as the Great Train Robbery.

Sixteen of us were scattered about the embankment and track that night, four of whom would never be caught.

The train robbery was the work of two different London gangs who came together for the 'Big One'. The 'big one' that Bruce would refer to as 'my Sistine Chapel'.

I was a member of neither gang, yet after everything I have read and heard since it is often difficult to believe that it was my friendship with one man, Bruce, and the work I had done as a legitimate builder for a train driver, that brought me to be lying on a grass embankment that August night.

My journey to the embankment can be traced back to 1949 and my first spell in Lewes Prison at the age of 19 as a YP (Young Prisoner). It was during my time in Lewes that I met a young ex-post office sorter by the name of Albert Kitson.

Kit, as we called him, was serving 18 months for taking part in the robbery of the post office where he had been working. Kit and I used to walk together during exercise periods, and more than once he made reference to the 'large sums of money' transported by British Rail.

The following year I met Bruce in Wormwood Scrubs Prison. I was back inside again with a three-month sentence for 'taking and driving away a motor vehicle without the owner's consent'. From the start it was clear that Bruce was a cut above the other cons. We became good friends and over time discovered a number of mutual interests. I told him what Kit had told me about the large sums of cash being transported by rail. It was a piece of information he never forgot. Our paths crossed during the ensuing years – in and out of prison – but we never got up to any villainy.

It was after a longer stretch in Lewes Prison, four years for burglary, that I concluded that it was time to have a go at honest employment and I found work as a carpenter. I had learned the basics of the trade in prison and the work really interested me. When I came out I went to live with a tough lady in Merstham, Surrey. Her name was Ivy and she was a good friend of Bruce. She was quite fearless and wouldn't shy away from a punch-up. But Ivy was a good sort and if you were a friend of Bruce, then you were a friend of Ivy.

Bruce would visit from time to time, usually arriving in a ritzy sports car of some kind and always impeccably dressed. He was moving up in the world of villainy and was beginning to build a reputation as the 'Prince of Thieves'.

In late 1957 I changed jobs leaving a muddy building site in Redhill for the cleaner work of erecting partitions in offices in central London. The job entailed travelling to London by train and it was on one of these journeys that I first spotted Charmian Powell, the future Mrs Biggs, then sweet 17. We were mutually attracted and in no time we were making mad and passionate love in hotels, empty train carriages and on the floor of the classrooms of the school where Charmian's father was headmaster. But you could say that fate and Latin played a part in Charm and I ever meeting. If she had not failed her Latin A-level, having passed in English and French, she was all set to go university in Birmingham. If she had, she would have never been on the train and our lives would have been very different.

In a romantic moment, Charmian and I eventually decided to elope, but like most young lovers we were hard up. Then, with a little persuasion from me, Charm dipped her hand into the cash box at work and filched £200 (now about £3,500). Just before Christmas 1957, off we went à la Bonnie and Clyde minus the firearms, with my good friend Michael Haynes, a man who was later going to play such a key role in my life and survival. We headed west from London as I had a fancy to see Devon and Cornwall again. I had been evacuated to Combeinteignhead in Devon at the beginning of the war and later, as the bombing got worse, to Delabole in Cornwall.

But before we got to Cornwall our money had run out. So Mike and I decided to try a break-in or two with Charm acting as lookout. Sadly, one snowy evening after a hair-raising chase through the tortuous roads of Swanage, our luck ran out and we were nicked. A string of charges followed.

Charm got her first – and only – taste of UK porridge in the women's wing of HMP Exeter.

On 1 April 1958, we appeared before the judge at the Dorset Quarter Sessions. A love story was presented to the court by our learned counsel, but the prosecutor declared us 'a threat'. Our fate was now in the hands of the judge.

After a break for lunch, the well-fed judge returned to pass sentence. Charmian and Mike were put on two years' probation, while I ended up with two and a half years in prison – not a bad result, considering. With remission I was looking at 20 months so Charmian and Mike would still be on probation when I got out.

And that's how it turned out. I was sent to Norwich to do my time, but regularly, once a month, Charmian came to visit. We sat holding hands and making plans for our future. We were going to get married and 'settle down'. We exchanged long and passionate letters. I thought my sentence would never end. At the time I could not have foreseen that I would be returning to Norwich almost 50 years later for what would be my last spell inside.

I was finally released on a cold, foggy morning in mid-December 1959. I had been transferred to Wandsworth Prison in London to finish my time and Charmian was waiting outside the gate to meet me. We made a beeline for our favourite hotel and booked in as Mr and Mrs Biggs.

It was late evening when we emerged and caught the train to Redhill. I had arranged to stay with friends until I could find a place of my own. I got a job with Reigate Borough Council working as a carpenter. Not very well paid, but plenty of tea and sympathy from the housewives.

From my wages I managed to rent a small furnished flat on Elm Road in Redhill where Charm and I spent as much time as possible together. We were keener than ever to get married but Charmian's father – far less fond of me since having to fork out the money his daughter had pilfered as well as her legal fees – was dead against the idea. In the end we decided to force the old man's hand. We would get Charm pregnant and present our case as a fait accompli.

The wedding took place at the Reigate Registry Office on 20 February 1960. For us it was the wedding of the year.

I changed my job shortly after and started working for an elderly Redhill building contractor by the name of Sid Budgeon. Sid allowed me to get in as much overtime as possible as soon there would be a third Biggs to feed.

Nicholas Grant was born on 23 July 1960 at Redhill County Hospital. The proud and happy parents could be seen wheeling his nibs through the streets of Redhill in an enormous plum-coloured baby carriage.

I was happy with the way things were going. I was being offered so much work that I decided it was time to set up in business for myself, hiring help whenever necessary. We also moved into larger premises at 37 Alpine Road between Redhill and Merstham.

When Nicky was nearly one year old, our close friends Ron and Janet Searle invited Charm and I to spend a week with them in a caravan in Hastings. Although I couldn't really afford to take the time off, I allowed myself to be persuaded to go.

We drove to Hastings in the Searles' car and for much of the time Janet was raving on about her pet subject, fortune-telling, trying to persuade us all to have our fortunes told.

The second day in Hastings, Charmian did go and see a fortune-teller. When she rejoined us some 20 minutes later she was visibly shaken. The fortune-teller had told her things that she thought only she and her mother knew.

Despite showing a lack of interest in all the hocus-pocus, the next morning, when everyone was asleep I went into town and found myself a fortune-teller.

The fortune-teller told me that I was a self-employed carpenter and that when I had worked for other people I had always had 'foreman trouble'. She said that I was on holiday, but could ill-afford to take the time off because of work commitments. I was with a wife – nine to ten years younger than myself – and had an only son who was just one year old. She saw me forming a partnership with a man who worked with 'bricks and mortar' (at that time I knew of no bricklayer that I would take on as a partner).

Until that point everything she had said had been totally correct. Her credibility took a tumble when she told me that I would 'travel extensively around the world and that I would have a child with a woman with long, black hair'. Now, I thought, we were really in the realms of gypsy flim-flam. But I was impressed. She told me I would never be rich but I would always be a good 'breadwinner'. Then, as I was leaving, she called me back.

'I have some advice,' she offered. 'If you want anything out of this life be sure you pay for it.'

A year passed and one day over lunch, Charm told me that she had run into an old school chum who had moved into the neighbourhood with her husband, Ray Stripp. Ray was a bricklayer and Charm had told her friend that I might be able to fix him up with some work. As history shows we became partners, splitting the expenses and profits down the middle. We went from strength to strength taking on more workers until we had a gang of ten. On paper we were making a good profit, but some of our clients were slow to pay and there were times when I found it difficult to meet my half of the payroll.

Christopher Dean, our second son, was born on 24 March 1963. A little beauty – and the image of his dad. Christopher brought with him additional expenses and one weekend in June I found myself particularly strapped for cash given how difficult it had been to work during the Big Freeze of '63. I decided to phone my old pal Bruce and see if he could lend me £500 – that would be about £10,000 today – to tide me over until better times.

'Normally, I would be only too happy to help you out,' Bruce said. 'But at this exact moment all my dough is tied up in a piece of business, something that I can talk to you about, only not over the phone.'

We made an arrangement for him to visit us at the weekend. He arrived at Alpine Road with his wife Frances and his baby son, by coincidence also called Nicholas. While the girls were in the garden cooing over the kids, Bruce asked me what I was up to. I explained I was painting an old boy's bungalow and replacing the windows, and that he had offered to take me out on his train.

'On his train?' Bruce asked.

I explained he was an engine driver, but due to his age was mainly involved in shunting. It was then that Bruce said that he was in a position to put me into his 'piece of business', details of which he could not give me right away. I thanked him for the offer but pointed out that I was now working for a living and was very happy with married life. I also wasn't keen to put my liberty at risk.

'I'm pleased to hear it,' Bruce said, 'but if you want to make one I can guarantee you a minimum of 40 grand for your whack.'

Forty grand was a lot of money to even dream about. It was enough money to buy four new four-bedroomed houses in the best part of Reigate. Worth about £750,000 in 2023.

'Jesus!' I replied. 'Can I have some time to think it over?'

'You can, but there's one simple condition. I need an introduction to the train driver.'

I phoned Bruce early the next morning and put my name on the list.

'I'm in,' I said. I gave him the train driver's address and told Bruce that I would be working there for at least another week.

A few days later, Bruce drove down with his brother-in-law, John Daly. They wanted to get a close look at the old man. The train driver – who I will call 'Peter', although he must be dead by now – saw Bruce and John pull up in Bruce's sporty Lotus. We went off to a nearby pub to discuss a plan of action.

My first priority was to see if Peter would join the gang. All he would have to do was to drive a diesel train for a mile or so for a straight £40,000. When I returned to the house, Peter was watering his garden – his pride and joy.

'What would you do for £40,000?' I asked casually.

'£40,000?' he repeated. 'Blimey, I'd do just about anything for that kind of money. Why are you asking?'

'Would you rob a bank?'

'Yes I would,' he affirmed after a moment's thought. 'Are you serious? If you want me to help you with anything like that, I'd be in like a shot.'

'I can't tell you anything yet. But if I ask you to join me, you will?'

Peter put his hand out and we shook on it. His interest in his roses had wilted somewhat. He kept asking questions – most of which I honestly could not answer.

The first time I met the whole gang was in the flat of up-and-coming racing driver, Roy James – 907 Nell Gwynn House in Chelsea, a block whose notable residents have included Diana Dors and Bruce Forsyth. The gang looked a pretty formidable bunch. With a few exceptions they were all big men and even though well dressed, the majority still had the distinctive look of villains.

The basic plan for the robbery had already been well established when I entered the scene. Jimmy White was the 'quartermaster' responsible for the provision of army uniforms and overalls to be used in the raid. Charlie Wilson was chosen to stock the hideout with food and drink. Roy James and the man I will call Mr One, a member of the gang who would never be caught, would take care of transport. And so forth.

Bruce formally introduced me to the gang and I was invited to tell the assembly what I could about the train driver. They asked questions. What kind of trains was he working on? How well would he hold up if he got nicked? No stone was left unturned.

Most decisions taken by the gang were made on a show of hands and a vote was called for as to whether the old man should be brought in or not. All hands were raised with the exception of one, Roy James. The gang listened as Roy argued that the old man had no experience in the world of villainy and 'had never been trampled on by a 15-stone copper'.

It was a strong argument and I knew from experience how ugly the Old Bill could get during an 'interrogation'. But where would we stand, countered one of the gang, if the actual train driver refused to cooperate? We had to have a back-up driver, it was that simple. On a second show of hands yours truly and Peter were voted in.

Now formally accepted, Bruce filled me in on the details of the plan and when the robbery would take place. I would have to take Peter to see the kind of train that he would be expected to handle and so a couple of days later we went to Euston station. I bought a platform ticket and sat on a bench close to a sleek diesel engine of a train preparing to leave. After a minute or two, Peter came along dressed in his railwayman's blue dungarees. He gave the driver of the train a cheery greeting.

'I'm going on one of these big buggers next week. I wonder if you'd like to give me a few tips?'

'Sure,' replied the driver, clearly only too happy to help one of his colleagues, 'hop up.' Twenty minutes later I 'bumped into' Peter in a café near the station. He was confident and clearly enjoying the part.

It was all arranged. Bruce would meet Peter and me at Victoria station at 8 am on Tuesday 6 August. So that we could get away from our homes for what might be as long as two weeks, I concocted a story that I had been contracted for a tree felling job 'somewhere in Wiltshire'. Peter was 'invited' to go with me as a cook and applied for two weeks' leave of absence from the railway. Charmian was disappointed that I was going to be away from home for my 34th birthday, which fell on 8 August, but I convinced her with the argument that I was going to be well paid for my labours and that we could celebrate upon my return.

Monday 5 August was a bank holiday. I had promised to take Charmian and the children to Brighton for the day. Early that morning my partner appeared at the house with a £50 cheque for some work we had done. He was to give me half the value of the cheque but only had £15 in cash. Before he arrived I had been studying the form and looking over the runners and riders scheduled for the races that day. Ray lived above a betting shop, and on the spur of the moment I decided to make a bet with the £10 he owed me. I wrote down the bet on a piece of paper. It was to be a £5 each-way double. Dameon and Rococco. Two horses at different meetings. Ray thought I was mad to be gambling such an amount (about £185 at today's values), especially on two horses that appeared on paper to have little chance.

We travelled to Brighton by train and had what appeared to be a happy family day. The fact that I was going off on 'the business' the following day was on my mind and I wanted to enjoy ourselves to the full. It just could be our last day together as a family for quite a long time. I tried to push these negative thoughts from my mind – I should be coming back from my trip with 40 grand!

There was horse racing in Brighton that afternoon and after looking over the runners and riders in the midday newspaper my 'special selection' was the favourite in the last race. I tried to get Charm interested in a ten quid 'investment' but we settled for a fiver. I went off to place the bet. After a dinner of fish and chips I bought the late evening paper to see if the nag had obliged; it had, and there was eight pounds to collect.

Standing in line at the betting shop to collect my winnings, I found myself looking at the day's other racing results. The name Rococco caught my eye. It had won at odds of 10 to 1. Then I saw Dameon, a 9 to 1 winner.

If Ray had placed the bet I had won over £600, but would only get £500, still over £9,000 at today's values, which was the bookmaker's limit on any one bet. I said nothing about it to Charm, but when we got home I urgently telephoned Ray to check that he had in fact placed the bet. He said he had and asked if I had won anything. I told him, and loud enough so that Charm could hear me, that I had indeed won and £500 to boot. I asked him to go to the bookmaker in the morning and pick up my winnings.

I rose early the next morning: I had a train to catch! A light breakfast, hugs and kisses. At Redhill station I was glad and relieved to see Peter was among the early morning travellers to London. We had previously agreed not to travel together. At least not as a pair.

During most of the journey to Victoria I was deep in thought. I had set out to borrow £500 and I had won exactly that amount. I remembered what the old fortune-teller had said: 'If you want anything out of this life, be sure you pay for it.' But the die was cast and there was no turning back. In truth, I didn't want to.

Bruce was waiting for us in a café in Wilton Road, next to Victoria station. He was with his brother-in-law, John Daly, and two other members of the gang that I had met at the gathering in Roy's flat. They were Jimmy White, the quartermaster, and the biggest man in the group who was one of the four men never to be caught, whom I'll call Mr Three.

After a sandwich and a cup of tea we climbed into a green army Land Rover which was parked nearby. Soon we were on the open road and heading for Bucks. The weather was still good and the day seemed full of promise.

It was mid-morning by the time we arrived at our destination, Leatherslade Farm, a smallholding that had been purchased by Bruce, located 300 yards off the B4011, the Thame Road, close to the villages of Brill and Oakley in Buckinghamshire. The nearest towns of note were Bicester and Thame.

We were the first to arrive; the rest arriving at staggered intervals. We explored the two-storey farmhouse and the various outbuildings. Precious little had been left behind by the former tenants. A rusty generator seized the attention of Jimmy who immediately set about trying to get it to work. Mr Three and I volunteered to fix lunch. Peter, for his part, found a deckchair and relaxed in the sun. He might as well have been in his own backyard.

During the afternoon, a second group arrived in an Austin goods platform truck that had been purchased from a government surplus contractor. Among the group were Tommy Wisbey, Jim Hussey, Bob Welch, Buster Edwards, Mr One and Mr Two, two other members of the gang who were never caught. On the way to the farm, the group had stopped off at a nearby town to buy further provisions. Bobby Welch, who liked a drink or two, bought a number of pipkins of ale, an act that subsequently led to his arrest and conviction. The pipkin of ale, with his fingerprints, is a prize exhibit at Scotland Yard's own private Crime Museum.

Roy James and Charlie Wilson arrived soon after in a second Land Rover, bringing yet more supplies. John Daly had thoughtfully brought cards and games to while away the time and I was one of the first to start a game of Monopoly along with John, Tommy, Charlie and Roy.

It was just after dark when Roger Cordrey, head of the South Coast Raiders, and the man who knew how to stop trains, arrived at the farm carrying a large suitcase. He was popular with his gang and received a vociferous welcome. By now there were 15 of us at Leatherslade Farm – only Gordon Goody was missing.

The 16 who would be at the track for the robbery would consist of Bruce and his gang (Buster Edwards, Charlie Wilson, Jimmy White, Roy James, John Daly, Mr One, Mr Two and Gordon Goody), of which Peter and I were also considered part, and Roger Cordrey's South Coast Raiders (Tommy Wisbey, Bob Welch, Jimmy Hussey and Mr Three). Despite being different gangs, many of the men had worked together before, although not Bruce and Roger. There was also a support team, but they never came to the track or 'entered' Leatherslade Farm.

At the time, Gordon, who had travelled to Northern Ireland to set up his alibi, was in Pangbourne, an hour's drive from the farm, at the home of solicitor's managing clerk Brian Field and his German wife Karin. Field had been key – and far more than the police ever suspected – in the planning of the robbery.

Gordon was waiting for a phone call from a certain informant. Described by some in the media and in various books about the robbery as the 'Ulsterman', this person was said to be working with the gang and the call would tell us when the extra big load of registered cash in High Value Packets (HVP) had been despatched. Who the 'Ulsterman' is – or was – I cannot say, and neither could Bruce, who never met him, but when the loot was eventually split into shares, the 'Ulsterman' got his full whack. Over time I now question if there ever was an actual 'Ulsterman', rather than a group of informants. The only people said to have met the 'Ulsterman' were Gordon, Buster and Field.

Gordon finally arrived at Leatherslade Farm just before 11 pm making a dramatic entrance, swigging from a bottle of Jameson's Irish whiskey.

'You can all relax,' he announced as he caught us trying on our army uniforms. 'The hit is off.' Groans greeted this piece of news. We had been raring to go.

Few of us felt like sleep that night. We sat around in the kitchen, chatting, playing cards, drinking warm beer and telling lewd jokes. It was late when we finally stretched out our blankets and sleeping bags in the various rooms of the farm.

Dawn broke with the promise of another warm and sunny day. I got up and made breakfast. Rural sounds were coming through the kitchen window, a mixture of livestock and the mechanical sounds common to farms.

It had been decided on the previous day that we should show as little movement as possible and be 'confined to barracks', only allowed to make use of the privy situated some 30 yards from the house.

During the morning that plan changed when a visitor turned up and knocked on the front door. Everyone slipped out of view and Bruce went to take care of the caller. It turned out to be Roland Wyatt, a neighbouring farmer who had become accustomed to hiring a meadow which formed part of the farm. He wanted to know if he could make a similar arrangement with the new 'owner'. Bruce gave the visitor a cock and bull story about being at the farm to take care of redecorating the premises before the new owner moved in. He promised to pass on Mr Wyatt's request.

The day dragged on. There was little interest in cards or other pastimes and it was difficult to concentrate. No phones or tablets to look at. Towards late afternoon we assembled in the kitchen to go through the plan one last time and make certain that everyone knew what they had to do. Subject to getting the green light, we would leave just after midnight and travel as an army detail on night manoeuvres.

Bruce would be dressed as the officer and would be carrying 'official papers' to show in the unlikelihood that we were stopped. Bruce's driver would be 'Corporal' John Daly and the rest of us ordinary squaddies.

At Bridego Bridge, where the railway goes over a quiet country road just off the B488, two miles north of Cheddington station, we would put on dark blue boiler suits over the uniforms and go about our various trackside tasks.

Gordon slipped out of the farm just before 10 pm to phone

Field from the phone box in nearby Brill. He was soon back with the news we had been waiting to hear.

'There's an unusually big load on the train tonight – and it's on its way.'

It is probably worth noting that there are many rumours surrounding the Great Train Robbery, and one was the assumption that all the money had been put on the train in Glasgow and was being sent to London to be burnt. In fact, as I discovered later, very little money had been loaded on to the Night Flyer Up Postal, consisting of an engine (English Electric Class 40 diesel locomotive – D326 [40126]) and five coaches, when it left Glasgow for London at 6.50 pm on Wednesday 7 August.

The Up Postal arrived at Carstairs, 28 miles south of Glasgow, at 7.32 pm where four coaches, that had left Aberdeen at 3.30 pm, were added to the back of the train. It departed at 7.45 pm. The engine and nine coaches arrived at Carlisle at 8.54 pm where three further coaches were added. It departed at 9.04 pm with still just 30 HVP mailbags on board.

Following other stops, the Night Flyer arrived at Crewe station just after midnight on the morning of Thursday 8 August. It would leave at 12.30 am with driver Jack Mills and fireman David Whitby now in charge of the engine. Both men lived in Crewe.

When the train left Crewe it consisted of the engine and 12 coaches, with 91 HVP mailbags now in place. It was scheduled to arrive at Euston station in London at 3.59 am on 8 August.

CHAPTER 3

THURSDAY 8 AUGUST 1963

Midnight came and went. I hardly had time to remember that it was my 34th birthday, yet by the end of the day it would be the one to remember!

As the Night Flyer Up Postal left Crewe station with Mills and Whitby in control, it was our turn to leave Leatherslade Farm. We got on the move slightly before 1 am. From what I remember it was a cool, dry, moonlit summer night with just a few scattered clouds. More importantly there was no sign of rain.

I was in the lead Land Rover, which was driven by John Daly. Mr One drove the truck. Besides the driver my Land Rover was carrying Bruce, Roger Cordrey and, of course, Peter, who was my responsibility. Most of the rest of the gang piled into the truck, with Roy James bringing up the rear in the second Land Rover with Gordon Goody, Jimmy White and Mr Two.

The country lanes were deserted, with not a sight nor sound of anything during the 50-minute drive to Bridego Bridge (Bridge 127), two miles south of Leighton Buzzard, off the B488. The only exception was a solitary hitch-hiker, but he would be key in reporting to the police his sighting of an army convoy of three vehicles. Another witness reported seeing three vehicles on the road between Cublington and Aston Abbotts at around 1.20 am.

On arrival we backed up the lorry between Bridego Bridge and a pond to the west of the track, so that it was in the right place to receive the mailbags. The Land Rovers were parked up close by.

Our first task was to put on our blue overalls, overalls being more appropriate for our trackside duties should we be spotted from a passing train, of which there were a number. All of us had balaclava-type masks for when the train arrived. I scrambled over the protective fence and up the bank to the track with Bruce and Peter.

Markers were unrolled to show Peter exactly where the train had to stop for unloading. We made our way up the track towards the gantry and Sears Crossing, a bridge which went over rather than under the track. Roy James left us to cut the telephone wires from the trackside boxes and then went off to help Bruce and John Daly to cut the public telephone lines that linked two nearby farms, Rowden Farm, near Bridego Bridge, and Redborough Farm, near Sears Crossing, to the outside world. Bruce then went back to get one of the Land Rovers so that he could take up his position further down the track, where the road to Ledburn crossed under the railway, a mere 800 yards from Leighton Buzzard station. From this vantage spot he could warn us of the train's imminent arrival while he enjoyed a fine Montecristo No. 2 cigar as he waited for the train and his destiny.

John Daly and Roger Cordrey had the most to do. To them fell the responsibility of stopping the train. John's signal with an amber light would slow the train at the distant signal, the dwarf signal, while Roger's red light would stop the train altogether by the home signal on the gantry. A distance of some 1,300 yards separated the dwarf signal and gantry.

We spent nearly an hour and a half trackside waiting for the train. During this time, other trains sped by on one of the four sets of tracks. The nearest track to me, to the west, was known as Down Fast, the fast track north to Scotland, next to it was Up Fast, the track our train would be on, and then the Down Slow and Up Slow. From the west we would have to cross one fast track to get to the train while Buster's group on the east would have to cross the two slow tracks.

At one point a freight train came to a stop directly under the gantry. Roger hid behind the signal while the rest of us crouched down on the bank listening to the conversation between the driver and his mate.

Having made various stops since Crewe, the train arrived at Rugby at 2.12 am and departed five minutes later with its full complement of 128 HVP mailbags finally on board. Whoever had the information about how much money would be on the train – 'Ulsterman' or not – had to know exactly what was to be loaded and where. Most of the money had joined the train in England.

It was just after three o'clock when Bruce's voice crackled over the walkie-talkie to warn us that the train was on its way.

'This is it! This is it! This is it!' Bruce yelled.

'Check!'

'Check!'

'Check!'

. . . came the response from the team.

The light on the gantry switched to red and Roger scrambled down to join Buster, Jimmy (White), Roy, Bob and Mr One and Mr Three on the other side of the track to where I was waiting with Peter, Charlie, Gordon, Jim (Hussey), Tommy and Mr Two.

The train came slowly, almost silently, to a stop. The time was 3.03 am. From where Peter and I were hiding there was only the sound of the diesel motor ticking over. A light went on inside the driver's cab, then a door opened and a shadowy figure descended from the train and headed to the foot of the signal gantry. It was David Whitby, the fireman.

Whitby went to the gantry to call the signal box and must have discovered that the line had been cut. He was starting back to the train when he saw a figure between the second and third coach, whom he would have assumed was a trackside worker. It was Buster Edwards. He said nothing but beckoned Whitby to follow him across the Down Slow and Up Slow tracks to the east embankment. There, Whitby was grabbed by Buster and bundled down the embankment where other gang members were waiting. He was quickly handcuffed and told to keep quiet. We were on the move.

Roy James and Jimmy White took up their positions to start uncoupling the locomotive and the HVP coach from the rest of the train, and most importantly from the 72 Post Office employees who were busily going about their business of sorting the regular mail, oblivious to what was going on just a few feet away.

Buster and Gordon now stormed the cab from different sides. The train driver, Mills, reacted instinctively and kicked out at Buster as he was coming up the ladder from the east. Gordon, who had entered from the other side, pinned Mills and spun him around and handed him to Mr Three, who in the heat of the moment and for no reason coshed Mills once, and once only, on the back of his head. He fell sideways to his knees striking his head against the solid steel cab wall as he went down; the action that did the most damage.

Mr Three should never have been behind Gordon because he

was meant to have followed Buster into the cab, but when Mills blocked Buster's way, Mr Three went around the front of the engine and followed Gordon into the cab.

Other members of the gang now moved into the cab from both sides.

'Get the old man up here!' a voice called, which I recognised as Gordon. I led Peter across the track to the ladder leading to the cab. The driver was back on his feet by now, looking groggy and bleeding from a head wound; Charlie, ever the gentleman, was mopping the blood with a handkerchief.

Peter had witnessed the scene and threw me a troubled look – he hadn't bargained for anybody getting hurt, but then neither had I. The coshing was regrettable but it was one blow and not the heavy beating the media likes to portray. While force was used to break into the HVP coach, you could never call the train robbery a violent crime compared with much that has gone on before and since. We had no knives or guns.

The blood coming from Mills's injury had made people nervous and Gordon took Peter by the arm and hustled him into the driving seat.

Behind us, Roy and Jimmy were waiting for the signal to complete the uncoupling of the engine and HVP from the other coaches. An express train whistled past on the inside track, nearly taking the two with it.

The word was passed to the cab that the uncoupling was complete but during the procedure, and unbeknownst to any of us, there had been a loss of brake pressure. Gordon gave Peter the order to get the train moving. The old man just sat looking steadfastly at the controls.

'What's the problem?' barked Bob Welch. 'Let's get going.'

'I'm waiting for the brake pressure to build. I can't take the brake off until I've got the right pressure,' Peter answered matter-of-factly.

'Get him out of here and get the driver,' Gordon exploded.

Peter began to protest, referring again to the necessary brake pressure.

'Fuck the pressure,' stormed Gordon. 'Get the driver up here.'

Peter was pulled out of the seat and Mills took his place. Gordon waved his cosh under the nose of the injured driver.

'Listen,' he said. 'Get this thing moving – but not too fast – and stop when I tell you.'

The pressure built – thanks to Jimmy finally closing the air pressure valve – but in more ways than one. Finally the large diesel lurched into life and began to move slowly forward. The time was 3.14 am.

Roy, who was riding on the outside of the cab, saw the markers first and shouted for us to slow. The large locomotive glided to a halt and the gang spilled out from the train on to the track.

Bruce was already standing waiting for us, cutting an elegant figure in his army officer's uniform rather than our blue overalls. He had watched the initial assault on the train from the Land Rover with John Daly.

We stopped the train exactly at Bridego Bridge, which we knew was little used at night. The bridge was just 38 miles from Euston, the train's final destination.

'Take Peter and wait for us in the back of the Land Rover,' Bruce told me.

Peter and I did as Bruce said, scrambling down the grass embankment to the road and over the tailboard into the back of one of the Land Rovers. At the same time, members of the gang were taking Mills and Whitby off the train and getting them to lie face down on the embankment.

From our position, Peter and I had a clear and unobstructed view of the bridge and the paralysed train. There was the sound of glass shattering as the assault team led by Charlie got to work. Charlie and Jimmy entered the HVP carriage through a broken window, while the rest entered through a rear gangway door. In less than a minute, the side door was open and the mailbags started to emerge.

We sat in awed silence witnessing the sacking of the train. The gang worked swiftly, passing the mailbags by way of a human chain to Jim and Bob who were loading the truck. I knew then that I was a privileged spectator to a historic moment, although at the time I did not know just how historic it was to be. The Great Train Robbery was now fact.

Dawn was approaching and Bruce called a halt to the plundering of the train, even though a few mailbags still remained. Mills and Whitby were moved from the embankment to the HVP coach with the five HVP sorters. Charlie asked Mills and Whitby if they wanted any money for their troubles, but they declined.

We removed our overalls and reverted to the role of soldiers. The 'work party' returned to the vehicles breathing heavily from their labours. The whole robbery – from the stopping of the train at Sears Crossing to leaving the scene – had taken less than 40 minutes, 24 minutes since stopping the train at Bridego Bridge. The time was 3.40 am.

Our small convoy made deliberately slow progress back to the farm, the truck sluggish with the weight of the mailbags and the gang. As I had had it comparatively easy, I was given the task of being the radio operator and tuned into the Old Bill's wavelength on the portable VHF radio we had brought along.

In comparison to recent events, the drive back was uneventful and as we drove up the lane leading to the farm, a rooster crowed. As far as I was concerned it was a new day in beautiful, bucolic Bucks.

As we reached the farm, the radio crackled into life for the first time that morning. It was a general call. A train had been robbed near Linslade. At first, Scotland Yard believed it was a break-in at Cheddington station. The time was around 4.35 am. The first senior police officer would get to the scene of the robbery at just after 5 am.

The truck backed up close to the door of the farmhouse and was quickly and quietly unloaded, the mailbags and their valuable contents being dumped unceremoniously on to the floor of the empty living room. One hundred and twenty bags all in all – nearly ten bags each! Later we learnt that it had been eight bags that had been left behind on the train.

The truck was parked in a lean-to shed – squashing a can of yellow paint in the process – and the Land Rovers placed out of sight. From the air or from the main road nobody would be able to tell that the farmhouse was inhabited, certainly not by 16 villains and some 120 mailbags that contained 636 individual high value packets.

Charlie and Roger were appointed 'accountants' to take care of the counting and distribution of the cash, but first it was decided that we should empty the sacks on the off chance that a homing device had been planted in any one of them. It took Bruce, Mr Two and me close to three hours to empty the sacks and pass the money to Charlie and Roger.

I assumed we would have our work cut out separating the 'wheat from the chaff' and made a comment of this nature. By way of an answer, Charlie opened a pocketknife and slashed open one of the bags. He took out a tightly wrapped bundle and ran his knife down the length of it, laying it open and exposing a wad of blue five-pound notes.

'It's wedge, Ron,' he said with shining eyes and an ear-to-ear grin, 'it's all fucking wedge!'

When our accountants reached the magic million we were all called in to admire the stack. Appreciative sounds filled the air and jokes were cracked.

Gordon was crooning one of his favourite Tony Bennett pieces, 'The Good Life', while Charlie was twisting to Gerry and the Pacemakers' 'I Like It'.

In total our haul was over one million in five-pound notes, over one million in one-pound notes, and over £174,000 in ten-shilling notes, and less than £20,000 in Scottish and Irish notes.

Peter was much more relaxed by now and smiling at one and all. He set about making 'a nice cup of tea' for 'his boys', as he now fondly called us.

Although there was general euphoria our guard didn't drop. There was always somebody monitoring the police traffic on the radio until the Old Bill took to using a code after suspecting that we might be listening in, but even then we constantly monitored the news broadcasts.

BBC Radio's first news broadcast about the robbery went out at 8 am. It told Britain:

'A Glasgow-to-London mail train was stopped and robbed in Buckinghamshire early today. It happened at Cheddington, near Tring, at about 3 am. The driver and fireman were attacked and injured; and two coaches of the train were detached.'

The original plan was for us to sit tight at the farm for some time – possibly a week or more. We certainly had the supplies for it and the farm was well off the beaten track and set well back from the road. Police broadcasts and news bulletins were to change that.

It was around midday when we heard on the radio that the

police suspected that army vehicles had been used in the robbery. Another report spoke of the likelihood that we were held up in a farmhouse somewhere in the vicinity of the robbery, perhaps 'within a 30-minute drive or 30-mile radius of Bridego Bridge'. A 'senior police spokesman', Malcolm Fewtrell, announced that a systematic search of farms and outbuildings would take place immediately.

For whatever reason, the police told the press that we had got away with 'over £100,000. By late afternoon we were looking at a pile of over £2.5 million. According to official records, our total haul that night was £2,631,784 of which only £343,448 was ever recovered. That represented over $7 million at the time and nearly £50 million at current sterling rates. If we had invested the money in a bank it would be worth over £130 million in 2023.

The money was split into 16 equal 'whacks' after Peter's £40,000 and £100,000 to be split by our 'lawyers' – Brian Field, John Wheater and Leonard Field – had been deducted. The extra whack was for the 'Ulsterman' and would be taken care of by Gordon. Each person took his share and packed it into kitbags, holdalls and suitcases. My whack filled two army kitbags, more money than I had ever dreamt of, over £147,000, about £2.7 million at today's rates. I gave Peter his money in a leather holdall.

'My word!' said the old man, his retirement suddenly looking a little bit more promising that the 15 bob a week promised by British Rail.

Decisions were still being taken as to what we should do next. As time was not on our side, we started to throw the empty mailbags down into the cellar and the cleaning of the farm began. Wrapping paper bearing the names of various well-known banks were incinerated in a small stove in the kitchen until Roy pointed out that the column of smoke pouring from the chimney on a warm summer's day might attract attention. The fire was quickly put out.

Peter was still troubled by the fact that he hadn't been given the time to drive the train and he assured me more than once that he could have done the job. Subsequently I was told that the engine had been modified in the weeks before the robbery, something we did not know, and no amount of waiting for the pressure to build would have helped Peter until the cap had been replaced on the valve.

Peter was a lovable man and I am happy that he never had his collar felt by the Old Bill. He would not have survived in the nick and it was nice to think that at least he and three other members of the gang got to enjoy the spoils from that night's work.

Looking back on it, the Old Bill would have known exactly who Peter was and where to find him, but I think that the powers that be – namely Butler – probably told them not to arrest him. Had he been in court with us, he would have been a very good witness for the defence because as a total outsider – with no criminal record – he would have told the jury how we behaved, which would not have matched the picture painted by the prosecution of us as dangerous, violent and greedy villains.

While it was felt unwise to use the Land Rovers, we decided to carry on with painting the truck in case it was needed as a last resort. Jimmy and a helper set to with brushes and a can of canary yellow paint to disguise the khaki truck. This yellow paint would be the undoing of Gordon at the trial after samples from the crushed can had been matched to those found on his shoes, only the shoes the police presented at the trial, which had been taken from Gordon's house, had never been anywhere near the farm. You can draw your own conclusion.

Quiet, chain-smoker Roger Cordrey put it to the gang that he could nip out on the bike he had thoughtfully brought along to see what was going on in the neighbourhood and buy a newspaper and some more fags. If Roger was anything he was unobtrusive, so there was no objection to him going for a spin, especially as we all had the concern of how we could get away from the farm. It was agreed he would return in the morning.

The gang gathered to discuss the options and what our next move should be. The original plan had been to lie low for a week or so. But one thing was for certain: the Old Bill was flat out on the case and the 'heavy mob' were involved. The unanimous decision was that we should get away from the farm and as soon as possible. Bruce encouraged everyone to wipe the place down.

'No dabs are to be left.'

As nothing could be done until the following day we sat around drinking warm beer. It was then that somebody remembered it was my birthday. Each of the gang congratulated me and I was asked what it felt like to finally have made the big time.

CHAPTER 4

AFTERMATH AND CAPTURE

Roger Cordrey cycled to Oxford, some 12 miles from the farm, and booked into a small boarding house from where he called his children and then Billy Boal, whom he asked to meet him on Friday with transport.

The Thursday evening paper told Roger everything he needed to know. He had been involved in one of the largest robberies ever. Given his reputation for being able to stop trains he knew it wouldn't be long before the Old Bill was knocking at his door. And if the Old Bill knew of his reputation so did some of his friends who went back on promises to help after seeing the papers and hearing the news.

Back at the farm we had awoken early. After breakfast the 'cleaners' got to work, washing everything with great care and attention. Bruce and John Daly set off on foot to hitch-hike and get a bus to Thame where they would arrange to get some extra transport to come out from London.

During the day we continued to listen to the news broadcasts. The police were certain that we were still in the area. All police units had been mobilised to take part in a search which would cover a 30-mile radius from the robbery site. The farm was just 28 miles from Bridego Bridge by road and 17 miles as the crow flies. The public were invited to get in touch with the police if they had seen or heard anything of a suspicious nature.

We were becoming more nervous and there was further speculation about what should be done in the event of the Old Bill turning up on the doorstep when a car came racing up the lane to the farmhouse. Everybody took up their positions as it stopped in a swirl of dust by the front door.

'I thought that might make you jump,' said a smiling Roger as he emerged from a Wolseley he had bought in Oxford to replace the bike. Roger was back for his whack, but the news was mixed. 'The Old Bill's flying about all over the place,' he reported, 'but at least there are no roadblocks.' He spread the evening and morning papers on the kitchen table.

The newspapers were calling the crime 'The Great Train Robbery', while the *Daily Sketch* went with the headline 'Balaclava and the 40 Thieves'. The *Daily Mirror* said: 'The (Scotland) Yard men agree, there has never been anything quite so big, bold and crookedly brilliant as The Greatest Train Robbery.'

After some discussion, Buster decided we should club together and pay a man to take care of the farm after we had left by picking up and removing everything we leave behind. Sadly, for most of us, the police got to Leatherslade Farm before the 'dustman'. Without the evidence they collected, or said they collected, at the farm, the Yard would have had no case, just speculation.

First to leave the farm were Roger, Mr Two and Jimmy, travelling in Roger's newly acquired car. Jimmy then bought an Austin Healey in the King's Road and returned to pick up Mr One and his whack.

Just after dusk, Bruce and John got back to the farm driving another Austin Healey. A middle-aged woman at the wheel of a van accompanied them. Bruce told Peter to get his bags; he would be travelling with John and the lady, who had been introduced to me as Mary Manson, who would take Bruce and John's share which was to be hidden amongst furniture in the back of the van. I would go with Bruce and my dough in the Healey.

We made our hasty goodbyes in the hope of never seeing one another again. And then we were on our way, the nippy sports car growling along the country lanes. Not a sign of the Old Bill.

On the way to Redhill, Bruce and I talked about our plans for the future. I visualised dribbling some money into my building business. I needed plant such as ladders and scaffolding and perhaps, later on, a smarter-looking van for Biggs & Stripp.

I asked Bruce if he was going to get out of the business.

'I don't think so,' he said with half a smile. 'I'll probably look around for something bigger and better.'

As we were making our way back to Redhill, Brian and Karin Field were arriving at the farm to help Gordon and Buster. They returned to the Fields' house (Kabri) close to Pangbourne, along with Charlie, Bob, Jimmy, Tommy and Mr Three for what I gather was a bit of a party. Leatherslade Farm had been abandoned.

Bruce and I made a short stop near London Airport so that I could tell Charm that her loving lord and very clever husband was on his way home. In a relieved but anxious voice she asked me if I had recently been in the company of a friend who wore spectacles. I told her I had and that he was in the car.

'I know,' she said.

Mary Manson had followed Bruce back from the farm and at Horley we stopped to go our individual ways. I shook hands with Peter and wished him well. We agreed not to be in touch until the dust had settled.

Charm was all done up in her Sunday best when Bruce and I arrived back at Alpine Road. She gave Bruce a shy hello and eyed the two kitbags standing in the middle of her neatly kept kitchen where she had even prepared something for us to eat.

'What's that?' she asked.

'Money. It's all money,' I replied, yanking open the drawstring on the kitbag and pulling out a few bundles of fivers for her to see.

We were all too excited to touch the food and eventually Bruce left, promising to give me a 'tinkle' in the near future. I wouldn't see my good friend for another 29 years, until we met again in Rio.

I would not see my brother Jack, either. Charmian waited for Bruce to leave before telling me that my brother – 15 years my senior – had died of a heart attack on the eve of the robbery. His wife, Winnie, had been in touch to ask if I could attend the funeral. Charm told her that I was somewhere in Wiltshire engaged in a tree-felling job, the story I had given her and Ray to account for my absence. Winnie suggested that Charm should contact the Wiltshire Constabulary to see if they could find me. All I had told Charm was that I would be in the vicinity of Devizes. Charm had contacted Redhill police station and asked for help in tracing her husband. The call had been logged in the 'Occurrence Book' and a search had been carried out in Wiltshire but there had been no sign of Charmian's 'clever husband'.

The next morning, after my first decent sleep in what seemed like weeks, we tipped the contents of the kitbags out on to the bedroom floor.

We went through the pile note by note, setting to one side any that were in any way suspicious. With a little reluctance we had to burn a pile of more than £700 in the kitchen stove – that is over £13,000 at 2013 values – later digging in the ash around the rose bushes.

I packed £40,000 in blue five-pound notes into a suitcase, £60,000 in mixed notes into another and the rest into a holdall. I had three 'minders' who I was hoping I could trust with my cash and made arrangements by telephone to meet these people the following day. Charm and I kept a modest amount to pay off some bills and to have a private celebration – for my birthday if anyone wanted to know.

Charmian's sister, Rosalind, was invited to babysit for us so that we could have our night out. We took a train to London where for the first time I was quite happy to join Charm window-shopping.

We were wandering around Soho when we saw a notice on a news-stand: 'Train Robbery Latest. Police Hunt the Weasel'.

Although Roy James's nickname had been The Weasel, this Weasel did not turn out to be anyone I knew, so I was not unduly worried. I bought the newspaper anyway. The Weasel was described as a well-known figure in the underworld and, as usual, the police were 'acting on a tip-off'. The news was not sufficient to put us off a splendid Indian meal. Wined and dined, we caught the last train back to Redhill without giving the robbery or the Weasel a second thought.

I was up bright and early on the Sunday morning and went out to buy all the newspapers, certain that they would give the robbery their full attention. From what I read, the Old Bill didn't seem to be making much headway with their enquiries, but much was being made of the 'battered' driver and a possible link to the London Airport job. There was also mention of a reward of £260,000 for any useful information about the robbery.

A friend in the building business turned up in his pick-up truck soon after 9 am and the suitcase containing £60,000 was put in the back and covered by a tarpaulin. I gave my friend a carrier bag holding £5,000 which was the amount agreed for him to babysit the money 'until further notice'.

I arranged to meet a second friend just after noon in the saloon bar of his favourite pub in Horley, a short distance from Redhill and not a million miles from Peter's home. I called a minicab and casually handed the driver a suitcase holding £40,000 to put into the boot of the car. When we got to the pub my friend was waiting for me, greeting me with a strong handshake and a warm smile. He was also to receive a £5,000 'drink' for his troubles.

With the money out of the house I started to feel more relaxed. I told Charmian to go and buy herself some new clothes and shoes from the £500 that I had won on the horses.

On the Monday I was back at work lying furiously about the tree-felling job. My partner, Ray, had told our motley crew of workers about my good fortune on the horses and it was pints all round at lunch. There was a lot of joking about the train robbery and, like most of the country, we toasted the robbers. As I got another round in, Sally, the barmaid, was ringing up a sale on the cash register. She was looking closely at a one-pound note that a customer had handed her, comparing it with a list of serial numbers by the side of the till. The fellow wanted to know why.

'I've got a list of numbers of notes that were stolen from the train and this might be one of them,' she told the customer.

'I wish it was,' he laughed.

I handed Sally a recently 'earned' five-pound note for the round. She tucked the fiver straight into the till drawer and was just preparing my change when the customer drew her attention to the fact that she had not compared my note with the list.

'I don't have to check money that Ron hands me; I know him too well,' she said.

That same Monday the police had been contacted by a farm

labourer and told about a suspicious-looking truck parked in a farm not 30 miles from the scene of the robbery. At first the police added the information to their list of calls but the caller was persistent. On the morning of Tuesday 13 August, the police found the farm. PC John Woolley was the first policeman to visit the farm.

'The place is one big clue,' the police later told reporters. 'We found the farm pretty much as they had left it,' Woolley recalled. 'Their vehicles were still in the yard, their foodstuffs in the kitchen, and the cellar was full of empty mailbags, overalls and masks.'

The evening papers also announced that chief of the Flying Squad, Detective Chief Superintendent Thomas 'Tommy' Butler, the so-called 'Grey Ghost', was now in charge of the train robbery enquiry. Police records show that on 10 August, they were given the names of Bruce, John Daly, Charlie, Bob, Wisbey and Hussey as the possible robbers.

The following evening I heard on the news that Roger had been arrested in Bournemouth. Roger's capture, along with a man called Billy Boal, whom I had never met or heard of, was a blow, but I still felt comfortable that I would not immediately be amongst the suspects. Charmian was not altogether sharing my confidence and when four cases containing £100,000 were found in the woods by Dorking – scant miles from where we were living – she really got an attack of the 'nadgers'. In one of the bags, the police found a receipt for Herr und Frau Field from the Hotel Sonnenbichl in Bad Hindelang in southern Germany. The Fields had stayed at the hotel for two weeks in February 1963.

Worse was to come, as four days after the Dorking find, the police discovered a substantial sum of money concealed in the panelling of a caravan in nearby Boxhill – and Jimmy White's fingerprints to boot.

Two weeks after the robbery, on 22 August, Charlie was arrested at his home in London. The arrest came on the same day that Scotland Yard circulated mugshots of Bruce, Jimmy, Roy, Buster and Charlie to the press. Now Charm and I were tuned into all news broadcasts on the radio and television. Families and friends of the men whom the police were hoping could 'help them with their enquiries' would most certainly be investigated and visited, and as I knew that I was on Bruce's prison record as one of his 'associates', it would not be long before the Old Bill came calling.

Inspector Basil Morris and Sergeant Church were from Reigate police station. They came to see me at 6.45 pm on 24 August just to make a few 'routine enquiries'. I tried to look pleased to see them and invited them through to the living room. Charmian offered to make a cup of tea and gave me a glum look as she went to the kitchen.

Inspector Morris lost no time in getting down to the nitty-gritty of his routine enquiries.

'Now, Ron. When did you last see this chappie Bruce Reynolds we're looking for?'

'Bruce? I haven't seen him for about four years or more,' I said, lying through my teeth. 'The last time I saw him was when we were both in Wandsworth. Bruce went out before I did and I haven't seen him since.'

The questions flowed and so did the lies. The inspector told me that the local police had been keeping tabs on me and that he, for one, was glad to see that I had 'settled down to life on the straight and narrow'. He said he didn't have a search warrant but would I mind if he had a look around.

He was a 'friendly' policeman with a disarming manner. He admired our kitchen but took the opportunity to check in the

Bendix washing machine which, he said, he had been thinking of getting for his 'better half'. He also checked out the stove where Charm and I had recently sent 700 quid up in smoke.

He checked the bedrooms, opening cupboards and wardrobes, then expressed a desire to take a look in the loft. I got him a stepladder and a torch and held the ladder while he climbed up into my workshop.

'Any sign of Bruce, Mr Morris?' I joked.

'No, Ron,' he answered evenly. 'No sign of Bruce.'

Next it was the garden that attracted Morris's attention and he made a beeline for the coal shed. I had recently had half a ton of coal delivered and upon seeing it the friendly inspector gave me a probing look. I admit a delivery of coal in early August may have been a little strange, but my coal was clean, so to speak.

'I think you're on the level, Ron,' Inspector Morris concluded. 'But I am going to ask you for a little favour. If this fellow Reynolds should get in touch I'd like you to string him along. He's on the run and he's going to need somewhere to hide. I think there's a good chance he'll be calling on you. If he does, give me a bell. I'll make it worth your while. You help me and I'll help you.'

The previous evening the police thought they had their man when they had swooped on the Grand Hotel in Leicester after a tip-off from the receptionist. They had dragged a man they believed to be Bruce from his bed at 2 am, only it wasn't Bruce, it was Gordon. Gordon was taken down to Aylesbury and interviewed by Butler, but then to his surprise he was allowed to go, Butler even giving him a lift into London.

Soon it was September and there was less and less mention of the robbery in the media, even after Leatherslade Farm was opened up to the public to visit. As far as Charmian and I were concerned, no news was good news. I went about my business as normally as was possible, returning to work on converting a house into three flats. The days were still warm – these were almost the halcyon days.

On the afternoon of 4 September, one of my painters asked if he could borrow the company van to take his wife to the pictures. I had no objections as long as he dropped me home and picked me up in the morning. He dropped me off outside my house. Alpine Road was deserted as I walked down the side of the house and went in by the back door. Two men were in the kitchen. The Old Bill!

One of them reached behind me and locked the back door, putting the key in his pocket.

'We are police officers,' he announced matter-of-factly. 'We are in the process of searching your house – we have a search warrant. We want you to be present when we take up the floorboards in the front room.'

This was not a time to be clever. It was a time when silence is often golden. I caught a glimpse of Charm who was looking very distressed. She tried to say something but was told to keep quiet. I could hear Nicky kicking on the door of his room and calling for me. It should have been playtime.

Burly cops with their shirtsleeves rolled up were attacking the living-room floor with crowbars. The policeman who had greeted me in the kitchen identified himself as Detective Inspector Frank Williams and began a search of my person during which he appeared to find nothing of interest.

'You are to be taken to the police station to make a statement,' Williams informed me. Another cop was told to fetch the car which was parked close to the entrance of the house. Then, wedged between Williams and another beefy detective, I was bundled into the car and driven off.

Later, I was to discover that one of the policemen to visit my house that day was a young detective called Jack Slipper. A name that I was going to get to know rather well in the coming years.

After leaving Alpine Road we took the wrong turning to go into Redhill where the local police station was located. I pointed this out to Williams.

'I know,' he said, with just the slight trace of a smile. 'We are not going to Redhill, we are going to the Yard.'

We drove along Frenches Road and past the Jolly Brickmakers. How long, I wondered, was it going to be before I saw these familiar sights again? I was clearly nicked. They don't send a car unless you're nicked.

At the Yard I was taken directly to see Butler. He pointed to a chair in front of his desk.

'Sit down,' he said. 'I have here a questionnaire. I'm going to ask you the questions and I want you to write down your answers.'

I told Butler not to waste his time.

'It's only for your antecedents,' he added, hoping to make it all look routine. 'Have you ever heard of Leatherslade Farm?'

'Of course I have heard of Leatherslade Farm; it's been on television every night for the last month.'

'Do you know Buckinghamshire well?' he pressed.

'Yes, I was stationed at two different camps in Buckinghamshire when I was in the Royal Air Force,' I admitted.

Butler started writing. Williams was at his side as a witness.

'Look,' I repeated, 'I told you I'm not answering any questions.'

Butler looked mean and leaned forward. 'All right, I know it's a big one and you've got to keep your mouth shut, but I'm going to charge you with the train robbery. I've got you by the bollocks, lad, and what I don't know I shall make up – do you understand what I mean?'

'Perfectly,' I nodded.

A fast car was ordered up and Williams was told to 'take this bugger to Aylesbury and charge him'.

Charged, I was and photographed and fingerprinted and locked in a dark, dank cell. I was the ninth person arrested in relation to the robbery.

'Turned out nice again!' I thought to myself.

CHAPTER 5

TRIALS AND TRIBULATIONS

The next morning I was up before the beak at Linslade Magistrates' Court, where I was remanded in custody to Her Majesty's Prison Bedford. So convincing was Tommy Butler's manner when he gave his 'evidence' that he almost had me believing the things that I was supposed to have said. Under oath, he declared that when I had been asked about the farm I had replied: 'No. Never heard of it. I've got no interest in fucking farms.' He also told the magistrate that he had no idea as to why I had refused to sign my 'statement'.

As I was led away to my cell, I heard a news report on the prison radio. It said that 'Ronald Biggs, a 34-year-old carpenter of Alpine Road, Redhill appeared before the Linslade magistrate . . .' I did not catch the rest as the screw conducting me down to the cell had butted in.

'We've got one of your mates here, Charlie Wilson,' he said.

'Charlie Wilson? Never heard of him,' I replied.

The next day when we were unlocked for exercise I saw both Charlie and Roger in the yard. We ignored each other until the exercise was over. Charlie then said in a loud voice for all to hear: 'Aren't you the bloke who's been charged with the train robbery?'

'Yeah,' I said, 'but I had nothing to do with it.'

'Incredible,' said Charlie. 'I've been charged with that too. Bloody liberty.'

Another person arrested and charged on 5 September was Christine Keeler, the most famous person in the Profumo affair.

Gordon surprised us by turning up in Bedford to visit Charlie. I'm not certain why he took the risk but he had a message for me from Bruce and that was to let his solicitor, George Stanley, take care of my defence. Until then, as a poor, struggling carpenter, I had been granted Legal Aid, but I decided to take Bruce's advice. Then, on 3 October, Gordon was rearrested.

One by one the ranks of the 'innocents' swelled. First Jimmy Hussey, then Tommy Wisbey, who was quickly followed by Bobby Welch. None of us had any idea what evidence there was against us or how they came to pick our names. We were allowed visits, but we were all extra cautious as it was suggested that the visiting cubicles might be bugged.

Charmian came to see me and I was glad to see that at least by appearances she seemed to be weathering the storm reasonably well. During her second visit she told me that one of her friends, Jean Jarrard, was having a fling with a cop attached to Scotland Yard. He told Jean, after a bit of priming, that the evidence against us were the fingerprints found at Leatherslade Farm. Bob, Tommy and Jim, who had been three of the 'cleaners' at the farm, wouldn't hear of it.

'It's all bollocks,' said Bob firmly. 'If the Old Bill produces fingerprints, then it's a fit-up.' Jim and Tom agreed.

They were almost right as even the forensic boys admitted that the house was remarkably clean from having housed a gang as large as ours. It was only after they had dusted the more unlikely places, such as the Monopoly set, which we could easily have taken with us, that they found anything of worth.

A total of 243 photographs were taken at the farm of 311 fingerprints and 56 palm prints. The three of the gang who arrived at the farm wearing gloves, and who had the sense and discipline not to remove them, were never caught, but that could have been for other reasons. What prints Peter may have left behind could not be traced as he had no previous record for them to be matched against, and the Old Bill initially did not know that they were looking for a second driver. The fact that they did know which prints to look for, however, made their job a lot easier.

Solicitor's managing clerk, Brian Field, and his boss, John Wheater, were arrested in connection with the sale of Leatherslade Farm, and at the beginning of December, Bruce's brother-in-law, John Daly, was arrested in Eaton Square. A week later, on 10 December, it was the turn of Roy James to fall into Butler's grasp after a dramatic rooftop chase in St John's Wood.

The police had even stumbled upon Bruce after a neighbour had reported a ladder propped up against a house. Frances Reynolds had opened the door to them, but Bruce had the presence of mind to take off all his clothes and play the part of the cheating lover. Franny explained to the slightly uncomfortable policemen that she was a married woman and her boyfriend had come to stay with her for a day or so, and that she would be ruined if his presence ever became known. The two policemen thoroughly understood, took their names and gallantly withdrew. It was not until they got back to the nick to check the names that they realised the names were not only false, but they had just had the world's number one wanted criminal and his wife standing in front of them.

With no Bruce in custody, but 19 other people being held on

various charges (but only nine of the 16 that had been at the track), Butler told the media that he was ready to start the court case.

During the time in Bedford I tried to get the group interested in an escape. The wall to the prison was not very high and there were more than enough of us to take care of the screws that supervised the exercise. But everyone still thought that they had a good chance of 'slipping out of it' – even when told about the fingerprint evidence – so the opportunity was lost.

Somebody was obviously reading my thoughts, because very soon we were transferred en masse to Aylesbury Prison. The hospital wing had been cleared of patients and we were put into cells that had barred observation flaps on the doors. Experienced screws were selected from different prisons around England to take care of us. Security, at first, was tight.

After a time, security in Aylesbury was relaxed and we spent our time over Christmas and New Year playing cards and chess, listening to the radio and getting to know one another rather better than had been possible at the time of the robbery.

Our legal representatives visited us regularly. George Stanley also had the pleasure of taking care of John Daly's defence. Stanley confirmed that the main evidence was the fingerprints found at Leatherslade Farm. Stanley suggested that I should admit to having been to the farm prior to the robbery, but only in my capacity as a carpenter, to construct a whipping post for 'kinky' parties. He told John to plead guilty and hope for leniency.

John seriously considered pleading guilty in the hope of copping a shorter sentence. We had to work on him to make him see that he was making the wrong decision. Finally he agreed. The only one who was obliged to plead guilty was Roger Cordrey, as he had been caught 'bang to rights' with his share of the loot.

The majority of the gang thought that they still had a reasonable chance of slipping out of the charges against us, a view that was not shared by Gordon, Charlie and Ronnie Biggs! We began to put together an escape plan.

God knows how or why, but Charlie had been put to work in a small kitchen in the hospital wing. His job was to prepare snacks and hot drinks for the screws. Two officers patrolled the prison yard at night and were accustomed to getting a mug of cocoa passed out to them through the bars of one of the cells. It was decided that these two screws would have to be drugged to facilitate our plan. Once the guards were in the Land of Nod, friends would come over the wall and Bob's your uncle. Roger, who had spent a large part of his life in the horse racing world, was consulted for information as to the best type of dope for the job in hand. He knew exactly what was required and from where it could be obtained: tasteless and colourless, satisfaction guaranteed. Charlie was enthusiastic: knocking the screws out by hand – or by dope – would give him great pleasure. That was until Brian Field appeared reading from his *Archbold's Criminal Law and Practice*: 'For administering a stupefying drug: up to 14 years' imprisonment.'

'Fuck that!' said Charlie.

The screws that took care of us in Aylesbury Prison were changed every month. Most of them were an unhappy lot and being away from their homes didn't do much to improve their humour. One exception was Paddy, a fine fella from County Cork. One evening when he came on duty he looked into my cell and saw that my table was laden with a selection of cold meat and cheeses plus a couple of bottles of Carlsberg 'Special Brew' lager.

'Sure, you fellas are livin' like lords,' said Paddy. 'I think I'm in the wrong game.' 'Y'know,' he said, lowering his tone, 'I've got a lot of admiration for you and your mates.' I felt I knew what was coming next. 'I'd be prepared to help you lads – if you needed anything. But I wouldn't bring in any guns or dope.'

'Come off it, Paddy. You know that we're not into anything like that. But I would be interested in getting hold of a miniature radio.' So we talked about a price and a place where the deal could be done. As I knew Aylesbury fairly well from my days in the Royal Air Force, I was able to arrange for a friend to meet Paddy outside a certain cinema. He would pass over a tiny 'Ruby' radio and receive an envelope containing £100, now worth around £1,800. Paddy was delighted – and so were Gordon and Charlie when I told them that we had a sympathiser in our midst.

Contact was made with a legendary key-maker, known as 'Johnny the Bosh'. He only had to know the make of the lock to come up with a blank key that was sure to fit. This information was duly passed out and the key was produced and handed to one of Gordon's pals. During the next couple of weeks, hacksaw blades, a one-inch wood chisel, a watch, the blank key and a set of needle files were smuggled into Aylesbury. All that we needed to put our plan into operation was a copy of the key that unlocked the doors to our cells.

Security slackened off during the months we spent on remand. The hearings at the Magistrates' Court were over and we had all been committed for trial. We associated most of the day, only being locked in our cells during lunchtime and after 9 pm. The screws were generally easy to get along with. Friendly screws often played games of cards or chess with us, and it was during one of these fraternal moments that Gordon was able to exercise his artistic skills.

As a guard and I sat facing each other, pitting our wits over the chessboard, Gordon came along, sketch pad in hand, and asked the screw if he had any objection to being drawn in this somewhat remarkable pose. Permission granted, Gordon started sketching away, telling us how he planned to publish a book of his drawings 'when he got out'.

The screw sitting across the chessboard from me was so engrossed in the black-and-white armies in front of him, that he paid no attention to the bunch of keys hanging from his belt: in the meantime Gordon was filling in the details. With the aid of his sketches and the needle files, Gordon produced the key we needed overnight. The following morning, whilst someone kept the screws occupied, Gordon tested his handiwork on the door of my cell. It turned the lock first time! It was a 'goer'!

Roger, Billy Boal (whose only crime was to give Roger a lift and help him hide the money, and who had been arrested at the very beginning along with Roger) and Brian Field shared a dormitory at one end of the first floor of the hospital wing. The door was not like the cell doors, which were faced with sheet metal on the inside. The dormitory door was fitted with a flimsy mortise lock and there was no metal facing. Anyone on the inside would have little trouble cutting the wood and removing the lock. As Roger and Brian were not anxious to participate in the planned escape, we reluctantly decided to invite Boal. Ever worried about the welfare of his wife and three children, he was only too ready to 'make one'.

Arrangements were made. Charlie's 'firm' would leave a car at a spot near the back of the hospital. Bill would quietly cut the lock from the dormitory door and get out, unlocking Gordon's cell, which was next door to the dormitory. Gordon would then unlock Charlie – who was on the same landing – and they would cop for the nightwatchman, tying him up. Then they would go down to the cells in the basement and unlock me.

Lying under a blanket, fully dressed, I heard the nightwatchman shuffling around, making his rounds. I could just imagine good old Bill at work on the door – using the chisel as I had shown him. Somewhere a clock struck eleven, then twelve . . . one . . . two. At three o'clock I took my clothes off and got into bed: something had obviously gone wrong.

For whatever reason, Bill chickened out and laid wide the plot to the chief screw. The screws moved in with a massive search of the cells and their occupants. 'Association' came to an abrupt end and the screws were no longer friendly. Most of the items that had been smuggled in were found and confiscated. All privileges ceased, visiting time was curtailed and foodstuff coming into the prison was restricted to the permitted amount. And for good measure, a pig of a principal officer came to the nick to take charge during the Christmas period.

God Rest Ye Merry Gentlemen!

Roger John Cordrey, Charles Frederick Wilson, Thomas William Wisbey, Leonard Dennis Field, Douglas Gordon Goody, William Gerald Boal, Ronald Arthur Biggs, James Hussey, Brian Arthur Field, John Denby Wheater and Robert Alfred Welch were charged on divers days unknown between the 1st day of May, 1963, and the 9th day of August, 1963 in the County of Buckingham conspired together and with other persons unknown to stop a mail train with intent to rob said mail. Against the Peace of our Sovereign Lady the Queen, Her Crown and Dignity. For that they: Roger John Cordrey, Charles Frederick Wilson, Thomas William Wisbey, Leonard Dennis Field, Douglas Gordon Goody, William Gerald Boal, Ronald Arthur Biggs, James Hussey, Brian Arthur Field, John Denby Wheater and Robert Alfred Welch on the 8th day of August 1963, in the County of Buckingham being armed with offensive weapons or being together with other persons robbed Frank Dewhurst of 120 mailbags contrary to Section 23 (1) (a) of the Larceny Act, 1916.

It did not seem important at the time, but we were charged with robbing the train of 'mailbags' and not money. The reason was that no money was found at the farm to be used in evidence, just mailbags. The trial proper began on 20 January 1964. The judge was Mr Justice Edmund Davies, a Welshman and one you would expect not to be known for his leniency in dealing with the likes of us. Yet on 30 September 1963 – less than two months after the robbery and six months prior to passing sentence on us – he had given his ruling on a case in the court of appeal. The man appealing took part with three other men in the armed robbery of the Royal Arsenal Co-operative Society depot in Surrey. During the robbery, a van driver, and father of two, was shot and killed. At the original trial the man who pulled the trigger was sentenced to death, later commuted to life, which turned out to be 16 years. The other three, who were also armed, were sentenced initially to 15 years each. The presiding judge stated that the gang was 'one of the most dangerous ever to be brought to justice.' Yet at appeal Justice Davies reduced their 'excessive' sentence to ten years!

Caught 'bang to rights', Roger pleaded guilty on the first day of the trial to conspiracy to stop the mail and receiving large sums of money from the robbery. He pleaded not guilty to robbery with aggravation. The court accepted his plea and he was returned to prison to await sentencing.

As the crime had been committed in the county of Buckinghamshire, the venue for the trial was set to be the county town of Aylesbury. The town's Assize Court was far too small to accommodate such a large number of accused, so the local Rural District Council Chamber was converted into the courtroom.

A team of carpenters were called in to construct an enormous dock that would be big enough to seat all of us and then as many again to accommodate the accompanying policemen.

Being in Aylesbury meant that it was easier to take the jury to visit Leatherslade Farm, which was key to the prosecution who would argue that if it was proved you had been at the farm, then you were a train robber.

Every morning, Monday through Friday, we would be handcuffed and locked into small individual compartments in a police bus, commonly known as a Black Maria. Then with a massive escort which consisted of at least four police cars and a dozen or so motorcycle cops, we would make the ten-minute journey from the prison to the council chamber.

After the morning hearing we would return to prison in much the same fashion for lunch. At the time we were still having our meals brought into the prison from one of the town's better restaurants and served by the proprietor.

At around 2 pm the routine would be repeated and we would be cuffed up and sent off to court for the afternoon session.

The court, packed with reporters, coppers, the public and the accused, would often become stuffy, particularly during the afternoon sessions. A string of bank clerks were early witnesses and they would be led painstakingly through their earlier statements to the police by the junior prosecutor, Howard Sabin. The aim was for the prosecution to prove that beyond any question of doubt, the train in question had been carrying a large sum of money which was subsequently stolen. At times it was hard to stay awake and more than once I saw members of the jury nodding off. My solicitor, George Stanley, had engaged Mr Wilfred Fordham, a barrister, to defend me. Fordham was a kindly old gentleman, highly respected in legal circles.

At one point, Fordham's absence from the proceedings, as he catnapped in court, was noted by his Lordship who sat drumming his fingers as he waited for my defence counsel to rejoin us. Charlie spoke to me about the matter.

Charlie was right, so I raised it with George Stanley. Stanley argued in favour of sticking with Fordham – a fine man if it should come to making a plea for leniency, he said – but it was finally decided that a QC would be brought in and Mr Fordham would stay on to assist.

I remember feeling distinctly more optimistic after my first meeting with Michael Argyle QC. At that time he was the Recorder for Leicester – dishing out bird! A young man, obviously well bred, exuding efficiency and Old Spice. This was more like it!

A hush fell over the court when on 22 January, Jack Mills, the train driver, entered to give his evidence. The judge glared in the direction of the dock as Mills made his way to the witness box and took the oath. He was invited by the judge to give his evidence seated and accepted the invitation. Aided by the prosecutor, Mr Mills described his misadventure when his train was stopped at a point on the line known as Sears Crossing. The hordes of reporters scribbled away furiously, not wanting to miss a word of the driver's whispered and damming testimony.

Mills was the key figure in manipulating the 'monstrous' nature of our crime. Without him it would have been nigh on impossible for the judge to get away with the sentences he later handed down. I never met Mills personally, so I can only base my impressions on hearsay, but I do know that when the robbery was planned there was never any intention that anyone would get hurt. As we were all wearing masks at the time of the robbery, Mills did not know who did cosh him or if they were in the court. They were not.

One of the people most troubled by Mr Mills's performance in court was the wife of my lawyer, Peta Fordham. Mrs Fordham, who went on to write one of the first books about the crime, *The Robbers' Tale*, revealed that in an interview with her five years before his death, Mills had admitted that he had been warned that his 'pension would be affected' if he showed any sympathy in court to the gang or suggested that we had treated him 'like a gentleman'.

On the 14th day of the trial, my old friend, Detective Inspector Basil Morris from the Surrey Constabulary, Reigate CID, appeared to give evidence.

The prosecutor took the inspector through the evidence he had given before a magistrate when I was first charged.

'Did you, Inspector Morris, ask Mr Biggs if he knew any of the men wanted for the train robbery in Buckinghamshire?' he asked.

'I did,' affirmed the inspector.

'And what did he say?'

'He said: "I know Reynolds, I met him when we were doing time together."'

The reply took the prosecutor by surprise; it was not the reply he was expecting or wanted. To enable the jury to return an impartial verdict, it is essential that there must be no indication that the accused has previously been to prison. Telling the court I had 'done time' was quite wrong. Those in the courtroom who were aware of this, looked at Inspector Morris in disbelief.

My lawyer hurried over to the dock to confer with me about 'the inspector's unfortunate remark'. I didn't hesitate to tell him I wanted a retrial. I imagined that if I stood accused alone I would have a better chance than standing cheek by jowl with a bunch of obvious villains. My counsel went off and entered into a whispered conversation with His Lordship, returning to say that the judge did not think that the jury had 'picked up' the inspector's reference with regard to me having previously been to prison. But I insisted. I wanted a retrial.

The judge gave the order for the jury to be taken from the court, then, when the last good man and true had left the council chamber, Mr Justice Davies turned his attention to the hapless detective inspector. I almost felt sorry for him, such was the dressing-down he received from the judge.

I was then discharged from the present trial without a verdict and ordered to be held in custody until the date of a new trial. I nursed a hope that my lawyers could get the venue of my trial changed – perhaps to the Old Bailey – where friends could possibly 'get at' someone on the jury to hold out for a 'not guilty' verdict. It was 6 February.

Next day, when the gang were carted off to court, I stayed at the prison. I was allowed to pass my days in the company of Roger who was not attending the trial as he had pleaded guilty. He was interesting, intelligent company, with an endless fund of anecdotes about his capers before the train robbery. Unlike me, in 20 years Roger had only one previous conviction, for embezzlement, that had landed him in Borstal.

Five days after Inspector Morris had made his blunder, the case for the prosecution closed. It was now up to the defence to make submissions to the judge and jury, offering arguments with regard to the innocence of their respective clients.

On Wednesday 12 February 1964 the defence began. The gang told their stories and produced their witnesses. If they were to be believed, few of the defendants should have been accused in the first place. Gordon couldn't have participated in the raid because he had been going about his business smuggling watches. Roy, late on the night of 7 August, had engaged in a long conversation with a friendly taxi driver which took them into the wee small hours of the morning of the 8th. And so forth.

Mid-morning on Valentine's Day, 14 February, Roger and I heard the main prison gate opening. We went to the window of the dormitory and saw a police car drive in. Minutes later John Daly, the man who wanted to plead guilty, came to the door, trembling and pale-faced.

'What's the trouble, John?' I asked. 'Are you ill?'

'No, I'm not ill. I've been acquitted!'

John's counsel had made a submission to the effect that the Monopoly set could have been taken to the farm after he left his prints on it. The judge accepted that and acquitted him.

Too bad I wasn't able to share the lucky Irishman's good fortune. My fingerprints were found on the Monopoly set but also on a sauce bottle (I never thought they would 'ketchup' with me). It was the sauce bottle that, the prosecution argued, tied me to the farm.

Most of the explanations given by the gang for their fingerprints being at the farm were, at best, ludicrous. My fairy story was quite pathetic. Charmian and I, the court were told, had been given the chance to buy the humble little house we were renting in Redhill. The owner, a retired policeman, had told us that if we could come up with £500 as a deposit we could pay the rest off weekly instead of paying rent. During a trip to London to visit my ailing father, I ran into an old prison chum named Norman Bickers.

It so happened that Norman had been invited to join in 'a little piece of business' – down the country somewhere. He was not at liberty to give me any details, but he was sure that I could take part in the venture. I would be away from home for four or five days, so it would be necessary to concoct some kind of a story to tell my wife. The tree-felling job was Norman's idea. He knew where I lived and he knew Charmian. It would be no problem to convince her that a few days away from home would provide us with the cash for the deposit on the house. It was arranged that I would not tell my wife about the job and Norm would pick me up in his car on the morning of 6 August.

Charmian (who had agreed to play her part in this pretty piece of perjury) waved us goodbye as we set out for 'somewhere in Wiltshire' to cut down trees. But instead of driving to Wiltshire we went to Leatherslade Farm. The place was deserted when we got there; but we saw an army truck parked in one of the outbuildings. Inside the house, which was unlocked, we found a great amount of food, sleeping bags and army uniforms. I didn't like the look of it. I imagined that there was some kind of plan afoot to attack a military installation. I got cold feet and wanted out. But, much like Goldilocks in the house of the three bears, we fixed ourselves something to eat. Hence my fingerprints on the ketchup bottle and a Pyrex plate. After the snack we looked around and found – of all things – a Monopoly set! I opened the box; I hadn't played Monopoly since I was a kid. We decided to get out and go straight back to London, where I spent the next few days with Norman's friend, Brian Morse – another ex-con – arriving back in Redhill on Friday 10 August.

Later, when called upon to substantiate my story before the magistrate, Brian and Norm lied skilfully and convincingly; working hard for the £1,000 apiece they were paid.

By now the gang, particularly Hussey, Wisbey and Welch, were feeling less confident about their chances of 'slipping out' of the case. There was some speculation as to what the sentences might be in the event of us being found guilty. According to *Archbold's Criminal Law and Practice*, the maximum term of imprisonment for robbery was 14 years, but there appeared to be no limit for 'conspiring to rob', the second charge against us. 'Conspiring to blow up a bridge', however, carried a maximum sentence of 15 years, so it was thought that our conspiracy charge was infinitely less serious.

The closing speeches for the defence began on 10 March and ended four days later. The following Tuesday, 17 March, St Patrick's Day, the judge began his summing up. It took six days. While he accepted that the prosecution could not prove who was at the track and at the scene of the crime, if it proved somebody was at Leatherslade Farm then that should be sufficient to prove the guilt of robbing Frank Dewhurst who was in charge of the HVP coach.

At 3.36 pm on Monday 23 March, the 49th working day of the trial, the jury retired to consider their verdicts. They deliberated over their task for 66 hours – then the longest in British legal history.

With the exception of John Wheater, the solicitor Brian Field worked for, all the accused were found guilty on the conspiracy charge. Roy, Charlie Wilson, Gordon, Jimmy, Bobby, Tommy and Bill Boal (who was nowhere near the train or the farm), were also found guilty of robbery with violence. After hearing the verdicts, the judge decided not to pass sentence until after my retrial.

On the morning of Wednesday 8 April I appeared once again before his Lordship, Mr Justice Edmund Davies, but with a different jury and at the Assize Court rather than the Rural District Council Chamber. The prosecution went through all the evidence, and some but not all of the witnesses were recalled.

Michael Argyle, peering over the top of his half-moon glasses, addressed the court with charm and eloquence in my defence, describing how I 'took fright' at the sight of the army uniforms at Leatherslade Farm. My case was looking reasonably good until Norman was called to support my alibi. He had mysteriously disappeared. A private detective was hired to find the witness, but to no avail.

In his closing speech to the jury, Mr Argyle made a splendid effort to convince them of my innocence. But, in view of the fact that I had pleaded not guilty, Mr Arthur James QC, prosecuting for the Crown, had the right to the famous 'last word'. And that word was, 'Bullshit!'

Mr Justice Davies finally summed up, eulogising at length my learned counsel's manipulation of the English language.

'But, ladies and gentlemen of the jury,' he went on to say, 'let us keep our feet firmly on the ground. What the Crown says is so-and-so. And what the Crown says is this, that and the other.' The jury gaped. Then, off they went to deliberate. It didn't take them long to come back with the verdict, just 92 minutes: guilty on both counts.

Only later did I learn that my defence team had not been told that two of the items my fingerprints had been found on (the Pyrex plate and bottle of ketchup) had been left by the owner of the farm, and not taken there by the gang. The third item was the Monopoly set, so arguably like John Daly, my case should have been dismissed and I would have no story to tell.

The next morning, 16 April, just over eight months since the robbery, we all left Aylesbury Prison in the Black Maria. This time we were not taken to the Rural District Council Chambers but instead to the old Assize Court and locked into chilly cells beneath the courtroom. A steep, narrow staircase led up to the dock where, one by one, we were called to receive our sentences.

Roger, who had pleaded guilty, was the first up the steps. The first to be sentenced out of what the judge described as 'eleven greedy men whom hope of gain allured'. Despite his guilty plea, Mr Justice Davies sentenced Roger to 'concurrent terms of

20 years' after which officers hustled Roger from the dock and down a second flight of steps that led to a different line of cells to where we were waiting.

Billy Boal, who was neither a conspirator nor one of the robbers, was next to be called for sentence. The judge announced he would 'extend some measure of mercy' on the grounds of Billy's age and that it was fairly clear that he had not played a very dynamic part in the planning or the robbery itself. Something of an understatement, yet His Lordship was still happy to hand down a sentence of 21 years on the first count and 24 years on the second.

The judge went on at length with a prepared text for each of us that was obviously aimed more at the general public's perception of the case than the man in the dock. He referred to the robbery as 'nothing less than a sordid crime of violence inspired by vast greed.'

The judge, now warming to his task had Charles Frederick Wilson before him, a man he intended to make sure would never get to enjoy any of his 'ill-gotten gains' from the robbery. On the first count Charlie was sentenced to 25 years and on the second count to a concurrent term of 30 years. Charlie was taken down to join Roger and Billy. It was my turn.

'Ronald Arthur Biggs, yesterday you were convicted of both the first and second counts of this indictment. Your learned counsel has urged that you had no special talent and that you were plainly not an originator of the conspiracy. These and all other submissions I bear in mind, but the truth is that I do not know when you entered the conspiracy, or what part you played. What I do know is you are a specious and facile liar and you have this week, in this court, perjured yourself time and time again, but I add not a day to your sentence on this account. Your previous record qualifies you to be sentenced to preventive detention; that I shall do. The sentence of the court upon you in respect of the first count is one of 25 years' imprisonment and in respect of the second count, 30 years' imprisonment. Those sentences to be served concurrently.'

The old boy's totally off his rocker, I thought to myself. Only spies get locked away for 30 years. With remission for good behaviour, I calculated, it meant that I was looking to do at least 20 years in the nick! Twice the amount of bird you might get for bumping somebody off. My earliest possible date for release would be February 1984. I would be 54.

Charmian stood above in the public gallery, pale and shattered. As I was led in the direction of the 'down' staircase I looked up and gave her a wave and a smile. I may have lost a battle, but I knew the war was far from over.

'What did you get?' asked Charlie as I joined him, Roger and Billy in the cells.

'Thirty!'

'Same as me. Bill got twenty-four and Roger got twenty on a guilty plea, for fuck's sake.'

Wisbey, Welch and Hussey, all sentenced to 30 years, joined us in swift succession. Then came Roy, bewildered with his 30 year sentence.

'Who's dead?' he asked. 'Did we kill somebody?'

Swashbuckling, Gordon Goody came down from the court tight-lipped, also with 30 years.

Brian Field was sentenced to 25 years' imprisonment for conspiracy with a concurrent five years for obstructing justice. Leonard Field – no relation to Brian Field – who was paid £500 to 'buy' Leatherslade Farm received a similar sentence. John Wheater, Brian Field's boss, who had been only marginally involved in the conveyance of the farm, was sent down for three years.

The gang was demolished. The villains had got their just desserts. Twelve 'greedy' men were to be jailed for a total of 307 years, although the total sentences were for 573 years but some sentences were to run concurrently. Newspapers sold like hot cakes.

The trial had lasted 51 working days over a period of 10 weeks. Evidence had been heard from 264 witnesses and an estimated 2.5 million words had been spoken. The words filled over 30,000 pages of foolscap paper. The 12 jurors, who were paid 50 shillings a day, had examined 613 exhibits and listened to the questions and speeches of the 21 barristers. The cost of the trial was estimated at £38,733 (over £700,000 by today's values).

Back at the nick, they were waiting for us. We were only given time to pick up our personal belongings and shake hands with each other. Then, handcuffed and under heavy police escorts, we were taken individually to different prisons around the country.

I wasn't told where I was going but from road signs I gathered that my new home – at least for the time being – was going to be Her Majesty's Prison in Lincoln.

At 'reception' I exchanged my sports jacket and cavalry twill pants for an ill-fitting 'Special Watch' prison uniform. The cons working in the area were friendly, almost reverent – never before had they seen anyone with a 30 stretch. I could even feel a certain sympathy from the screws.

For some time there had been various mentions in the newspapers about the possibility of a parole scheme being introduced into the British penal system. Under this scheme, prisoners would be eligible for parole after serving one third of their sentence. Remission, on the other hand, offered a third off the total sentence for good behaviour. Although it was clutching at a straw, I told myself that such a scheme would come about.

Perhaps I would see a light at the end of the tunnel after I had served ten years or so.

On the day we were sentenced, our respective counsels lodged appeals against the severity of the sentences. I didn't entertain high hopes that there would be any reduction – in fact, we were running the risk of having the sentences increased. For the time being, I decided to play it cool.

In Lincoln I was allowed to exercise with other Special Watch prisoners and offers to help me escape were soon being made. But I decided to wait until the appeal had been heard before making any moves to 'have it away'. In any case, after less than two weeks in Lincoln I was transferred without explanation to HMP Chelmsford where the wall was higher, but the food was better.

Early in July, again under maximum security conditions, the gang was reassembled in London at HMP Brixton. On arrival we were placed on Rule 43, which meant that we were to be held incommunicado. We were allowed to exercise, but never more than two or three of us on the yard at any one time. We were supposed to walk separately, in silence, but we took little notice of the screws trying to impose this order.

One member of the gang who decided to play it even cooler than me, was Charlie, who didn't even bother to appear at the Court of Criminal Appeal when the hearing began. Charlie had a plan and that plan included staying put in HMP Winson Green, Birmingham. If he attended the appeal he ran the danger of being transferred to a different prison.

The appeals were over. The three judges again accepted the premise of the prosecution that although the robbers were not identified, the fingerprint evidence was sufficient. However, Roger and his friend Bill Boal had their sentences reduced to 14 years.

In Boal's case, the court saw that his physique and temperament did not fit him for a part in the robbery.

The two Fields were 'lucky'. Their appeal against conviction on the conspiracy charge were allowed as 'no facts had been established that they knew of the intention to stop and rob the train', and they left the court facing only five years. The rest of the appeals were dismissed – including Charlie's, which was heard in his absence.

The judges stated: 'Last year's £2,500,000 raid was warfare against society and an act of organised banditry touching new depths of lawlessness. In our judgement severe deterrent sentences are necessary to protect the community against these men for a long time.' Our leave to appeal to the House of Lords was refused.

But the best was yet to come. The next day I was transferred to HMP Wandsworth, Britain's answer at the time to Alcatraz. As far as HM Government was concerned, this was to be my home for at least the next 20 years. Not a happy prospect if you want to get out with all your marbles intact. In the event, Wandsworth was to be home for just a few days over one year.

CHAPTER 6

ESCAPE: THE MAKING OF THE MAN

Had I not escaped from Her Majesty's Prison in Wandsworth, South London, there would never have been a 'Ronnie Biggs' to talk about and that is something that is sometimes overlooked.

At the time of the robbery, no one person involved was any more famous than any other. That is at least as far as the general public were concerned, although I am sure that the Yard had its favourites. Admittedly some of us did get a head start with the media: Roy James for being a very promising driver, me for the mistrial, and Bruce and Buster for still being at large at the time of the trial.

But while the British public could name the gang to a man during the trial of 1964, 60 years on – and thanks mainly to the media – the names to stick are 'Biggs' and 'Buster'. Those of the right age will remember Charlie for his escape to Canada and his murder in Spain, and hopefully Bruce as the brain, but the other names have or are being forgotten with the passing of time.

You don't have to be very clever to realise that anybody

sentenced to 30 years is going to at least consider the idea of escape. Normally, the thought went as far as getting over the wall; what you did after that was a bridge to be crossed when you came to it.

When I was first sentenced I was given about five minutes to talk to Charmian before being taken off to the cells. She was upset and crying, but I told her not to be like that as she, more than anyone, should know that I was not going to stick around and spend a lot of time in prison. I would be out the first chance I got.

I wasn't being totally sincere with Charm or myself, as at the time I honestly did believe that a parole scheme would come about and if it only meant doing ten years then I was going to do those ten years and get them out of the way as fast as I could and enjoy the money. The only way to do that was to keep my nose clean. That is what I tried to indicate to the authorities when I got to Wandsworth, but they took it with a pinch of salt.

All the members of the gang were aware that whoever escaped first would have the best chance of getting away. Once a couple of us had got away the security would become much tighter. Yet at the time, surprising as it may sound, all of us would have considered that escaping from prison was something of a doddle. If it was easy to stop and rob a train, it was even easier to escape from the nick. In the 1960s it was not a question of 'if' we would get out, but 'when'.

Charlie was the first to walk. And walk he did after being 'abducted' from Winson Green Prison in Birmingham on 12 August 1964. Three men, described as 'strangers', somehow got him over the prison wall and into a waiting car – wearing only his vest – all in under 15 minutes without leaving the vestige of a clue. He was on the run for over three and a half years before being recaptured in Canada.

On the same day as the appeal had been turned down I was transferred from Brixton to Wandsworth, a prison I knew well and hated. But being sent there had its advantages as I knew its ropes.

In a short time I had a miniature radio smuggled in and every Saturday afternoon, Joe, the landing cleaner and a fellow con, would deposit a bucket of murky water with a floor cloth and scrubbing brush outside my cell door with a view to having a 'scrub out'. Down in the depths of the inky water would be lurking a tin of crab, lobster, corned beef, peanuts and half a bottle of whisky. The empty tins and bottles went out the same way.

I was put to work – for a few brief hours each day – in the mailbag shop, hand-sewing mailbags for the GPO. I was considered a 'security risk' and categorised as a Special Watch prisoner. There were 30 or more cons in this category, most of us with a history of having broken out of one nick or another. We had coloured patches sewn on to our jackets and trousers and we were denied certain 'privileges' such as evening classes and 'open' visits. We worked immediately in front of a watchful prison officer.

Almost as soon as I arrived in Wandsworth I began receiving offers to help me escape, but I turned them down. One of these offers came from the prisoner who was working beside me, Paul Seabourne. Paul was on the tail end of a four-year sentence with less than a year to serve. He had a good reputation among the other cons and was known to be 'as game as a bygone' having escaped from Wandsworth during the sentence he was serving.

Paul and I became good friends. I liked his dry sense of humour. I turned down his first offer to get me out, using my argument about the introduction of a parole scheme and getting out legally after ten years or less.

It eventually got to a point where Paul and I started to annoy each other, him wanting to get me out and me refusing. He told me that he was simply against the idea that I had been handed a 30-year sentence for robbing a train.

Paul also loved the idea of getting me or anyone else out of Wandsworth. I think to him it was a way to fuck with the authorities. To stick it to them on a grand scale.

I was delighted that on the Glorious Twelfth, Charlie had been 'spirited away' and was not in the slightest bit surprised. The Home Office was far less elated and orders were given to double up on the security on the train gang, especially when less than a week later they uncovered a plot to free Gordon from Strangeways in Manchester.

A screw was posted outside my cell door full-time, peering at me through the Judas flap at 15-minute intervals. I could hear him coughing, sneezing, farting and humming to himself. His chair creaked with every movement, and he would have conversations with passing screws or the nightwatchman and I could hear him messing with his Thermos flask and sandwiches. At first I asked him politely to make less noise, but it was all to no avail, so I became more abusive.

As a result I started being subjected to frequent 'changes of location', sometimes at midnight or later – the 'idea' being that this would confuse would-be rescuers.

After a few weeks of the 'extra security measures', including being escorted by two screws wherever I went, even taking a crap, I felt that my health was being affected. I asked Governor 'Gusty' Gale to relax the pressure, showing him my trembling hands. He said he was very sorry, but his orders were from the Home Office and those orders were quite clear.

Later, in the exercise yard I told Paul that if the offer was still open I wanted him to get me out. From that moment in the yard, Paul and I started plotting, considering every possible angle to put a plan together of getting me over the wall that was going to work.

The idea of a removal van came to mind, and I asked Paul just how tall the average van was.

'Not tall enough to reach the top of the wall if that's what you're thinking,' was his immediate answer. 'But I like the idea.'

We made some calculations using my experience in the building trade to find out the exact height of the prison wall by counting the number of brick courses. It was over 25 feet high.

At this time another friendly face appeared in the Special Watch section of the mailbag workshop. His name was Eric Flower. Eric was a pal from the early days in the boob. We had been Young Prisoners at Lewes in 1949.

Eric had been sentenced to 12 years for conspiracy to rob, armed robbery and robbery with violence, and had lodged an appeal against the severity of his sentence, while knowing full well that he stood little or no chance in having it reduced. As a prisoner on appeal, however, he was able to receive visitors on a daily basis and I immediately saw how this could be very useful with regard to passing messages in and out of the prison.

Another member of the mailbag workshop that I extended an invitation to do a bunk was Roy Shaw. He had been sentenced to 15 years for the robbery of a security van, and a further three years for grievous bodily harm. Roy partly blamed the length of his sentence on the Great Train Robbery, with longer sentences becoming the norm.

I told Roy of my plan as we stitched mailbags, and that to be part of it he would need to come up with £10,000. Roy weighed up the pros and cons, but realised in the end that he would need a lot more money to keep on the run. He wasn't wrong, and by chance prior to my escape, he found himself transferred to Parkhurst on the Isle of Wight and would not have been around on the big day. Next time I saw Roy was in Rio when we were both as free as a bird!

During the weekdays, Special Watch inmates like me were exercised in a yard that was flanked by the main prison wall. On the other side was a narrow service road which ran around the prison and on to the main road and freedom.

Exercise took place in the afternoon in the form of two one-hour periods: from half past one until half past two and from half past two until half past three. A senior prison officer was always in charge of the exercise and he would appear in the workshop just before 1.30 pm to make the random selection of half the number of Special Watch cons for the exercise period. Those passed over at this time would then automatically be taken into the yard at 2.30 as the first batch returned to the workshop. As we could not guarantee being picked for the first period we would have to be 'missing' from the workshop at 1.30 pm on E-day.

As soon as I had decided to go over the wall I embarked on a get-fit programme, as I was quite a bit overweight. I obtained books from the prison library and had a one-hour workout every evening. At night I listened to my miniature radio tucked under my pillow and only just loud enough for me to hear. An Australian pop group, the Seekers, had a hit at the time which was my inspiration: it contained the line 'There's a new world somewhere, they call the promised land.' Years later I was to meet them in Melbourne when I was working as a carpenter at the Channel Nine TV station.

Charmian knew about the escape plan and was excited about the possibility of seeing her loving lord in liberty. A month or so before Paul was due to be released, Charm received a communication from a friend of ours, Brian Stone. Brian was in HMP Brixton on remand facing some spurious cheque charges and needed some financial assistance. I gave Charmian the green light to arrange a lawyer to defend our friend and soon enough there he was sitting beside us in the mailbag shop!

Despite the circumstances of our meeting, Brian was 'over the moon' with the four-year sentence he had received as he had been expecting to go down for a much longer stretch.

I had figured that Eric and I were going to need a little help on E-day. There would be four screws in the exercise yard and it was a certainty that they would come running as we started scaling the wall.

I talked it over with Eric and Paul and it was decided that we would ask Brian to mind us as we went into action. Brian didn't think twice when I put it to him, but he suggested that there should be a second 'minder' to tangle with the screws.

I decided, at Brian's suggestion, to have a wee word with a young lad from Glasgow. I told him that I needed someone to help me go over the wall. I stipulated that I didn't want any violence and all he would have to do would be to grab a screw and hang on. I told him I would pay him £500, the equivalent today of over £9,000, for his help.

'I don't want your money, Biggsy,' said the Scot. 'I'll do it for the prestige.' The brotherhood of prison life really does exist.

Days before Paul's release, we were doing dummy runs, rehearsing ways and means of avoiding the first exercise period. Dwelling in the bog seemed to be sound, a 'sudden excruciating pain in the gut' was another sure-fire way to be taken to the prison hospital for a dose of 'white mixture', a concoction that was administered for practically everything.

As Eric was able to receive visitors every day, he got his friends and family to arrive at 1.30 pm on the dot, thus avoiding the first call. There was also a storeroom in the workshop where one could go to have a pair of scissors sharpened or get more mailbag thread and 'not hear' the first call for walkies. On one of his visits, Eric was able to smuggle in a small ladies wristwatch that was to be vital for timing ourselves in the exercise yard.

It had been arranged that on the day Paul would go into action at exactly 3.10 pm, giving us enough time to make sure we were in the yard, even with delays. We discovered that it took approximately half a minute to get from the toilet block to the main wall at a point between the two screws.

When I had finally given Paul the word that I wanted to escape, he made two stipulations. Money to cover his expenses and an introduction to 'someone who you can call your friend'. I assured him there was cash available and he would be working with a very staunch friend, Mike Haynes.

The eve of Paul's release arrived and there was the customary leg-pulling by the screws. 'You'll be back!' and so forth.

Paul lost no time in contacting Charmian and we soon began receiving 'progress reports' via Eric's visitors. Our 'bird' was dragging. E-day was set for Wednesday 7 July 1965.

As it turned out E-Day was a typical English summer day. The forecast was rain!

When my cell was unlocked soon after 1 pm the screw found me doubled up in agony, gasping for medical attention. To say it must have been something I ate wasn't that far-fetched in Wandsworth! Two screws were summoned to escort me to the sick bay. The quack had seen it all before and as I had expected prescribed a good dose of 'white mixture'. Miracles of miracles it worked and by 2.30 pm I was fully recovered and back in the mailbag workshop, sewing away.

Eric was smiling after having spent the last half hour with his loved ones while Brian was looking relieved after having spent a similar length of time on the crapper. Wee Jock also looked confident as he emerged from the storeroom.

At 2.30 pm, as expected, the call went up to put our work away and line up for exercise. Before 2.35 pm we were in the yard and conforming to regulations, walking around the footpath in pairs. Eric and I together, Brian and Jock a few yards ahead. The wall was almost within touching distance.

Dark clouds lowered above us and it began to drizzle.

Fuck!

The discipline officer – the screw in charge of the exercise – gave a signal to the other three screws to take us back into the prison wing for 'indoor exercise'. I protested, pointing out that it was only raining lightly, but as I was speaking the heavens opened and it started to piss down. Eric and I exchanged dejected looks as we were returned to the workshop.

At the very same moment the escape team was trundling towards the prison in their converted furniture van. But when Paul saw the rain he knew from experience that we would be taken off the yard. Given Britain's inclement weather we had foreseen the situation and it had been decided that should rain 'stop play' we would carry out the same procedure the following day.

Happily nothing we had done had attracted any attention so the escape was very much on. There was still the frustration of knowing that we had nearly done it and would have to do it all over again. We would all have to be missing from the mailbag workshop the next day when the screws chose the cons for the first exercise period. Not one of the four of us could afford to be there until well after 1.30 pm. I was logged on my prison record as arriving from my cell at 2.20 pm.

The delay gave Paul some extra time and he visited phone boxes in the direct vicinity of the escape and disconnected the mouthpieces to stop people telephoning our getaway to the police or reporting a suspicious-looking van. We discovered later that not even a prison of the importance of Wandsworth had a direct line to the police. When I did go over the top, the screws, like everyone else, had to call 999 and this meant a 20-minute delay until the cops arrived.

Thursday 8 July, one year and 11 months to the day since the robbery, the sun rose brightly over London and I sensed that this was going to be the day. Charmian, who must have been getting fed up of traipsing off to museums with the kids as an alibi, set off for Whipsnade Zoo in Bedfordshire. She also thought that after the disappointment of Wednesday this would be the day.

Never had the exercise yard looked so good. I felt like peeing with pleasure – so we headed for the toilets, where – surprise, surprise – Brian and Jock were to be found just shaking the drops off.

With his back to the screw, who was watching closely to make sure that no one was having a crafty smoke, Eric checked the time by his watch and gave a nod. It was close to 3.10 pm. The four of us joined the other cons on exercise.

As we drew level with the wall I heard the sound of a heavy vehicle on the other side. I stopped to tie my shoelace, looking up at the wall. Suddenly a head in a nylon stocking appeared. A split second later the first of the rope ladders came snaking down the wall. As Eric and I made for them the screws came running, blowing their whistles. Brian and Jock went into action.

As I cocked my leg over the wall, Paul, the man in the nylon mask, greeted me.

'Hello, you big ugly bastard!' I gave him a slap on the back and looked down at the melee in the prison yard. My boys were hanging on to the screws as if they loved them.

'You're too late,' Brian shouted, 'Biggsy's away.'

The red truck was parked close to the wall, something that would be unthinkable today, so it was an easy matter to drop on to the roof. A large rectangular opening had been cut in the van to allow a five-foot hinged platform to be pushed up through the roof giving Paul those vital extra feet needed to reach the top of the wall and throw down the rope ladders. On the floor of the van were old mattresses for us to jump down on to. A getaway car, a blue Ford Zephyr, was parked nearby with Paul's trusty friend, Ronnie Leslie, at the wheel. Two other cons seized the opportunity to follow us over the wall and because of this Paul never got to burn the truck as he had planned.

Besides Ronnie Leslie, a motor mechanic who had worked on converting the van, there was a third member of the escape team, Ronnie Black, a Ron whom I had had my doubts about.

Black had spent time with me in Wandsworth where he had been a bit of a hothead. The last thing I wanted was to have any kind of violence or guns. No guns and no violence was a strict rule and Paul had grudgingly agreed to go along with this. I got pissed, therefore, when I heard the rules had been broken and there had been a shotgun involved. But Paul just offered to put me back inside.

As Eric and I scrambled into the car with Paul and the two Ronnies, the other two Special Watch cons, Robert Anderson and Patrick Doyle, came racing to the car looking for a lift.

'Let 'em in,' I shouted. They piled in and we zoomed off full of the joys of being sprung.

We had made it!

We had done it!

We had fucking escaped from Wandsworth!

Despite the initial euphoria we still had a long way to go.

The car raced around the perimeter wall, all seven of us piled inside. It was the only route to freedom and the main road. As we sped off, our route was nearly blocked by a prison work party with a dustcart. Happily the screw, not knowing who we were, pulled them off the road and waved us through. If he had left the cart in the road our exit would have been blocked.

We drove on, four of us desperately trying to tear off our tell-tale Special Watch uniforms. A police car passed us going in the other direction, but there never seemed any danger of being stopped.

Even without being chased we went through with Paul's plan. It took us to a quiet cul-de-sac close to Wandsworth Common where we dumped the Ford Zephyr and ran up a footpath leading to a second car. If the Old Bill had been in pursuit we would have run down the alley and hoped they did *not* have a second car waiting.

As the second car had been hired on a dodgy brief, we told the two opportunists they could use it after they had dropped us off and go as far as they liked until the next day, when a scream would go out for it. The first to be dropped off were the two Ronnies at Tooting Bec station. The five of us then went on to Dulwich where Eric, Paul and I left the car close to our final destination. Our address was not something we necessarily wanted to broadcast to our uninvited guests who, without a plan, were more likely than us to get picked up.

When I was in hiding I read that our guests had been caught after three months. One of them, Robert Anderson, turned up on Frankie Fraser's doorstep.

'On the afternoon of the escape I was sitting in an office listening to the details of the escape on the radio when there was a knock at the door,' Frankie later explained. 'The door was opened, and standing there was Anderson. He said he had been told that if he was in London and needed any help, to call at the office. Well, to say he needed help is a major understatement.'

After all these years I can't help thinking about the king-sized bollocking the governor at Wandsworth must have got for the manner of my escape. That was fine with me because he had not believed me when I said I did not want any special treatment but wanted to be treated like every other con. He had said that it could not be. When I told him that everything he was doing was going to drive me over the wall, he saw this as insolence. It was not. I was trying to be perfectly honest, man to man, and show that it would be too much for me to endure. In the end I think I proved my point.

Charmian heard of my escape on the four o'clock radio news when they first announced that four men had gone over the wall of Wandsworth, one of whom was 'believed' to be train robber Ronald Biggs.

CHAPTER 7

RON ON THE RUN

The hideout was the upstairs flat of a semi-detached house in Camberwell Grove, a quiet road north of Dulwich. On that lazy summer afternoon the road was deserted and Paul, Eric and I appeared to be just three men going about their business.

Two young people were at the flat when we arrived: Paul's brother-in-law, George Gibbs, and his wife Jean. Eric threw me a furtive glance indicating that he was far from happy about 'unknowns' being on the scene.

'George is sound,' Paul assured us, 'and so is the girl.' It was now just after 3.30 pm.

'Open up the champers, for Christ's sake!' I exclaimed.

We celebrated and toasted Paul. Another bottle of champers was cracked as we sat around the telly to catch news of the escape. The escape was described as: 'One of the most daring jail-escape plots of the century.'

Although for the moment we were safe, I could see that Eric wanted to arrange somewhere more secure for us. He had friends in East London, well-connected friends, and as soon as it was dark he slipped out to make a phone call to one of them, a certain Freddie Foreman. Eric had worked with Freddie, whom I had never met, but Fred was already friends with Bruce, Buster, Tommy, Gordon, John Daly and Jimmy Hussey. Eric returned looking elated – his friends would be arriving in less than an hour. Now it was Paul's turn to look troubled. He wanted to know more about Eric's pals.

'I promised to get you out and I did,' Paul said. 'You would be as safe here as anywhere.'

Eric could not agree. 'Paul,' he said, 'the Old Bill is going to turn over every drum in South London. They must know that we're not far from the boob. My people will have us safely down in the country by tomorrow.'

I had to admit that the idea of getting off the manor appealed and I was certain that Eric wouldn't be putting us in the hands of mugs. We also knew that Paul would be the number one suspect for putting together the escape. Paul didn't seem too worried about the possibility of getting his collar felt, but as Eric was quick to point out, if the Old Bill were looking for Paul it would lead them to us.

With the arrival of Eric's friends, the once spacious living room looked crowded. Both men, Freddie and his right-hand man, Alfie Gerard, were twice the size of Paul and unmistakably villains. Paul was wearing his worried look again. He had recognised one of the men. When the chance came he drew me into another room.

'Look,' he said, 'I know Alfie and I can tell you he's bad news. They're not here to do you any favours and they know you've got lots of dough tucked away.' He produced a pistol. 'Take this to look after yourself. You're out, now make sure you stay out.'

I refused to take the gun. I told Paul I didn't need it and that I could take care of myself better without one.

Freddie and Alfie got into the front of the car which they had parked a short distance along the street. Moments later Eric and I slipped into the back and crouched down on the seat. We were tired; it had been a long and exciting day.

Morning noises filled the room, but they were not country noises, but city noises. We were not 'in the country' but in a humble tenement building in Bermondsey.

An elderly docker was our landlord for the next few days. We were provided with clothes, good grub and booze, and a record player, plus a pile of LPs that had been knocked off from a shop in the Charing Cross Road. Life was starting to look considerably better than it had done a few days earlier.

If Lady Luck was looking after Biggsy, she wasn't as kind to the other people involved. Days after we moved on from Dulwich, as Detective Chief Superintendent Tommy Butler and his Flying Squad crew were raiding every hang-out where he thought Eric and I might be found, Paul was arrested. Paul was to serve four and a half years for getting me out of prison, but many more indirectly for later crimes because the authorities were always out to get him for springing me.

Paul knew he would get caught, but he didn't care. My freedom was his reward. His only charge for getting me out of prison were expenses – which were virtually nothing – and some money for Ronnie Leslie. When I got over the wall I had to force £1,000 (about £18,000 today) on Paul as a show of gratitude, but he only took it because of his old lady.

Ronnie Leslie got three years for helping Paul, while Brian Stone and his mate Jock were given an extra 12 months apiece for tackling the screws.

A week or so later we were moved on from Bermondsey to a spacious apartment in Camberwell owned by Freddie's sister-in-law. While we were there we were introduced to a friend of Alfie's named George. This sharp-looking fellow represented an 'organisation' capable of taking care of travel arrangements for people like Eric and me. Thomas Cook they were not. With great self-assurance, George outlined a 'package deal' which consisted of temporary passports, a boat trip to the Continent, a car transfer to Paris, plastic surgery, ('complete facial reforming by one of the most famous names in European cosmetic surgery', was how he put it), real passports in our 'new image', and airline tickets to 'anywhere in the world'.

The price? A mere 80 grand, over half my share from the robbery. Nearly £1.5 million at today's prices. A bargain, George assured me, as a lot of people would have to be paid off. With a bit of haggling the price fell to £40,000 (£750,000), £20,000 down and the rest after the ops in Paris. There was also the question of a further £15,000 for the safe passage of Charmian, Eric's wife Carol and the kids to join us at our final destination. A cool £55,000 was spent, nearly one million pounds at today's rates and roughly a third of what I had netted from the robbery.

In 1996, under the 30-year rule, it was revealed that in July 1965 the then prime minister, Harold Wilson, pressed for a novel way of preventing us train robbers from laundering our money. He suggested to the Treasury to secretly prepare replacement banknotes and suddenly withdraw all former currency. Banks would then ask customers to account for their money in order to exchange old notes for new. Wilson's idea was that the money we had all kept under the mattress after the robbery would become useless. Thankfully, Wilson's idea was rejected by the Whitehall mandarins as impossible to effect, so money, for the moment, was not my problem.

The 'organisation' I talk of had nothing to do with the train robbery – despite what people would like to believe – or my escape from Wandsworth, but is a body that helps those with the right connections. It almost certainly got Buster out of Britain, and more than likely Charlie as well. But I am only guessing. Freddie had explained how he helped organise Buster's return in his biography *The Godfather of British Crime*.

My contact with Charmian was at first restricted to calls to phone boxes in and around London, the numbers of which she had jotted down in the weeks before my escape. I have always assumed that Charmian's movements would have been monitored yet, despite the escape, Scotland Yard never contacted her directly.

As the preparations for the move to Paris would take some time, our minders decided that we should make another move. Again, just after dark, we were picked up and spirited across London to new digs. This time we would be sharing a room with a private detective! An Irishman. The apartment was in a house somewhere between Putney and Richmond which belonged to friends of Alfie. Everyone was in the villainy business, including the Irish detective.

Our host made us very welcome and the grog flowed. The detective entertained us into the wee small hours with hilarious tales about his clients and work. Although we were enjoying the company, we were not getting any exercise to speak of. It was still summertime and I was hankering to feel the sun on my body.

Leafing through a copy of the *Evening News*, I spotted an ad: Bognor Regis: 3 bedrooms; garden; quiet, secluded neighbourhood. I showed it to Eric and he was as enthusiastic as me.

We put the idea to Alfie who growled a bit, but finally agreed to see what could be done.

All went well. After the trip to Bognor lying in the back of Alfie's car, we found ourselves in a comfortable, fully furnished two-storey house, exactly what we had been hoping for. There was a small garden surrounded by a high wooden fence with flowers and plants galore. This, we decided, was more like it. It was late July 1965.

A plan was made for Eric's wife to come down to take care of the shopping, cooking and washing. With the arrival of Carol to take care of these chores, life was almost idyllic.

After a hearty breakfast we would lie in the garden sunbathing and listening to the radio. The Dave Clark Five were also feeling pretty good at the time, their song, appropriately 'Catch Us If You Can', riding high on the charts.

One night the door to my room flew open and a body landed on top of me.

'You're nicked, you bastard!' It was Charm. My cup runneth over.

Once again we were nearly one big happy family, although Charm for safety had left the kids back in London. The only thing Charm and I couldn't do was go for a walk on the beach. But we talked and made our plans for the future.

The second anniversary of the robbery came and went and later I discovered that Tommy Butler now believed Eric and I were in South Africa, a place we had been considering.

George came to visit us on a couple of occasions to discuss details of the plastic surgery. He took photographs of Eric and me on the first visit and returned with suggestions from the surgeon who was going to wield the knife. Eric was only to have a nose job, but I was going to have the works.

George also informed us that our sojourn to Bognor was coming to an end, so we started making the necessary preparations to move back to London. In mid-September the 'holiday' came to an end and after three months of hiding behind net curtains it was time. Little did I know that those early autumn days of 1965 were going to be the last time that I would set foot on British soil until I returned 13,087 days later in May 2001.

Eric and I transferred back to the flat in Camberwell, minus the wives and kids. Now that we knew that we were on the point of departure the time seemed to drag. We wanted action.

Early one morning that October, Alfie turned up with two parcels of clothing. The clothes were second-hand and consisted of flannel shirts, jeans, donkey jackets and gumboots. We were supposed to look like seamen.

We dressed quickly and were soon on our way in a black van which had been parked outside the building. Freddie was at the wheel and from him came the instructions.

'When you're dropped off, walk straight through the gate. The mate of the boat on which you're travelling will be waiting. He'll take you aboard and hide you. Now however bad you feel, stay put. Even when the boat docks. The mate will tell you when it is okay to go ashore. When you leave the boat walk straight out of the dock gate and turn left. Keep walking. Someone will come along driving a yellow DAF and offer you a lift into the city. He will take you to a motel where George will be waiting.'

As we left the van close to London Bridge, Fred wished us well.

The mate, a Dutchman, was waiting just as he had said. He spoke little English but had enough international sign language to get us to follow him. Other than the three of us there was no other sign of life. We went aboard the cargo ship unchallenged. Down in the hold we scrambled over sacks of what smelled like rubber and with the aid of a torch the mate conducted us through to the bow where a small area had been left clear. The mate indicated that this was to be where we would spend the journey.

After what seemed like an age, the boat's engines began

to throb and we were under way. The trip was not as rough as had been expected but it seemed to take forever, especially as we had no idea of time.

Finally we became aware that the boat had docked and eventually the sacks hiding us began to fall away. It was our friend, the mate.

'Come. Leave now!' he beckoned in faltering English. We clambered over the sacks on stiff legs and up on to the deck. It was early morning and the boat was as deserted as when we had embarked. The mate smiled and shook hands pointing to the dock gates as he did so.

There was nobody to be seen and the dock gates were wide open just as promised. We turned left, as per instructions, and before we had gone more than a couple of yards, along came a yellow DAF.

'Hello, boys,' called the driver. 'Going into town? Perhaps I can offer you a lift?'

His name was Peter and it turned out he had been the captain of our vessel. With typical Dutch humour he asked if we had enjoyed the crossing. He laughed when we told him we did not even know where we were.

'Antwerp! You're in Antwerp. I'm sorry that we won't have time to look around, but your friend is waiting.'

George was indeed waiting at the motel. He was immaculately dressed with Lisa, his 'gorgeous piece of German crumpet', at his side. He wrinkled his nose as we approached.

After a quick shower, a shave and some fresh clothing we were ready for action, the first step of which was a slap-up breakfast while George outlined the next leg of the journey, which would take us to Paris.

We would be travelling in two cars. Eric would be with

George and Lisa in George's Mercedes and I would travel in a Ford Zephyr with an English couple, Bill and Veronica – trusted friends of George – and their two young daughters. We were given false passports, mine in the name of Ronald King, a sports master by profession.

'We'll drive ahead,' George told us. 'When we come to the frontier the gendarmes will only be interested in one thing – Lisa's legs!'

I was told that I would be in the back of the Zephyr with the kids and all of us were to be asleep.

Crossing the frontier proved no problem. Bill presented the passports and a gendarme peered into the back of the car. It was by now way past midnight and the three innocents were fast asleep.

We had made it to France. After a brief pit stop for a beer and a snack we pressed on for Paris.

Bill pulled up behind George's car in a tree-lined avenue with the Eiffel Tower looming high above us. A man stepped out of the shadows and went to George's car and got in. The Merc pulled away and we followed though the quiet Paris streets.

Our new hideout was a fourth-floor apartment on the Rue Vivienne and the person who would be taking care of us from here on was 'Henri', the man who had emerged from the shadows. Henri was well dressed and appeared to be in his mid-fifties. He was powerfully built, not the kind of man you would choose to pick a fight with. He had a bone-crushing handshake, a big smile and an even bigger heart. He spoke English with a heavy American accent which made it impossible to pin down his origins.

The apartment was small but comfortable and well stocked with food and drink. Henri was to visit daily with bread, milk and the newspapers. Within a day or so George came calling and told us we would be taken to the clinic to discuss the forthcoming surgery.

It was cold and snowing heavily but Eric and I were thinking of sunnier climes, as after the ops we would be free to go anywhere. We both discussed the subject of where 'anywhere' would be until one Sunday afternoon I read an article describing the pleasures that Australia had to offer and in particular Bondi Beach and Sydney, and the sun-kissed Sheilas. I handed the article to Eric and without hesitation we agreed that we could do with some of that. So Oz it was.

Eric and I began to look forward to Henri's visits. We could hear him as he hauled his bulky frame up the wooden staircase to the flat where he would arrive breathless. Every day he would follow the same routine, slumping into a chair from where would come the by now familiar phrase: 'God dammit boys . . . I quit!'

George turned up a couple of times, bringing mail and presents from home, where our wives were 'over the moon' with the progress we were making.

Although it was against 'orders' we did go out at night from time to time. We went to see Les Folies Bergère where Eric was nearly selected to join the girls onstage in the can-can. Mostly we would go to small bars and jazz clubs where we could pass unnoticed as a couple of British visitors enjoying the Parisian nightlife.

Finally we were taken to the Clinique Victor Massé in Henri's old Citroën Deux Chevaux and he was clearly nervous about his 'hot cargo'. Hunched over the wheel like the getaway driver in a bad B-movie, Henri's nerves took him through a red light on more than one occasion.

Marcel, let us call him, would perform the operations. I had my doubts about him being 'one of the most famous names in

European cosmetic surgery' but pressed on. He examined us and made a few notes. A date was fixed.

Our 'cover story' for the clinic was that we were a pair of Canadian tax dodgers – not that anyone seemed to worry. Whilst I was being prepared for surgery a doctor spoke to me in French. I apologised and told him that I did not speak any French. He looked bemused: 'But it says on your card that you are from Quebec?' I put on my best sick smile and explained that my mother had taken me to the English-speaking provinces when I was a small child. I got a feeling the doctor did not believe me.

My mobile stretcher was wheeled off to await my turn in the operating theatre. A sexy nurse dug a needle in my arm and hooked me up to some sort of contraption. She took my pulse, her hand cool and efficient.

'You are very calm,' she said. 'That is good.'

I was just about to invest further in this conversation when the doors to the theatre swung open and there was my old mate looking a very sad and sorry state. I wanted to laugh. Only his blood-suffused eyes were visible – and they were visibly distressed – and two bloodied prongs projecting from the area that had been his nose. A muffled voice came from behind the bandages. 'Don't let them tell you it doesn't hurt.'

Before you could say 'knife' or check my pulse I was on the operating table and starting to feel woozy. Bright lights, voices, someone breaking up the cartilage in my nose with what felt like a hammer and chisel. The blood was running down my throat. 'You won't feel a thing,' they had said. 'Liz Taylor does it all the time . . .'

Henri arrived the following morning to pick us up and take us back to the apartment. As usual he was smiling broadly, thanking and bull-shitting the surgeon.

Back at the apartment Henri set out our antibiotic tablets and painkillers, fussing around us like a mother hen. The pain from the first surgery eased off after a couple of days and eating and drinking became less difficult. George paid us another visit to talk about the second part of my surgery. A permanent facelift. He and Henri pooh-poohed my misgivings about further suffering. 'The worst,' they assured me, 'was over.'

It was about this time that our friend Henri told us that his name was not 'Henri'.

'That's the name that George chose for me. Do I look like the kinda guy that would have a name like "Henri"? No! I'm gonna tell you guys my real name. It's Barney.' He gave us his best Anthony Quinn smile and stretched out his hand. 'Shake hands with Barney. An' don't forget it!'

Barney went with us to the clinic to have the casts removed and was very impressed. At first it was strange looking at and feeling my new nose. It wasn't exactly what Marcel had promised, but if I had my reservations, Eric seemed to be more than happy with the results of his op.

Far too soon I was back at the clinic getting a thorough medical examination before surgery. I could not help wondering why all the fuss if the worst was over.

I regained consciousness at one point and found myself lying in a bed in a ward with the faithful Barney sitting beside me in a chair. Unbelievable pain was raging in and around my head. Pain like I had never experienced before.

Barney was smiling just before I vomited into his lap and went into oblivion again. When I came around the second time, everything had been cleaned up and there was no sign of Barney. The pain was unbearable, any and every movement sending shock waves of agony through my head. I could see French windows at one side of the ward and I began to think about getting up and throwing myself into the street. Luckily, just trying to sit up was out of the question.

I made a supreme effort and managed to press a bell push that was suspended above the bed. Somewhere a bell rang and at the same time a light came on in the middle of the ward. A door opened an inch or so, then a hand appeared and switched the light off. I rang the bell again and the same process was repeated. I gave up on the idea of asking for help and tried to sleep. Only Edgar Allan Poe could do justice to the night of torment that followed. If I had taken the gun that Paul had offered, I might well have used it that night!

Two days later I was released from the clinic and given a huge supply of antibiotics. It was four of this, six of that and two of those. When Eric saw the results he was very impressed.

After a week I returned to the clinic to have some of the stitches removed – there were 140-odd in my face to tackle – and this was a fairly bloody business. The healing was a slow and painful process.

When the swelling and discolouration left my face, Barney took us out to have our hair cut, telling the open-mouthed barber that I had just undergone brain surgery. From there we were taken to a photographer to have photos taken for our new passports. The scars on my face were still vivid and a black pen was used to give me some sideburns and hide the tell-tale marks. The photographs were sent on to George and he turned up at the apartment a couple of weeks later with the 'goods': the new passports, crisp and freshly issued by the Foreign Office, plus a one-way ticket to Sydney for Eric – it had been decided that he would go a couple of weeks before me as a trailblazer.

George also brought more mail from our wives, money and a

Christmas present from Charm – a gold watch. She didn't know it at the time, but the organisation had planned their own present and that was for her and the boys to spend Christmas in Paris.

Three days before Christmas it was time for Eric, now 'Robert Burley', to leave Paris. Eric set off for Sydney and one day later had rung through to say he had arrived safely.

Charm and the boys also arrived safely in Paris for Christmas. Barney brought me the glad tidings and told me that he would take me to meet them as soon as it was dark. Many precautions had to be taken to make certain that they had not been tailed.

Barney finally stopped the car near a cinema and pointed to a car parked nearby. It was the same Ford in which I had made the trip from Antwerp to Paris.

'There's your old lady and your kids,' said my friend reaching out to shake my hand. 'Merry Christmas! I'll see you guys later.'

Charm and the boys had been driven from London to Dover where they had caught the boat to Ostend before driving on to Paris. They were travelling on passports in Charmian's maiden name and did not attract any attention during the festive season.

It was wonderful to see Charmian and the boys again and there was much hugging and kissing. Nicky appeared to be a bit bewildered by his father's 'new look' and had to be convinced that I really was his father, but he was soon over it and chatting excitedly. When he could get a word in, Chris, now close to four years of age, also had much to say once he accepted it was his dad!

We booked into a modest hotel, the Hotel Cécilia at 11 Avenue Mac-Mahon in the centre of Paris, and spent the next five days having family fun. We went to the parks and the zoo. In the evening a babysitter would come in so that Charm and I could enjoy the nightlife of Paris. We did our Christmas shopping and

Charmian bought me a pair of very expensive crocodile shoes 'to travel in'. The shop assistant told me to take shoes that were half a size smaller than I usually took, so that by the time I had worn them in, they would fit more snugly. They felt tight, but I took the advice.

We were having a wonderful time: going to shows and eating at famous restaurants. This was the life, but I knew it could not last forever. Sure enough, just after Christmas, Barney appeared at the hotel with the news that it was time to move on.

Early the next morning, Wednesday 29 December 1965, George arrived with my new passport and the ticket to Sydney. I had some misgivings about the passport as it was quite obviously brand new and didn't have any stamps in it whatsoever.

'How did Mr Furminger get out of England and into France without a single stamp in his passport?' I asked George.

With a butterfly or two in my stomach I said my goodbyes to Charmian and the kids and reassured them that we would all be together again and hopefully soon. Nobody was looking particularly cheerful – least of all Nicky who was coming down with the measles.

George and I set off alone for Orly Airport and the flight to freedom. It was goodbye Europe, hello brave new world. There seemed to be very few people at the airport that day and my misgivings about the passport returned. George shook me warmly by the hand and I went to meet my doom.

To my surprise passport control barely glanced at the passport and handed it back to me wishing me 'Bon Voyage'. I gave George a wave and headed for my flight to Zurich – the first leg of the journey 'down under'.

I travelled as the writer Terence Furminger, a man who had been paid £1,000, about £18,000 today, for the use of his documents. To all intents and purposes Ronald Biggs no longer existed. I had perfected the escape. The only flaw to the plan were the crocodile shoes. They were already starting to pinch and I hadn't even got to the plane.

CHAPTER 8

TIME DOWN UNDER

After a stifling stopover in Darwin to go through immigration formalities, the plane finally touched down at Mascot Airport in Sydney. It was New Year's Eve 1965 and I had been flying for over 33 hours.

I crushed my swollen feet back into my crocodile shoes and limped to the customs area. All that I could think of was that all of my more comfortable shoes were in my suitcase.

'Anything to declare, sir?' said the official in an unmistakably Aussie twang.

'Yes,' I replied. 'These shoes are killing me. Please let me get at some old ones.'

I had already kicked off my crocodile shoes and was eager to make the change. Suddenly there seemed to be something more serious to deal with than my feet. Not only were the shoes made from crocodile skin – which put them in a special class – but even if they did let them into the country there would be import tax to pay.

'If you let me get at a different pair of shoes, you can keep these or throw them away,' I offered. 'I'll never use them again.' The offer was enough. I was cleared through customs, shoes and all.

'Welcome to Australia, Mr Furminger!'

Now I was bouncing along in the old Hush Puppies. I had made it to the promised land. I was in bloody beautiful Australia, a world away from Wandsworth Prison. Catch us if you can!

I took a taxi to Kings Cross and found the Wentworth Hotel where I had arranged to meet Eric.

'Mr Burley checked out two days ago,' the desk clerk apologised, 'and does not seem to have left a forwarding address.'

Worse was to come. The hotel was fully booked for New Year's Eve. With a lot of persistence the staff managed to track down a room at a hotel nearby. I left a message at the Wentworth in case Eric returned.

There was no air conditioning at the hotel other than an old-fashioned fan that whirred above the bed. But the room was clean and spacious – and the fridge was stocked with cold beer. Still doing mental handsprings I opened a 'tube' and guzzled the contents. Happy New Year, Ron!

After a long and much welcome shower I got dressed and decided to look around 'the Cross'.

With my scars and Paris pallor I probably looked a bit weird to the Aussies. I visited a few bars and found out all about 'ponies' and 'schooners' and 'grogged on' into the evening. By midnight I had joined up with some British sailors and their girlfriends, singing and sharing their champagne. We went from 'Waltzing Matilda' to 'We'll Meet Again' and back again.

I slept well and woke up early, the sun shining through the blinds. Today was a day to tour the city and get my bearings. I wanted to see some of the Sydney shoreline and especially Bondi Beach.

I got the first taxi that came along.

'I'd like to hire you for the whole day,' I said. 'Perhaps you could show me all the places of note in Sydney, but especially the beaches.'

'I'm your man,' said the driver enthusiastically. 'The first thing we will do is to turn off this bloody meter. I hope you'll excuse the smell of drink, but I've been on the piss for most of the night.'

There were no worries. I had also been on the piss too so I appreciated the man behind the wheel as my kind of cab driver.

The cabbie was Stan. Born and bred in Sydney, he was a family man with four kids. He had a keen sense of humour and soon we were chatting away like old friends. His passions were horse racing and Chinese food, so we decided that after the tour we would go to a track called Randwick and then on to one of Stan's favourite Chinese restaurants.

I told Stan I was a writer and that I planned to stay in Australia for about six months. As I didn't have a fixed abode, I asked my new friend if I could possibly have my mail sent to his home. He readily agreed.

. 'I'll take you to a pub near the Cross where we cabbies get together. I go there practically every day so everyone knows me and that's where I can hand over anything that comes for you.'

When I got back to my hotel there was a message from Eric with a telephone number where I could contact him. We had a brief but euphoric conversation and an hour later my friend was knocking at the bedroom door.

'Bob Burley?'

'Terry Furminger? You made it, you old bastard!'

When Eric's funds had begun to dwindle he had found himself a room in a boarding house and had even got himself a job as a petrol pump attendant in a service station. Eric was looking a picture of health and already had a deep tan.

It did not take us long to find a furnished house in Botany Bay (where else!) and settle in. Our next-door neighbours were the owners of the house and offered to take care of any chores. We bought an elderly Morris and spent some time tarting it up. Eric, who knew about these things, happily took the engine to pieces. Sunny and happy days; all that was missing were the wives and kids.

Back in the UK, a waxwork of Charlie and I had been unveiled at Madame Tussauds, while on 4 February 1966, Gordon, Roy, Tommy, Hussey and Roger were all being reunited by being transferred to HMP Parkhurst, on the Isle of Wight. Less than two weeks later, on 11 February, John Wheater, the solicitor who had purchased Leatherslade Farm for Bruce, was released from prison – the first person convicted of the Great Train Robbery to be so.

February 1966 also saw the broadcast in West Germany of *Die Gentlemen bitten zur Kasse (The Gentlemen Require Payment),* a three-part mini-series based on the Great Train Robbery. It had a 90 per cent audience share, the highest in German TV history. It was also the most accurate portrayal of the robbery, but nobody at the time noticed. Two months later *The Great St Trinian's Train Robbery* premiered in London and became one of the most popular films of the year. All of which kept the robbery very much in the news.

As cash was getting low at the start of 1966, I wrote to Charmian to send me more. We decided it was unwise to transfer money via the banks so we opted for the old prison trick of smuggling in money and letters. Banknotes or letters would be tightly folded lengthwise until they became narrow strips. The strips are then glued between two pages of a bulky magazine. Charm was no stranger to these little subterfuges and soon enough my Aussie chum, Stan, was calling to say that there was mail for Terence Furminger.

The second time my dutiful wife sent me a copy of *Country Life* it unfortunately caught the attention of Post Office inspectors, who were obviously interested to know why anybody would send money in this fashion. The first hint of trouble was a call from Stan.

Although Stan did not have our address he did have our phone number and that was enough to give Eric the nadgers. It was clear that we would have to 'shoot through' as the Old Bill would certainly be wanting to have a little chat.

Eric had bought the Morris in a false name, so there was no way the car could be traced and we hoped our landlord would not remember the car's registration number. We loaded up the Morris with our worldly possessions and headed out in the direction of Melbourne.

Eric was all for putting as much distance between us and the Sydney 'demons' as possible, so when we got to Melbourne we decided to press on. It was late at night when we arrived at the outskirts of Adelaide, 860 miles from Sydney.

I liked the 'feel' of Adelaide immediately. It had a certain atmosphere of calm, especially a beach area called Grange. We bought a newspaper and scanned a number of ads for room and board. One was for 'Surfside', a guest house owned and run by a young Australian called Gavin Jones. His price was five dollars a week – in advance.

The other guests were a mixed bunch. English, Australian and New Zealanders, mostly young, mostly nice. I have many fond memories of the time spent there.

Eric had kept the name of Bob Burley, but I was now operating as Terence King. We both got jobs without any trouble, Eric as a service-station attendant and me as a joiner in a furniture factory where I sweated for peanuts. But I didn't mind as we were having a ball and as a lifestyle it was certainly more appealing than HM Prison.

Money having changed hands in England, in excess of £55,000 and over a third of what I had netted from the robbery, the organisation was in the process of preparing travel documents and tickets for our families to join us. Charm would be travelling as Mrs Margaret Furminger, which worried Eric somewhat. But she would be bringing some much needed cash, as it was difficult and dangerous to send money out through the post.

Having 'lost' the Morris in a road accident, I bought another car from one of Surfside's boarders. It was a Holden, an Australian car, and in reasonably good condition.

Word reached us in April 1966 that Carol, Eric's wife, had arrived in Sydney with their daughter. Eric drove like a man possessed as he raced to pick them up, clipping hours off the time it had taken us to get from Sydney to Adelaide.

It wasn't long before Eric moved from Surfside into a small flat close to the gas station where he was working. I stayed on and it was about this time that the cook was sacked. A fearless Australian lady took her place by the name of Anne Pitcher. Anne and I became good friends and not long after her arrival at Surfside we took over the management.

Then 21 April 1966 saw the arrest of Jimmy White in Littlestone-on-Sea in Kent after nearly three years on the run. In June, Jimmy was sentenced to 18 years for his part in the train robbery, a fact that reflected just how unjust our 30-year sentences had been.

It was June when I got the news that Charmian was on her way to Australia. For security reasons it had been decided that it would be best for her to arrive in Darwin where I would go to meet her, 1,900 miles north of Adelaide. From an Australian motel guide I found what would be the perfect place for her and the boys to book into, the Koala Motel.

Charmian, Nick and the boys started their journey down under on 10 June by taking a ferry to Ostend and then a car to Brussels. They then flew to Zurich to connect to the BOAC flight on its way to Darwin.

The day that I was due to travel I became sick. I developed a high fever and arrived in Darwin feeling pretty groggy after a four-hour flight. I spoke to a number of taxi drivers but not one of them had ever heard of the Koala Motel. Later I discovered that the motel was still under construction. That's builders for you!

As there was some kind of convention going on in Darwin I considered myself lucky to even find a room. I flopped on to the bed and promptly fell asleep. When I awoke it was already past the time when Charm's plane was due to arrive. I grabbed a super-quick shower, dressed and called a cab to take me to the airport. The passengers were already leaving when I arrived. I looked about for Charmian and the boys, but there was no sign of them. I was thinking that they may have got a taxi and gone off in search of the Koala Motel when I saw her through the glass doors. Charmian was standing by her luggage, talking to an airport official. There was no sign of Nicky or Chris. As I stood undecided what to do, she turned and looked in my direction, but gave no sign that she had seen me. She was looking troubled.

I turned away abruptly, telling myself that she had been detained. I went out of the airport feeling sick and desperate. After what seemed liked hours, a van with some people in it came through a gate at the side of the airport. I was convinced it was Charm on her way to be locked up for the night. Back at my motel I spent a fretful night wondering what the hell I should do. If it had been discovered that Charm was using a phoney passport, she would obviously be charged with something and possibly make a court appearance. Wild ideas were going on inside my head.

Early next morning I called Eric and told him that Charm may have been taken into custody. He was shattered by the news. If Charm had been nicked, the Old Bill would know that we were in Australia. I told Eric I would get back to him later and hung up. I had had an idea. I would call the airline and see what they had to say with regard to the whereabouts of one Mrs Margaret Furminger. I rang and got an efficient-sounding lady on the line.

'Hello, I wonder if you could help me. I'm trying to find out if a Mrs Margaret Furminger arrived on the BOAC flight via Zurich last night?' There was a suspicious pause.

'Hello . . . Yes, Mrs Furminger did arrive and she is staying at the Fannie Bay Hotel.'

I thanked her for her help and hurried out of the post office from where I had made the calls. The woman had sounded a little too ready with the information for my liking and I had a sneaking feeling that she had not been alone.

Over a much-needed beer I studied a map of Darwin and found that the Fannie Bay was situated on the edge of town. I made up my mind to go out to the hotel.

As I got out of the taxi the first thing I saw was the Old Bill! There were plain-clothes coppers everywhere! As I walked down the path to the hotel I passed two beefy chaps with short haircuts. I was doing my best not to turn green. The receptionist smiled.

'Can I help you?'

I noticed other big men with short haircuts standing around.

As soon as I asked for Mrs Furminger, I told myself, these bastards were going to pile on to me. 'Yes,' I found myself saying. 'Could you tell me if there is a Mrs Furminger staying here?'

'She is, sir. She's on the second floor. Would you like me to call her for you?'

Nobody moved and a few brief moments later there was Charmian and the boys hurtling down the stairs and into my outstretched arms.

We hugged and kissed and cried with happiness, oblivious to the onlookers. Nicky and Chris were tugging at me for my attention, wanting to show me the drawings they had done on the flight.

I was right about the men with the short haircuts. Darwin was hosting a major convention for senior policemen, and that was the reason all the hotels were full. When I had seen Charmian 'look through me' she had been preoccupied with the fact that there was nowhere for her and the kids to stay and there had been talk that she would have to spend the night in the local police station! A vacancy at the Fannie Bay Hotel was found at the last minute.

It was 14 June and it was fabulous being together again, all the agony of the previous hours now forgotten. We went to the beach. I swam and played with the kids, chasing them and giving them 'bear hugs'. Back at the hotel I phoned Adelaide and brought Eric up to date with the glad tidings.

Charmian had arrived with a little over £7,000 (about £130,000 today). After lunch we went to a number of banks and changed a couple of thousand pounds into Australian dollars and then went shopping for a car. We had decided that we would buy a station wagon and make a slow overland trip down to Adelaide via the Gold Coast. It would be our first holiday since we went to Hastings five years earlier.

It did not take us long to choose a vehicle. A brand new, white, Holden station wagon took our fancy. As I didn't know how to drive a car we went for a test drive with Charmian at the wheel. We would take it. It came out about A$3,000 (about £25,000 today) including the tax and insurance. We loaded up with an array of stuff we thought we might need: blankets, jerry cans, water bottles, a cool box and so on. Then we went back to the hotel and picked up the luggage.

We drove out as evening approached, the sky streaked dramatically with red and gold. We stayed close to Darwin on the first night but the first big dot on the map was to be our target for day two. It was a place called Daly Waters.

As it got dark on our first full day behind the wheel we calculated that we must be somewhere near Daly Waters in the Northern Territory. We stopped where there was some light and sound coming from a bar of some kind. I went to investigate. The people in the bar stopped talking as I entered.

'Could you tell me where I might find the Daly Waters Hotel?' I asked politely.

The barmaid looked me over. 'You're in it, mate.'

Early next morning we were on the highway and the sun was shining fit to bust. The station wagon had an automatic transmission so once we were out in the middle of nowhere I had my turn at the wheel. Zipping along Highway 1 – nothing to it – Charm gently nagging, the kids loving it every bit as I was. It was hot and it was dusty, but we didn't mind as we were having the time of our lives, marvelling at the flocks of coloured birds, the billabongs, the 'roos and the emus.

We trekked on across the Northern Territory on Highway 87 and everywhere we stopped, Charm turned heads with her Pommy accent and beehive hairdo.

Looking at a map I discovered that our route east would take us close to Mount Isa, a copper mining town where I knew a couple of friends from Adelaide had gone to work. On the spur of the moment I suggested we should make a bit of a detour and give my chums a surprise.

It was early afternoon when we drove into Mount Isa. After we had booked into a motel, I left Charm with the kids and went off in search of my friends. I had no trouble locating the mine where they had told me they were working, but I got little or no help from the personnel department.

The department that day consisted of one bloke who was sitting behind a desk writing. He hardly looked up from what he was doing when I entered his office.

'We don't give out information about our workers,' the man said flatly.

'But I'm a friend,' I insisted.

'So you might be,' said the man, still writing. 'On the other hand, you could be a debt collector or a copper. Sorry, mate, can't help.'

'Thanks very much! But if by any chance you should see either of my pals, please tell them that Terry King is at the Paramount?'

The man showed no sign that he had heard me or cared, so it was a pleasant surprise when later that evening Mel Kidd and Dave Stone showed up.

Several years later, when I was hiding from the police in Melbourne, I considered making my way to Mount Isa. By then, the policy at the mine rather appealed!

From Mount Isa we headed across to Cairns on the Great Barrier Reef. We stayed a couple of days, going off on tours in the glass-bottomed boats, oohing and aahing at the coral formations and the brightly coloured fish. The kids played happily on the beaches, already tanned and glowing with good health. It was a big improvement on Bognor.

Somewhat reluctantly, we left Cairns and began the long trip south to Adelaide. We took the highway along the coast, making overnight stops in Townsville and Mackay, with an extended stopover in Rockhampton.

We continued our adventurous journey down the coast to Sydney, where we stayed the best part of a week, then across country to Adelaide via Melbourne. The trip had taken us just over a month – long enough for Charmian to get pregnant!

We had a jubilant reunion with Eric and Carol, the kids resuming the brief friendship they had with Kim in the UK. One big happy family.

In Adelaide, we rented a spacious house in an area called Glenelg and spent nearly all our remaining cash furnishing the place. Wall to wall carpets, 'Danish' furniture and so forth.

We were following the news from England, where the football team was winning the World Cup. This at least gave us some bragging rights over the Australians!

It had been suggested that Charmian could take part in the activities at the guest house. Her job was to serve food to the guests and clear the tables, not ideal work for somebody in her condition, yet even despite the heat she managed to battle through until she was nearly seven months pregnant. But the guest house with or without Charm was not paying, so reluctantly I passed on my share of the business to Anne and found a job as a carpenter.

The kids had taken to their new lifestyle like fish to water and soon made friends with other children in the neighbourhood. Nicky was six years old at the time and had accepted his new surname, King, without question. We had told him that I was on secret government work and it was necessary to live with a different name. He was a bright little chap and caught on quickly.

Life was almost a bowl of cherries. With plenty of overtime I was earning good wages, setting money aside for Charmian's forthcoming confinement. At weekends we would go with the 'Burleys' to one of the many beaches in the area or to 'hotels', as the pubs were called, and grog on while the kids ran wild.

In Britain, prison breaks were in the news again after the Russian spy, George Blake, escaped from Wormwood Scrubs. He was next seen in Moscow.

Farley Paul, our third son, was born in Glenelg Community Hospital on 21 April 1967, Paul being in honour of Mr Seabourne without whom there would have been no Farley. After a few drinks with the lads to 'wet the baby's head', I went to the hospital to visit my wife and the latest addition to the Biggs family. Charm was sharing a room with another lady who had also given birth. When I arrived, the other happy father was in the room, gazing proudly at his handiwork cradled in his wife's arms.

'Terry King,' I said warmly, extending my hand to the fellow, 'Congratulations!'

Mrs Charmian 'Furminger' was quick to cover my blunder. 'You and your silly jokes, Terry! Why don't you tell the gentleman your proper name?' I laughed it off, but I saw how easy it was to slip up using an alias. I needed to be more careful.

Farl was a great kid. He rarely cried or made a fuss. We all loved him! But not long after Charm left the hospital we received a bit of a blow. It came in the form of an anonymous letter. The police, it said in poor handwriting, were aware that I was in Australia. It was imperative that we should move out of Adelaide as fast as possible and change our names again. It was something of a mystery because we thought the only people who knew our address were immediate friends. I was all for ignoring the letter, but Charmian didn't want to take the chance. We discussed the matter with Eric and Carol. Charmian was right they said, we had to 'shoot through'.

Heartbreaking though it was, I went out and sold the station wagon for just A$900. At a different used car dealer, I bought a furniture truck for A$600 that looked as if it had been assembled soon after the discovery of Australia. But it suited my purpose and it left me with $300 for gas and other expenses. Soon after dark, Eric backed the truck into my garden. Then, as silently as possible, so as not to alert the neighbours, we loaded the truck with our belongings and stole off into the night and out of Adelaide.

Next morning, Eric and I arrived on the outskirts of Melbourne. Eric was just about wrecked after the 500-mile drive. We found a warehouse where, at an exorbitant price, I was able to leave the furniture. After a meal and a wash and brush-up, we set about finding new accommodation for my family.

In the newspaper I saw something I fancied. It was a two-bedroomed house with a 'beautiful garden' and a telephone. I rang a number and made an appointment with the estate agent.

I introduced myself as Terence Cook, giving my profession as an architect. My wife and children, I said, were on their way to Australia from England and I was anxious to find somewhere nice and comfortable for them. I was very sorry, but I couldn't provide any references because I had only just arrived myself. The estate agent was uncertain, but as I looked like an honest person he didn't think that would be a problem. He picked up a pen and asked, 'What is your full name?'

'Terence King,' I replied.

The man looked up in surprise. 'I thought you said your name was Cook?'

'I'm sorry,' I stumbled, 'I have a double-barrelled name, it's King-Cook. For practical purposes I mostly call myself Cook.' Mistake number two, but luckily the agent kept writing and an appointment was made to see the house in Hibiscus Road, Blackburn.

A pleasant Australian couple, Bert and Joan Shepherd, were the owners of the house. I told them much the same story as I had told the estate agent and was accepted as the new tenant.

I suggested to Eric that we pass the night in a cheap hotel, but he was all for getting back to Adelaide without a rest. We made better speed with the van now that it was unloaded.

Back in Adelaide we both slept through the rest of the day at Eric's flat. That same evening we were going to pick up the rest of our goods from the house at Glenelg and repeat the performance. And, after another 500 bone-shaking miles in the 'beast', with Charmian, Carol and the kids following in Eric's car, we trundled into Melbourne a second time.

Our new landlady had left the house spick and span and, by the time we got the furniture arranged, our new home looked very cosy. We had told the older boys that they were going to have a new surname, Cook. The next day, leaving Charm with the children, including Farley who was barely three weeks old, I returned to Adelaide with Eric and Carol and took the truck back to the dealer and swapped it for an automatic Ford Falcon, whose flying days were evidently long past. But somehow I got it – and myself – back to Melbourne.

As 'Charmian' was such an unusual name and we wanted to break off as many ties as possible with Adelaide, it was decided that Charm would change her name to Sharon. So we became known as Terry and Sharon Cook. We made friends with some of our neighbours. Lawrie and Rhona Black, who lived next door, were particularly friendly and helpful – always ready to babysit if we wanted to go out for the evening. The neighbours on the other side of our house were quite the opposite. They showed a hostile attitude to the 'bloody poms' who had moved in next to them, a hostility they would continue long after I had gone. But we took the good and the bad in our stride. We had settled in nicely. The kids were in a school just around the corner and I had found a job as a carpenter. We acquired a friendly yellow Labrador bitch, named Sadie, and it looked as if we were set to live happily ever after. As time went on we exchanged the much-maligned Falcon for a smart green Holden.

To help out with the housekeeping Charmian took on evening work, which varied from packing biscuits at the Brockhoff Biscuits factory to packing tissues at Bowater-Scott. She was none too keen on the work, but I think she liked the chance to have a natter with other women.

For Christmas 1967 we drove down to Adelaide to spend the holidays with Eric, Carol and Anne. A good time was had by all, but perhaps foolishly we returned the following year for New Year when a surprise was awaiting us. Eric's mate Alfie Gerard was also paying a visit, the same one who along with Freddie Foreman had taken Eric and me off Paul's hands when we escaped. Ronnie Everett and Jerry Callaghan who had fled Britain after a run-in with the police accompanied Alfie.

Much to Charm's distress, I changed my job on a number of occasions. I had a stint as a maintenance carpenter at the television studios of Channel Nine. It was our economic situation that finally dragged me away from Channel Nine where there was rarely any overtime to be had. I found myself another job at Associated Insulation, this time erecting office partitions. The pay was better and the hours longer. Another year slipped by.

During the time we had been in Australia, we had seen a number of news items regarding the gang. In September 1966, Buster Edwards had given himself up to the police and been sentenced to 15 years' imprisonment, half what we had received two years earlier, but somehow Buster had persuaded judge and jury that while he was 'in the hierarchy' he was 'not one of the leading planners' of the Great Train Robbery. Mighty Paul Seabourne, who had been given four and a half years for getting us out of Wandsworth, didn't stay free for long after his release. He went back with ten years for holding up an armoured truck. And about the same time, 'Gentleman' George, the Mr Fixit who had made all our arrangements, was given a long stretch for a piece of business that had gone badly wrong. Then, after we had spent a happy Christmas and New Year, we heard the news that Charlie Wilson had been recaptured in Canada by Tommy Butler supported by the Mounties. That was 25 January 1968. Butler apparently now believed that Bruce was back in the UK, but like Charlie he was somewhere in Canada.

As 1968 got under way, I was working on suspended ceilings at an immense shopping centre that was under construction. One morning, I noticed two men carrying a large sheet of glass. The fellow at the back looked a lot like my good friend, Mike Haynes. I got down from the scaffold where I had been working and went to get a better look. Sure enough, it was Mike! I couldn't believe it. I sneaked up behind him, grabbed his arm and said, 'You're nicked, Haynes!'

We were both completely knocked out by our chance encounter. Mike and Jess and their two children, Tracy and John, had emigrated to Australia only a short time before. During the lunch break we got together, still 'mind-boggled' by our encounter. That evening, we all got together at Hibiscus Road – there was a lot of drinking to do and the girls had plenty to talk about! It turned out that the Hayneses lived not very far from our house, on Latimer Street in Noble Park, so we got together quite frequently, becoming better friends than ever.

There was more bad news to come. On 8 November 1968, Bruce was caught in Torquay. As in my case, Bruce's fingerprints had been found on the Monopoly board and a bottle of tomato ketchup. He pleaded guilty on the understanding that Frances and Nick would not be prosecuted and in January 1969 received a sentence of 25 years. Bruce's wife Frances had her story published in the *Sunday Mirror* in London and in *Stern* in Germany, and subsequently in March 1968 over four consecutive weeks in an Australian women's magazine.

The magazine, *Woman's Weekly,* had been delivered to our home with the newspaper and Nicky was leafing through the pages.

'Look, Mum,' he said. 'Here's a picture of Dad!'

Charm hastily relieved Nick of the magazine, telling him that it was just somebody who looked like me. But she was worried – and so was I when I got home from work and saw the article.

A bright young girl called Marjorie, who had been a guest at Surfside, also saw the story and thought that Terry King looked a lot like the photograph of one of the wanted men. She showed it to Anne Pitcher's son-in-law, Max Philips, who agreed there was a strong resemblance. Max was a newscaster with a small radio station near Perth and decided to announce his suspicions over the air, which resulted in a visit from the police who were more than interested in hearing what Philips could tell them about Mr King.

While we had been doing our thing in Melbourne, Eric had gone into business with Alfie and his chums. They had set up a trucking company in Adelaide and were doing nicely. The article in the *Woman's Weekly* didn't please them even though it said: 'At the time of writing Biggs is still at large. He is believed to have been narrowly missed by the police in Belgium last month at a place where Reynolds stayed while on the run.'

Without knowing that our clever little guest at Surfside had recognised me, they assumed that somebody would. It was just a question of time, they said, before the Old Bill would find out that I was in Australia. Eric and his friends – who also had good reasons to avoid contact with the police – decided that it would be prudent to abandon everything and shoot through again, advising us to do the same. Even though we knew that other people in the neighbourhood would see the article I was for riding out the storm. The months crept by and we started to relax again. Eric and friends first tried Melbourne, against our wishes, and then moved on to Sydney.

I changed my job again. Still in the office partitions and suspended ceilings business, but this time as a foreman, cracking the whip over a fairly motley crew of 30 carpenters and labourers. I tried to be a good foreman. I didn't dock anyone's time for being late or absent if they had an excuse. I had been one of these poor buggers myself once.

Charmian was still working at the Bowater-Scott factory and we were becoming a bit like ships in the night as with only one car I would return home just in time for Charmian to shoot off for her night shift, having already prepared dinner for me and the kids and prepared Farley for bed.

In February 1969 we did treat ourselves to a night out and went off to see a new film. *Robbery* was a heavily fictionalised account of the train robbery with Stanley Baker playing a character based on Bruce. Luckily nobody was obviously me.

In July 1969 I nearly managed to kill myself and end the Biggs story early. I had had a bit of a tiff with Charm and had stormed off in the car having had a drink or two too many. I managed to total the car by running it into a street light and also did a good job on both my jaw and teeth, which would trouble me for the rest of my life. Luckily I managed to stagger away from the scene of the crash before the police turned up, as I still had no licence or papers.

One October evening I received a telephone call from a friend who was aware of my true identity. He asked if I had seen the six o'clock news. I told him I had arrived home too late to catch the headlines.

'Make sure you see the nine o'clock edition,' he said seriously, 'it concerns you – and it is not good.' I got the boys to bed before nine and sat on the edge of a chair to watch.

Earlier that day, 16 October, a Reuters correspondent named Reeves had dropped in at Melbourne Police headquarters in Russell Street snooping around for news. He happened to see a memo to the effect that it was suspected that I was living in Melbourne with my wife and children. Mr Reeves sent out this little gem of information as a news item and in no time the rest of the media picked it up.

Channel Nine showed mugshots of Eric and me, together with our general description and the information that the police believed I was working as a carpenter in Western Australia. The train robbery story was rehashed and the public was invited to contact the police in the event of having any information that might lead to our capture. This time, the shit had well and truly hit the fan.

Charmian paled when I told her the bad news. 'What are we going to do?' she asked. Once again I was all for 'sweating it out'. I was sick of running. I even considered giving myself up. But Charmian wouldn't hear of it.

Early the next morning, a Friday, Charmian backed the car out of the garage and drove to our local newsagent. She bought both Melbourne dailies and they told her more than she or I needed to know. Our story was all there including the name and ages of the kids, and that included Farley. Charmian drove straight back to Hibiscus Road.

I grabbed my bag, kissed the kids and jumped into the passenger seat of the Holden. Our lovely little boys were still sound asleep when we left. I hoped and prayed that I would be able to come back to them. We had a plan. Charmian would drive me to a motel on the outskirts of the city. There I would wait to see if the situation got any worse. In the event of little or no reaction to the news, we would meet at eight o'clock at a certain Chinese restaurant.

Charmian drove me to the Alexander Motel in an area called Essendon, not far from the airport where I had been working until the previous evening. I kissed my tearful wife goodbye and watched her drive off, then turned and booked in at the motel under the name of Arthur Robert Carson.

In her heart Charmian knew it would probably be only a matter of time until the police found the house, but she decided to carry on as if everything was normal. Back at Hibiscus Road she got the kids washed and dressed and dropped Nicky and Chris off at Blackburn North School. She then drove to the hairdresser with Farley for her normal Friday appointment. If the staff had seen anything in the morning papers, they did not say anything.

Charmian returned to the house, but there was still no sign of the police so she went and picked the kids up from school and just as I had, she picked up a copy of the evening paper. The news was more or less a repeat of what had already been published and added nothing to what we already knew.

Charmian left the kids at home and drove to the nearest public phone to call me. She was put through to 'Mr Carson' and updated me on the lack of police activity or any activity, for that matter. A case of no news is good news so we planned to meet at the restaurant at eight o'clock as planned.

At around 7.15, Charmian set out for the Chinese restaurant. She was going to bring me a few more shirts, my electric razor, that I had forgotten in the rush, and some family photos. As she turned right off Hibiscus Road, all hell broke loose and about a dozen police cars converged on her from every direction. The doors of the car were pulled open and four armed officers, guns at the ready, piled in. They wanted me 'dead or alive', they said. Charm got cross at the sight of the firearms. 'My husband isn't here,' she told them.

After some discussion, Charmian was allowed to return to the house to check on the children who were to be looked after by our neighbour. She was then taken first to Russell Street Police headquarters, Melbourne's equivalent of Scotland Yard for the Victoria Police, and then to 43 McKenzie Street, the headquarters of the then Commonwealth Police, Australia's equivalent of the FBI.

Ignorance being bliss, at the motel I emptied out my case and packed it with the clothes and personal items I might most need. I planned to leave the motel when it was dark and keep my appointment with Charmian at the Chinese restaurant. I didn't plan to return, and even left an unpaid bill of about £3 and a couple of suits. I wanted to travel light. When there was no sign of Charm by nine o'clock I guessed that she had been taken into custody.

I thought of turning up on Mike Haynes's doorstep, but dismissed the idea instantly: the Old Bill was probably grilling him at that very moment. Finally I decided to grab a cab and pay a visit to the friend who had tipped me off the night before. He was not expecting me. In fact he got a bit of a fright when I tapped on his bedroom window. But he was more than ready to help and two days later I found myself in a cosy little holiday home called Blue Waters, high up in the Dandenong Mountains that flank one side of Melbourne.

I was provided with plenty of food, magazines and a radio. Much to my joy, I heard that Charmian had been released after spending the weekend in custody and reunited with the children.

My friend came to visit with further good news. Charmian had sold her story to the Packer group of newspapers for A$65,000 (over £500,000 today), although the tax man was going to grab $40,000 of that, leaving Charm with just A$25,000 (still about £200,000 today). In her story Charmian said that before she arrived in Australia she had received a postcard from me that simply said: 'The weather is glorious, the opportunities are marvellous and the natives are friendly.' It became one of the top ten most popular quotes in Australia in 1969.

The not so good news was that the hunt was very much on. Victorian Chief Superintendent Jim Milner was in charge of the operation. He made frequent statements to the public – and me – via radio and television, telling us what moves were being made to 'catch the train robber'. Railway stations and airports were under close watch. Roadblocks had been set up. 'Biggs was desperate and without friends,' according to Mr Milner, who promised that I would be locked up 'within 24 hours'. Fresh evidence was presented to the news-hungry press corps, including the clothing I had left behind at the motel.

A few days later my favourite cop came on the radio and telly to say that the search was going to swing in the direction of the

Dandenong Mountains, the 'perfect place' for someone to hide. My pal had also heard Milner's pronouncement and soon showed up at my little hideaway. I would have to find another refuge.

It was a Sunday evening when I knocked on Mike Haynes's door.

'Christ Almighty!' exclaimed my old mate, 'I thought it was the law! Come in!' They had kept up with the news and thought that the Old Bill would be paying them a visit any moment. It would be very risky for me to stay with them. But they were friendly with a young English couple whom Mike thought could put me up for a week or two.

The couple, George and Janet, agreed to let me stay until the heat was off and that evening, when it was dark, I walked to my new digs. My hosts were quite nervous about their lodger but, said George, they were taking the chance because I was Mike's friend. Janet prepared the spare room, hoping I would be comfortable, and then showed me where everything was that I might need. They both had jobs and would be out of the house all day. I would have to fend for myself.

The 'demons' were still very active in the area. Through the net curtains I could see patrol cars cruising around the neighbourhood. Then, much to my delight, a couple of desperados escaped from Pentridge, Melbourne's grim old jail, and the police turned their attention to their capture.

Eric Flower, alias Bob Burley, was arrested in Sydney on 24 October, one week after I had gone to ground. Days later, Alfie Gerard's friends met a similar fate, and soon it was Alfie's turn. A neighbour had spotted him sunbathing in a back garden. The good lady, mistaking Alfie for me, phoned the cops and 'Biggs' was pounced on.

I also learnt that Charm and I had made the cover of *Private Eye,* a magazine I always enjoyed when I could get it.

Eric, Alfie and his friends having been arrested were all extradited back to Britain in mid-December. Eric was sent back to Wandsworth to finish his 12 years, while the other three stood trial for assault.

As the weeks passed, the police pressure seemed to ease off. As the police had not visited the Hayneses, we decided that it would be safe for me to move in with them. There was more room, a garden that wasn't overlooked, and I would be with people whom I considered to be 'family'. My plan at that time was to lie low for a few months then make my way up north.

Although Charm had been charged with illegally entering Australia, she was still permitted to go about her business and was being well advised by lawyers hired by the Packer group. The police kept watch on her, following her wherever she went, and a squad car could always be seen close to the house. But, with the help of friends, we managed to communicate, although it was to be nearly three months before we could physically meet, and then at first it was just for one hour. I was thinking particularly of Charmian and the kids at Christmas. Although there was a fine 'Christmas spirit' at the Hayneses and an abundance of everything, it was difficult to be 'merry'. New Year's Eve was even less jolly as my friends went off to spend the evening with Charmian. At midnight I raised a glass of champagne to absent friends and loved ones, listening to the neighbours singing 'Auld Lang Syne'.

It was during this period that Mike very generously offered me his passport. That literally opened new horizons. Mike and I were quite similar in general appearance and height; the only real difference was the colour of our eyes, his being brown and mine blue. But it was an offer I couldn't refuse.

I was again in a position to go anywhere in the world. But where? Mike, Jess and I discussed the subject for hours. I would have to think about a suitable disguise if I was hoping to get out of the country. I had gained quite a bit of weight since I had gone to ground so we decided that I would become a fatty. From then on, much to Mike's delight, we ate pasta practically every day.

I was still in a dither about where to go until one evening Jess arrived home with a pile of travel brochures. I picked up the one that was on top of the pile. It was from VARIG Airlines and showed the beautiful Bay of Guanabara and Sugarloaf Mountain in Rio. 'I want to go there,' I said without missing a beat.

All three of us had precious little knowledge about Rio, Brazil or South America. All we knew was what we had learned from the *Mission Impossible* television series: cruel dictators, corrupt officials and incompetent soldiers.

I did, however, know their music, and in Paris, Barney had introduced me to the wonders of bossa nova and in particular a man called Tom Jobim.

A map was produced to work out the best way to get to Rio. A boat to Panama, then a plane 'flying down to Rio' – Mike made it sound so easy.

I needed a haircut and Mike, who had been in the army and had a bit of experience, offered to do the honours. Soon I was sporting a 'short back and sides'.

Returning to the passport, I found – as good luck would have it – that Mike's photograph was quite loose and easy to remove. The difficult thing was going to be reproducing the embossed Foreign Office stamp which in those days appeared on the bottom right-hand corner of the picture.

That evening, under the cover of darkness, Mike and I went to a shopping mall where I made a couple of dozen passport pictures. The next morning, at my instigation and expense, the Haynes family went off camping for the weekend. I needed to be alone to work on the passport. Having got Mike to stock the refrigerator with beer, I got to work as soon as they were gone. I had never considered taking up forgery, but by Sunday afternoon I was satisfied with my labours. The new Michael John Haynes had a passport. When Mike saw the result he was very impressed. It was bloody near perfect.

Charmian had been able to lay her hands on some cash that she was to receive for the story, but not too much or it would have raised suspicion. She had been told of Operation Rio and managed to get $2,000 (about £17,000 today) to me without too much trouble. With part of the money Jess went to a travel agency and booked a sea passage to Panama in Mike's name. I would be sailing on the RHMS *Ellinis*, a Greek liner of the Chandris Line, in less than a week.

During my time with Mike and Jess I had not totally wasted my time, and by putting pen to paper I hoped that I could leave Charmian with a little insurance policy. Over what would be 77 typed pages, I told my story to date. Charm was to hang on to the manuscript, complete with my fingerprints and signature, and sell it to the highest bidder once I was safely away.

CHAPTER 9

PACIFICS: MELBOURNE TO RIO

As I had left most of my clothes at the hotel, I had precious little to put in the much-travelled suitcase which Mike produced for the trip. My bits and pieces just about covered the bottom of the case but little else. Mike threw in a sleeping bag and the old clothing that he and Jess no longer needed. Thinking that it might come in handy, I packed the magnifying glass which I had used to work on the passport. One of the locks on the case was broken, so we secured it with a piece of cord on one side. Not exactly what the well-dressed traveller would use, but functional.

When the day arrived to embark aboard the *Ellinis* – 5 February 1970 – both Mike and I were more than a little apprehensive. Fortunately, the ship was to sail in the evening so we would be able to leave the house under cover of dark. The plan was for Mike to go through passport control as the passenger, while Jess and I went aboard as visitors to see him off. I had stuck Mike's picture lightly back into his passport. Once we were all on board, I would take the ticket and passport, swap the photographs and assume my new identity. We opened a bottle of brandy 'to calm the old nerves', as Mike put it. I had a last get-together with Charmian to say goodbye. She was enthusiastic about the plan, but sad to see me go. It had been nearly four agonising months since the police had raided the house.

Charmian and I had no idea when we would meet again. We kissed and hugged each other. It would be four years almost to the day when I was next to see her and that was under very different circumstances.

Everything went according to plan on the day. Mike had no trouble going through passport control. Wearing horn-rimmed glasses and a check cap I went up the gangplank of the *Ellinis* with Jess steadying herself on my arm. We met Mike on deck, all of us nervous but flushed with success and brandy. I took the ticket and passport from Mike and went off to find the cabin I would be sharing with three other people. As luck would have it, it was empty. I locked myself in the toilet and swapped the photographs in the passport, taking particular care in how I stuck down my photo as I didn't want anyone to see the pencil marks on the reverse side. This was in the days when there was no plastic film over the photo, and I flushed the torn-up pieces of Mike's picture down the toilet and rejoined my friends on deck.

The Hayneses could not stay very long. They had made plans with Charmian to see The Modern Jazz Quartet and didn't want to miss the concert or the alibi. We said our fond farewells.

I watched and waved my friends ashore, then mingled with the other passengers on deck. They were a mixed bunch as the *Ellinis* was bound for Southampton via Sydney, Auckland, Tahiti and the Panama Canal. The ship's siren blew and a general call went up for visitors to go ashore. Families and friends left the ship and gathered on the quay calling last-minute messages to departing loved ones.

My cabin mates were a lot younger than me: two Aussie university graduates, Bill and Greg, on their way to Canada, and Peter, a wiry Italian-Yugoslav, also Canada-bound. Greg produced some 'coldies' and opened up the conversation. He was more talkative and humorous than his friend. Peter was quite a card and as friendly as only the Italians can be. He had been working as a labourer in Australia.

Soon we were under way and the boat came to life; the evening meal was served and the bar was open. We opted for a liquid dinner and grogged on into the night, finding out about each other. After half a dozen tubes we were all getting along like long-established chinas, and before the evening was over, Greg paid me the highest compliment that any Australian can pay an Englishman: 'You're not a bad bloke – for a Pommy.'

(I would be unaware for some time that on 28 February, Jack Mills, the driver of the train, had succumbed to lymphatic leukaemia. As the coroner was to make very clear, his death was in no way a result of what happened at the robbery despite what people continue to portray. Just two year later, on 6 January 1972, David Whitby, who had been in charge of the train along with Mills, collapsed and died of a heart attack at his house in Crewe. He was just 34, and he had become the forgotten man of the robbery.)

I rose early the next morning and went on deck – I had to meet the public sometime. Other early risers smiled and said good morning; the disguise seemed to be working. A bell sounded which announced breakfast.

We were steaming towards Sydney, the first stop on the voyage. Greg and Bill were full of plans to go ashore and have a last gut-full of fair dinkum Australian piss. But I feigned sickness, making appropriately nauseating sounds in the bathroom.

Well sloshed, my cabin mates returned to the ship just before we were due to sail. When I heard the blast on the ship's horn advising visitors to leave, I started to feel 'much better'.

Crowds of people were on deck as the *Ellinis* slowly drew away from the quay. Other passengers had joined the ship in Sydney and there was a similar scene to the one in Melbourne, with well-wishers waving and shouting from the dock.

There was a certain feeling of excitement in the warm summer evening air now that we were leaving Australia and New Zealand would be our next stop. A sing-song started as we passed beneath Sydney Harbour Bridge and it was not long until it seemed that the whole ship was singing 'Waltzing Matilda', roaring out the words of the Australian 'national anthem'. I couldn't sing. I had a problem with a lump in my throat. I had a feeling that I would never see this lovely promised land again – and I was going to miss it. The date was 7 February 1970.

I was not keen to go ashore in New Zealand either. It was still too close to Australia for comfort. But my cabin mates and others were going off to do a bit of rubbernecking and I was obliged to join them. It was a sunny afternoon, so I was able to put on a pair of shades for the outing.

That evening, so that the people could get to know each other for the Pacific crossing, the official 'captain's party' was held with everyone turning out in their crumpled finery. I stood at the side of the dance floor with Greg and Co., swigging Greek plonk from a paper cup, checking out the Sheilas. Greg summed the ladies up as 'a fuckin' grim lookin' bunch', but an unaccompanied girl in a white dress caught my eye. Unmistakably English, almost prim, not unlike a young Joyce Grenfell. Her name was Molly Evans. When I asked her to dance, she warned me that she was not a very good dancer. She was not much of a drinker either and, a little later, she warned me again; she was not very good in bed.

A day or so later, sunbathing with Molly after a swim, she surprised me by whispering in my ear: 'I know who you are!'

Warning bells were clanging.

'Really? Do tell me, who am I?'

'You're Bruce Reynolds!'

'Bruce Reynolds! I think you'll find he's in jail for the train robbery.'

'Well,' Molly insisted, 'if you're not Reynolds – you're Charlie Wilson!'

'And if I'm not Charlie Wilson, I must be Ronnie Biggs?'

'Yes! That's who you are!' she said as her eyes brightened. 'But don't worry, I won't tell anyone, Mike – and I'll help you if you need money or anything.'

Before I had gone aboard the *Ellinis*, I had imagined that my chief obstacle would be the Master at Arms. I had visualised an unpleasant snooper, in all probability an ex-detective, who would recognise me instantly from wanted notices. I needn't have worried, there wasn't a nicer person on ship. He was an easy-going young Dutchman, courteous and friendly, who occasionally joined us for our informal parties in the cabin prior to dinner.

It was just before dawn when the ship docked in rainswept Tahiti. The Aussies and I felt that we needed more sleep. Later Molly and I mooched around the island in the rain until we got bored and went back to the ship early for afternoon tea.

The voyage progressed. We were on our way to Panama where I would be saying goodbye to my new friends. Most were going on to the US, Canada and England, but there were two I knew who would be leaving the boat in Panama: Frank, the Spaniard who shared my table, and an attractive but rather serious German girl, named Rosie, whom Frank had befriended. They were en route to Caracas.

In October 2010, the *Mail on Sunday* published a couple of photos of me on the cruise. One photo showed me, Bill, Molly, Greg and Peter enjoying a drink, and another of Molly and me getting some food. While the *Mail* had the year right, it being 1970, they did not spot the subtlety of my disguise of piling on the pounds. Instead they decided my beaming round face and trendy sideboards were 'swollen from plastic surgery'. I know the surgery in Paris was primitive, but I think after four years the swelling might have gone!

Just before we docked in Panama, immigration officials came on board to interview travellers about to disembark. Offering up a silent prayer, I presented my passport. There was a problem: I didn't have a visa to land in Panama. I explained my reason for leaving the ship and said that I was unaware that I needed a visa 'just to pass through'. I was granted a stay of seven days but was obliged to pay a US$200 bond, about $1,500 today, which would be refunded when I could show my airline ticket out of Panama.

Two hundred dollars was about all the money I had and I needed that to cover the cost of a flight. The official was adamant; he would have his bond. I was wondering how I was going to manage when there was an announcement over the Tannoy that Michael Haynes was wanted in the Purser's office. I dragged my feet. Had somebody recognised me? Was I about to be arrested, as Dr Crippen had been in 1910? There was a message, but it was from Charmian who had managed to radio $200 to the *Ellinis* and which was now at my disposal.

I picked up my suitcase and prepared to leave the ship. It was early evening and many passengers were going ashore just for a look around. Molly, Greg and Bill went ashore with me. After I had booked in to a ramshackle hotel and unburdened myself of my equally ramshackle suitcase, we went off to a bar for a few last jars together.

After handshakes and back-slapping, my Aussie friends returned to the ship to give Molly and me a last chance to be alone. During those last few weeks, Molly was feeling less and less like returning to the love of her life in the UK. She fancied the idea of going on to Rio with me.

In spite of Molly's insistence to join me on my South American adventure, I managed to get her back to the ship before it sailed. She was young and pretty, I told her. She should go back to England, marry her man and settle down to the kind of life that she was obviously cut out for.

Like many of the people I have met on my journeys, I often wonder whatever happened to Molly. Jack Slipper said that he did track her down and interview her in South London after my arrest in Rio. He described her as 'a very smart, respectable woman in her thirties'. She did not hide from Slipper that we had become close.

Molly and all the friends I had made on the crossing gathered at the stern of the liner, waving and shouting their goodbyes as the *Ellinis* slowly inched away. The Pommy contingent was singing, 'Maybe It's Because "He's" a Londoner'. The quay was deserted and suddenly I felt very alone.

The next morning I met Frank and Rosie at the KLM office where they were in the process of arranging their flight to Caracas. Frank invited me to stop off at Caracas on the way to Rio and spend a week or two with him and his brother. So the ticket I bought was for Caracas, Rio and Montevideo, the latter to serve as a red herring if and when the police traced me to the *Ellinis* and as far as Panama.

With ticket in hand, I went to the immigration office to collect the 200 bucks that I had left as a bond. The agent wished me good luck on my trip south.

One footnote to the *Ellinis*. Years later I discovered that one David Bowie had written the track 'Aladdin Sane' while travelling on the ship from New York to the UK in December 1972, two years after I had been on board. He credits it as much on the album. Perhaps I was 'a lad insane'.

When I arrived at Caracas Airport, the first thing I noticed was a lot of policemen. Many of them were wearing plain clothes, but it wasn't difficult to pick them out. However, I went through customs and the passport checkpoint without a hitch and joined Frank and Rosie, who, having arrived a couple of days earlier, were there to meet me. I found out later that the cops had been on the lookout for a Commie terrorist and had no interest in a mere British train robber. I had arrived in Venezuela illegally, but at the time I had no idea how important that would turn out to be.

I stayed in Caracas for around two weeks, enjoying the hospitality of Frank and his brother, Carlos. When Frank started work, I found myself in Rosie's company a fair bit and we became fond of each other. She had split up with her husband in Australia and was seeking a new life in South America. She wanted me to stay in Caracas and I was tempted – I had been offered a job with a work permit and other papers in the name of Michael Haynes. But nothing could change my mind: the plan was to go to Rio de Janeiro and flying down to Rio de Janeiro I would go.

CHAPTER 10

MR HAYNES SETTLES IN RIO

On Sunday 11 March 1970, I landed at Rio de Janeiro's old Galeão Airport after the overnight flight from Caracas. It was early in the morning, sunny and already very hot. Once again I felt my heartbeat accelerating as I stood in line for my passport to be examined. It had been five weeks since I left Melbourne.

During the flight I had struck up an acquaintance with an elderly American gentleman named Bill and now, trying to appear quite at ease, I was chatting away 19 to the dozen with the old chap as we waited our turn behind a group of nuns. Subconsciously, I think, I hoped the nuns might bring some added heavenly protection. I need not have worried, my passport was stamped and returned with hardly a glance from the immigration official. I was in Brazil. I had done it again! I felt the same rush of adrenalin and euphoria that I had experienced when I escaped from Wandsworth and when I first arrived in Australia. It was the beginning of another new phase to my life.

Bill was only going to be in town for a couple of days. He was on his way to Argentina and had broken his trip to deliver a letter to a friend of his wife who lived in Rio. Bill was already booked into the Luxor Hotel on Avenida Atlantica (now Mercure Rio), the Copacabana seafront, and suggested I should find a room at the same place. In the taxi we drove along Botafogo Beach, which in places seemed within touching distance of the massive Sugarloaf Mountain. It was the same view that had first attracted me to Rio on the brochure I had seen in Melbourne, and every bit as impressive.

The prices at the Luxor were not impressive in a good way. I left my case with Bill and went off to find something more downmarket and within my limited means. A couple of blocks back I found what I could afford: a fleapit, the Hotel Santa Clara, at three dollars a night. The doorman-owner was a swarthy Portuguese who smelled of sweat. After we had laboured over a sign-language deal, a bulky black lady, also smelling of sweat, showed me to a room. The window looked out on to the wall of a neighbouring building. The furniture was old, the washbasin cracked, and there was an unpleasant, sweaty-sock smell in the air. But it was all I could afford and I had known worse. It was to be 'home' for the next couple of months.

I lunched with Bill and afterwards went with him to deliver the letter to his wife's friend, who lived within walking distance. Nadine Mitchell was her name, a beautiful American lady in her late fifties. A Christian Scientist and an English teacher, Bill had described her as 'quite a gal'. She had been 'married' to a Brazilian army colonel, who had died, and so she now considered herself to be a widow.

When Bill left, apart from Nadine, I knew no other English-speaking person in Rio and it was no easy matter getting to grips with the Portuguese language. Asking for a beer, I was offered milk, wine and Coca-Cola. I was pleased, therefore, when I met Adauto

Agallo, a clerk at the American Express office in downtown Rio. He was a young Brazilian who could speak English fluently and we soon found that we had a mutual interest in jazz.

I had gone to the Amex office in Rua Mexico, not far from the American Consulate, to see if I could receive mail there. The smiling Adauto told me there was no problem. By a happy coincidence, he lived only a stone's throw from the flea factory where I was staying. Sunday afternoons, Adauto told me, were dedicated to serious drinking and jazz, so I took him up on his offer to visit him at home.

I met and liked his family and friends, particularly a young medical student called Mauricio, who laughed a lot and could also speak fairly good English. He called me 'Gringo'. One evening, following an afternoon of slugging back a goodly number of gin and tonics, I agreed to go with Mauricio and a couple of his friends to a 'special' nightclub. The club was out in the sticks and I didn't have a clue where we were, but it appeared to be a popular place. The 'Gringo' was introduced to the proprietor, who spoke a little English, and a table near the raised dance floor was quickly arranged. The music pounded, the strobe lights flickered and the booze flowed. I was enjoying myself immensely. Mauricio drew my attention to a slender young girl dancing alone and smiling in our direction.

When I awoke the next morning, I found myself lying on the floor of a hotel bathroom. I remembered the smiling girl and dancing with her. I remembered taking a couple of drags at the cigarette she was smoking and telling myself that it was marijuana . . . Never again, I vowed.

The following Sunday, Nadine asked if I would go to church with her. After the service she introduced me to a number of the congregation, including Werner and Joyce Blumer, a Swiss stockbroker and his wife, leading lights in Rio's Christian Science community.

Everyone was very friendly, especially the Blumers. When Werner learned that I knew a thing or two about carpentry he invited me to his house to take care of a number of things that needed repairing. He had a fully equipped workshop, he told me, so tools would not be a problem, and I jumped at the chance to earn some extra cash. Satisfied with my work, Werner suggested that I should move in with them and be part of the family. There were only two rules, said my new boss: no girlfriends and no alcoholic beverages on the premises.

Back in Melbourne, Charmian needed a new start and moved the family about six miles north from Hibiscus Road to Towong Court, where she would live for the rest of her life.

It was about this time that I met an attractive mixed-race young lady named Edith. She was Adauto's sister-in-law and worked for General Electric as a bilingual secretary. She was 27. We started out as 'just good friends', but when our relationship developed into an intimate one I told her my story, including the fact that I had a wife and children in Australia. We became closer friends than ever, Edith wanting, above all, to see me reunited with my family.

A month after my arrival in Rio, on 20 April 1970, Detective Chief Superintendent Tommy Butler, the 'Grey Fox', died. Even on his retirement from the force a year earlier he had vowed that he would still search for me. Forgotten and unnoticed, Bill Boal also passed away. He died in prison on 26 June having been accused and sentenced for the train robbery. His misfortune was to be with Roger Cordrey at the time of his arrest. Admitting Bill was innocent would have brought into question much of the prosecution's evidence against Gordon and the rest of the gang.

As fate would have it, on the day that Butler died, *The Sun* newspaper in London finally published the 77-page manuscript that I had left with Charmian. Charm had managed to get a lawyer to negotiate a good payment from the new Murdoch paper. The money, Charmian sensibly turned into a trust fund for the boys that would help go towards paying for part of their education.

The publication of my story in *The Sun* stirred up a storm on both sides of the equator, with the authorities still assuming I was hiding out in Australia. A furious commissioner of police in New South Wales, Norman Allan, called Scotland Yard when he learnt the Yard itself had confirmed to the paper that the manuscript was genuine. He expressed amazement that Scotland Yard had supported *The Sun* in this way and pointed out that, whilst police in both countries still could not find me, a solicitor had been able to receive a manuscript with my fingerprints and signature on it. In Allan's opinion, the Yard were helping to finance my escape and even 'giving comfort and aid to an escaped prisoner'.

In the middle of 1970 I got to understand just how passionate the Brazilians were about their football. The World Cup kicked off in Mexico on 31 May, with England as the reigning champions, and Brazil not sure what to expect from its team. But they started and played well and this was the first World Cup that Brazilians could watch live on TV. I had some good-natured banter during the Brazil v England game on 7 June but a week later England were knocked out by West Germany, and the week after Brazil were crowned world champions for the third time. It was a great time to be in Rio.

In early September, six months after arriving in Brazil and still living with the Blumer family, the time came to renew my visa. I did not want to attract the attention from the Brazilian authorities by overstaying my welcome and that meant that I would have to leave the country, if only for a couple of hours. After consulting a map, I decided to take a bus to Argentina. Werner provided me with an advance against my salary which enabled me to buy the bus ticket and still have money for other expenses.

I got off to a bad start, finding that my seat on the 1,000-mile journey to Porto Alegre was next to a very large Brazilian lady. During the night, when she stretched out, she overflowed into my seat, making it impossible to get any shut-eye. I spent the night sitting on the steps by the door of the bus. At Porto Alegre, in the south of Brazil, I had to change bus and was grateful to find myself on a much less crowded one. It was still many hours and over 650 miles to Buenos Aires, but at least I could get some shut-eye.

It started to pour with rain as we left Porto Alegre. The bus lurched and shimmied on the muddy highway, finally slipping off the road and into a ditch. All the *hombres* were called upon to get the bus on the road again, even the sleeping Gringo in his suede shoes.

Treading warily, I made my way to the rear and joined in the heaving and shoving. We were winning!

Suddenly, and without warning, the driver hit the gas and the bus slewed back towards the ditch. I leapt aside to avoid being knocked over and landed up to my knees in soft, wet red mud. Soaked and muddy, I returned to my seat in the hope of catching an extra 40 winks while I dried off.

We would arrive at the Argentine border at about five o'clock in the morning, an hour, I thought, when frontier guards could be caught napping. Leaving Brazil presented no problem. The driver collected our passports and took them away to have *'saída'* stamped into them. I relaxed – it was going to be easier than I thought. The driver returned and the bus proceeded across a bridge into Argentina, stopping at the Argentine checkpoint. Here we were taken off the bus and herded into a large, well-lit office where we stood in line waiting to be attended by a solitary official sitting behind a small desk.

The line moved quickly, the official appearing to only give a cursory glance at the documents before stamping them. When I reached the table, however, he gave me a long, hard stare. He took Michael Haynes's passport and began going through it slowly, page by page. He returned to the page with the photograph, looking from the picture to me. He did this several times. He then picked up a paper knife and attempted to raise the corners of the photo. Still not satisfied he went through the passport a second time, stopping at a page where there was an entry in red ink. At one time, the real Michael Haynes had crossed from India into Pakistan and had been suspected of trying to smuggle a Land Rover, hence the entry. The official pointed to the page, said something in Spanish, and looked at me enquiringly. I shook my head.

Then, with a flourish, he stamped the passport with an *'entrada'* and scribbled his initials beside it. He fixed me one last time with a long, hard stare, tapping the passport against his hand for what seemed like an eternity before handing it back to me without further comment.

The trip continued without further drama and I arrived in Buenos Aires looking a picture in my by now dry pants which were pink from the knees down with shoes to match. One of Nadine's friends in Rio had kindly suggested that I could stay with her relatives in Buenos Aires and had given me some small presents to deliver to them. I found the address without much trouble and received a warm welcome. They took me around to places of interest and various bars and restaurants.

One afternoon while downtown, close to the only overseas

branch of Harrods, I spotted a familiar face, and one I knew would speak English. It was Sarah Vaughan and I was a huge fan. She was happy to stop for a chat and I even asked for her autograph which she signed on a page of my passport!

I didn't stay much longer than a week in Buenos Aires, returning to Rio by a bus that took a different route to the one that I had arrived on. I didn't fancy a second encounter with the same official.

Back in Rio and the bosom of the Blumers, I picked up from where I had been before my excursion. I wrote to Charmian, describing my 'near thing' in Argentina and its laxative effect. At that time, Charmian and I were kicking around a few ideas and making uncertain plans to reunite.

One of Werner's partners in the stock market, a middle-aged American named Scott Johnson, was also in need of a carpenter and I started working for him at weekends. We became pretty good friends and frequently went to the samba clubs in Rio. Scott was pretty well off, drove a Ford Cutlass and was extremely popular with the attractive young girls who flocked to the *samba* clubs. I really enjoyed these evenings. The beer was cold and the prices were as friendly as the girls.

Everything seemed to be going well. With the extra money I had been earning working for Scott I was able to buy myself some new clothes and other small luxuries. Although I was happy with the Blumers, I was keen to rent a place of my own and regain my personal freedom. Scott had told me about an apartment in Rua Siqueira Campos in Copacabana which belonged to one of his friends. He was confident that he could get it for me at a low rent. He could; the rent was about £70 a month.

One sunny morning in February 1971, I received a phone call from Adauto. A letter had arrived at the American Express office and he had taken it home for me to collect. His wife would be there if I wanted to pick it up. Olga, all smiles as usual, handed me a fat envelope bearing Charmian's unmistakable handwriting. Not wanting to be away from my job for too long, I left, happily tearing the letter open as I went. The opening line of the letter stopped me in my tracks: 'Wherever you are and whatever you are doing, sit down . . . our darling son Nicky has been killed in a road accident . . .'

I felt physically sick and faint, completely stunned by the terrible news. I don't know why but I felt I had to talk to somebody. In a trance I got to a bar and sat down. I tried, but it was impossible to read any more of Charmian's letter. I could only cry silently. I saw a payphone on the wall and got up to phone somebody – anybody. I dialled a number and heard Adauto's voice. I did all I could to force myself to speak, to say his name, but I was unable to utter a sound. I hung up and stumbled out of the bar. Still in a trance I wandered aimlessly. Then, through the haze, I decided I would go to the British Consulate and give myself up.

A short bus ride later, I found myself standing outside the British Consulate in Flamengo. The journey, however short, had given me time to get over the initial shock and regain part of my composure. I went to a bar and gulped down two large brandies. From where I stood, I could see the Union Jack hanging in front of the Consulate building. All I had to do was walk in through the door and announce who I was. Instead, I crossed the road and sat down on a bench in Flamengo Park and read Charmian's letter from beginning to end.

Charmian gave me details of the accident, which had occurred on 5 January, and said she felt heavily responsible because she had been driving when the tragedy occurred. She was in no way responsible. The crash had happened less than 30 yards from the Hayneses' front door.

Charmian had just dropped Mike and Jess off after the New Year break when the car was hit by another vehicle going straight across a junction which was Charmian's right of way. Charm's car somersaulted twice. Farley had been badly cut in the crash and his left eye and forehead gashed, while Charmian and Chris were both badly shaken. Nicky, however, had been hurled from the car and landed on the side of the road. Blood was pouring from his mouth and Charm realised he must have suffered terrible internal injuries and cradled his head in her lap. It took 20 minutes for the first ambulance to arrive which took Nicky, Charm and Farley to the hospital while Chris stayed behind with Jess Haynes who, along with Mike, had witnessed the crash. Mike went in the ambulance with Charm, who was sure that Nicky had died during the drive to the hospital; a fact confirmed by the doctors who could not resuscitate him.

Charm was numb, but had little time to feel sorry for herself. She had to turn her attention to Farley who was in considerable pain and being stitched up, although thankfully he would be OK and recover in time. Nicky's funeral had taken place in Melbourne on 10 January, over a month before I got the letter.

I sat in the park thinking things over and re-reading the letter and came to the conclusion that the last thing I should do was to give myself up. It was not what Nicky or Charm would have wanted.

Life continued, but Nicky's death at the age of ten had left me devastated. I found it hard to garner any enthusiasm for anything. When carnival came around, my first in Rio, Edith got tickets for us to see the parade. I was not really in the mood to watch a parade but Edith and her chums insisted that I needed something to lift me out of the doldrums. I'm glad I went. It was – and is – a wonderful experience.

Each day I thought more and more about getting back to Australia and to do so I had to keep 'my' passport up to date. To do that, and not attract unnecessary attention, I had to make a second trip out of Brazil.

I had been in Brazil for almost a year. Loath to return to Argentina, I decided in March 1971 to take a bus to Corumba, a town on the Bolivian border.

During the long, dusty journey, the military and civil police stopped the bus at least half a dozen times. The police either boarded the bus or took us all off for a more thorough search, but whichever method they chose they always demanded to see every passenger's identity and travel documents.

As I got to the police post in Corumba and saw the photographs on the walls of the cocaine busts that had recently been made, I realised that I was using a well-trodden South American drug trail.

At the Brazilian-Bolivian border, a friendly Brazilian policeman stamped the *'saída'* into my passport and advised me to stay on the other side of the border for a couple of days before re-entering Brazil. He was clearly used to 'tourists' who needed to re-validate their visas.

A bus took me over a bridge into Puerto Suárez on the Bolivian side of the border. It was very different from my arrival in Argentina – I was in Bolivia and I had not even been asked to show my passport. I found a cheap hotel and booked in. With great difficulty, I asked the proprietor where I should go to get an *'entrada'* stamped into my passport. Every evening, he told me, the man responsible for the border could be found at a nearby bar where he had his dinner. This was the *hombre* to speak to.

I had no trouble spotting my man, another *Mission Impossible* type. I soon discovered that he was running a nice little scam shaking down 'tourists' like me who required his initials in their passport so that they could return to Brazil. He started out at $100 (about $600 today) for the *'entrada'* and *'salida'* stamps – plus his initials – but grudgingly settled for $20 when he found I was not kidding about my worldly wealth.

Two nights at the Mosquito Motel had been two nights too many; I was glad when I got back to Corumba and caught the bus back to Rio, even if Rio was over 1,200 miles and a number of police searches away.

When I had chosen Brazil as a refuge, I was quite unaware that the country was under a strict military dictatorship. A communist witch-hunt was on and anyone found without some kind of identification was hustled off to the nearest *delegacia* for some heavy questioning or worse.

Soon after my return from the Bolivian trip, thanks to Scott's diligent work, I moved into a twelfth floor, fully furnished apartment in Rua Prado Junior in Copacabana, a short walk from the beach. I was still unhappy, but gradually the pain of losing Nicky eased and I picked up the pieces of my life. I worked long hours during the week and relaxed on the beach at the weekends with Edith and her friends.

About the middle of 1971, Edith went off on a long vacation to England and the US, so I started frequenting Adauto's Sunday afternoon jazz sessions again. On one of these visits I was introduced to a lively, friendly Brazilian fellow called Paulo. He spoke English quite well, having lived in the US for a couple of years and I found him interesting company. He was also a samba enthusiast and we made an arrangement to go to his favourite club, the Bola Preta (the Black Ball) the following Friday.

The Bola Preta had a reputation for 'hot' samba and was popular with people of all ages, colours and creeds. We got there early so that we could be sure of a prime table near the dance floor and ordered a couple of beers. Among the dancers I noticed a small young woman with long black hair and an enchanting smile. A young Brazilian guy accompanied her, but before the evening was over I had a chance to exchange a few words with her. Her name was Raimunda Nascimento de Castro, she said, with the same wide smile, and she would be happy to meet me at the club the following week.

It was a fine romance until the day that Edith was due back from the US. Raimunda had left her baby-doll nightdress on the bed and I suggested that she might like to take it with her in case Edith, who had a key to my apartment, turned up without warning. Raimunda exploded, giving me the ultimatum that I had to make a choice between her and Edith. I chose Edith and the fiery Raimunda stormed out of my life in a huff.

Whilst I had been dallying in Rio, Edith had not been wasting much time in New York and had met and become fond of a hotel manager, something she made no mention of on her return. I noticed, however, a distinct change in her.

Edith headed back to New York, but promised to be back for my birthday on 8 August. A few days after her departure, Scott gave me a call and, discovering that Edith was away, suggested a night out at one of the samba clubs. I was all for it and we made arrangements to meet at the Bola Preta. A couple of pretty girls at a neighbouring table were showing obvious interest in the two big gringos and at Scott's invitation they came across and joined us. The one that I took a fancy to was Ana Paula. We drank and we danced and eventually went back to my apartment to get to know each other better!

Then 8 August came and went and there was no sign of Edith. I telephoned her home and her eldest sister Zelia answered. From the start of our affair, Zelia made it clear she didn't approve of Edith being involved with a married man. I asked her if she had any news of Edith.

'Haven't you heard?' she asked.

'I haven't heard anything,' I replied. 'Edith said she would be back before 8 August but I haven't heard anything.'

Zelia could hardly wait to tell me. 'But Ronnie, Edith got married last week. Didn't you know?'

'What! Who to?'

'A German, someone she met when she was in New York last year.'

I was amazed by the news. Edith had mentioned meeting somebody and it had crossed my mind that she might have had a fling, but I found it unbelievable that she had actually gone and got married. Zelia must be lying.

But Zelia wasn't lying. Edith flew back to Brazil a week later to collect her clothes and to quit her job. She phoned me before returning to New York and said tearfully that she had made the decision to marry on the spur of the moment. She hoped I would understand. I said I did and wished her good luck and much happiness. She had been a fine friend and I was going to miss her.

Unwilling to make another trip out of Brazil after my previous experiences, I allowed the validity of my visa to expire in September 1971. Charmian was still nursing the hope that I would be able to get back to Australia, but the more I thought about it the less likely it seemed to be a good idea. My return to Australia, even if possible, could only be disruptive as far as Chris and Farley were concerned and my presence was sure to create complications. I outlined these misgivings in a letter to Charmian.

It was a Saturday, and although we were well into winter it was a warm, sunny day. I had just finished tidying up the apartment when someone rang the bell. I opened the door to three young hippies. They had heard that I was looking for a carpenter and were applying for the job. When they called I had little work on, but I invited the group in so that I could write down their details. I opened a couple of beers and asked about their experience as carpenters. Out of the blue one asked me if I had any objection to him rolling a joint and I told him to do his own thing. He rolled a long thin 'cigarrinho'. The joint finished, he lit up and took a couple of long tokes before passing the cigarette on to me. I hesitated for a second, then took the joint from him and took a drag on it and passed it on to his pals; it duly came around again and I had another puff. The joint was smoked down to the end and the hippies got up to leave. I thought they looked a bit uneasy on their feet and asked myself why anyone bothered to smoke the stuff. All I felt was a slight nausea. When they had gone I cleared away the beer bottles and put on a record. It was *Jazz Samba* with Stan Getz and Charlie Byrd, a record I particularly liked and often played. Then I stretched out on the settee to relax.

What followed defies description. I've been told that I went on an 'astral voyage', but whatever it was it was no ordinary trip. I was omnipotent – until it was time to turn the record over. The floor had turned to cotton wool. The experience was so extraordinary, if that's the word, that the next morning found me knocking on the boys' door for more of the shit. I was hooked.

It was Ana Paula's birthday on 8 September. I was going to take her to dinner and we had arranged for her to arrive at my place around seven o'clock. About six the doorbell rang and I presumed that Ana Paula had arrived early, but it wasn't Ana Paula, it was Raimunda with her wide smile.

'*Como vai, seu vagabundo?* (How are you, you bum?)', she asked.

In no time we were on the bed and talking about old times. I was really getting carried away when I remembered Ana Paula. It was ten to seven. Hastily I explained the situation to Raimunda and asked her to come back the next day. She called me a son of a bitch, but promised to return. Through the spy hole in the front door I watched her walk down the corridor to the lift. Almost as soon as she got there the door opened and out stepped Ana Paula.

She entered the apartment sniffing the air like a pointer. 'I can smell a whore,' she said. I tried to talk my way out of it but Ana Paula was a bright girl and she knew very well what the score was. We talked about our relationship over dinner and we decided quite amicably to go our separate ways. Two days later Raimunda moved into my apartment and my life.

Until her arrival, the apartment was – to say the least – untidy. Then one day, while I was at work, Xuxu (shoo-shoo, a small, green vegetable) as I called her, had the apartment clean, polished and in apple-pie order. As I looked around admiring her handiwork, she appeared with a glass of cold beer and invited me to sit down and switched on a table lamp. I was surprised to see that the white bulb had been replaced by a blue one. Then she put on a lazy samba record and began to dance to the music, letting down her long black hair. Artistically, she stepped on to the marble coffee table and slowly started to strip off her clothes. We got on very well together and she was fun to be with.

At what I thought was an appropriate moment, I told Xuxu my true name, the reason why I was in Brazil and the fact that I had a wife and children in Australia. Raimunda took this piece of news in her stride and it appeared to make little difference to our relationship. She showed a lot of interest in my children and told me that she herself had a young son who was living with his father, a doctor, in Maranhão, in the north of Brazil.

*

Around the end of 1972 I received word from Mike Haynes that he needed his passport back: he was planning to return to England with his family the following year. He had applied for a new passport, claiming he had lost his old one, but his application had been turned down. He would have to find the old one, he was told.

I was wondering how I could get the passport back to Mike when at a party I was introduced to a Brazilian girl who worked in tourism. She told me that she would be taking a group of Brazilians to Australia in February 1973. I explained to her that I had friends there – perhaps she would be kind enough to take some small presents. She agreed and when she travelled she took a small package which among other things contained Mike's well-travelled passport – minus the pages relating to my exit from Australia and the subsequent trips around South America.

Mike and his family returned to the UK in July 1973. Like Molly he received a visit from Jack Slipper after I had been found in Rio. Mike was questioned and made to give a lengthy statement, but was never prosecuted in the UK. He was in Australia and spent time in Beechworth Prison.

The months passed, bringing financial ups and downs. More than once the power was cut off when I failed to pay the electricity bill on time, so I was very pleased when the Blumers called me to work on an art gallery they were in the process of setting up. It was during this period that I met Joyce Blumer's sister-in-law, Phyllis Huber, an attractive and intelligent lady in her late twenties. She had been well educated and spoke English with an American accent.

She invited me to dinner where I was introduced to her hippie friends, Brazilians and Americans. After the meal we sat around talking, drinking cheap wine and smoking grass. I enjoyed the company and I became a frequent visitor to Phyllis's apartment. It was there that I met a young Englishman of White Russian extraction by the name of Constantine Benckendorff – 'Conti' to his friends. Over a joint or two we became quite pally and started going around together. He got interested in a stoned-out idea that Phyllis and I had to set up an interior decorating business we planned to call 'Planet Venus'.

I had told Phyllis my real name and why I was in Brazil, but she wouldn't believe me! I also trusted Conti enough to reveal my identity to him. It blew his mind but he said that he was ready to help me in any way possible.

A little less than a year after she had moved in, Raimunda asked me if I minded if her mother came to stay with us for a while. There was only one bedroom in the apartment but Raimunda said that her mother would be quite comfortable on the settee. We wouldn't even notice she was there, she promised. So I agreed.

A couple of weeks later, Dona Maria arrived in Rio after close to three days on a bus, accompanied by Rosangela, Raimunda's 15-year-old adopted daughter, who would also be quite happy to sleep on the floor of the living room and go 'unnoticed'. It soon became clear that all three of the ladies had the same insatiable thirst for the Brazilian television soap operas, which further induced me to seek the company of my grass-smoking friends. The 'blue lamp' cabaret had sadly closed.

One evening I returned home to find Raimunda, her mother, Rosangela and two other females who I didn't even know, all soaking their feet in bowls in preparation for a manicure session. The air was a mixture of cigarette smoke and nail-varnish remover fumes and the telly was going full blast. The next morning I had a bit of a showdown with Xuxu and ended up by saying that the time had come for Dona Maria and Rosangela to return to

Maranhão. Raimunda's reply was along the lines that if her mother and adopted daughter had to go, then she would go with them. A few days later I took all three to the bus station and waved a sad 'goodbye' as they set out on the long journey north.

Scott had just bought a rooftop apartment and planned to make extensive changes, so I was invited to take charge of the job. We started going to the samba clubs again at the weekends and it was on one of these jaunts that I met a 19-year-old bank clerk named Lucia Pereira Gomes – pretty, long-legged and sex-mad. It was something of a whirlwind romance and we spent as much time as possible together, mostly in bed. She didn't move in with me but she did bring some clothes to the apartment and left them in the wardrobe.

Around this time, I received a desperately unhappy tape from Charmian telling me how much she and the boys were missing and needing me. There was further mention of me getting back to Australia. The content of the tape left me deeply depressed and thoughts of giving myself up began to enter my head again. Charmian and my children were unhappy and so was I. The only way to put our lives in order, I decided, was to go back to prison.

I talked the matter over with Conti, who thought I had to be potty to be thinking of going back to the nick. But he knew I was serious. During the time I had been free, the long-awaited parole system had become a reality. In theory, certain cons would be considered for release on parole after completing one third of their sentence. By this time, the members of the gang who had been sentenced to 30 years were already eligible for parole and their cases were no doubt being 'considered'. Had I not done a bunk in 1965 I would have been standing alongside my colleagues, also cap in hand. Now, if I went back to jail voluntarily, I decided, it could weigh heavily in my favour in front of some future parole committee.

Roger Cordrey had been released in April 1971 while Buster and Jimmy White, who had been convicted after the rest of the gang, got out in April 1975. Roy James was the first of those to receive a 30-year sentence to be paroled. He was released in August 1975 having spent nearly 12 years in prison.

Conti was going back to spend the Christmas of 1973 in England. I asked him to do me a favour.

'When you get back to London,' I said, 'I'd like you to make a few discreet enquiries to see if you can find a paper interested in buying the story of my return.'

One evening, after a not very happy Christmas, I arrived home to find Raimunda sitting in the living room. She said she had decided to come back to me, she was 'my woman'. However, she wanted to know what was the 'shit' hanging up in the wardrobe. Inadvertently I had left the front door open, and almost on cue, Lucia came into the apartment with her best friend, Ana. I sensed that an ugly situation was about to develop and herded Lucia and her friend out of the apartment. I apologised to Lucia about the unexpected turn of events and told her that I would explain everything the following day. Then, while she waited in the corridor, I put her clothes into a suitcase and took it out to her. Raimunda's anger had subsided and I found her weeping when I went back into the living room. A long conversation followed, during which I told her of my decision to give myself up, outlining my reasons. She said that she knew that I was unhappy and that I had to do what I thought was best. But she wanted to be with me until I left Brazil; she loved me.

Xuxu was back in my life!

CHAPTER 11

CAUGHT: SLIPPER DROPS HIS CATCH

In January 1974 I received an excited phone call from Conti. He had met a *Daily Express* reporter, Colin Mackenzie, at a cocktail party in London and it was almost certain that his paper would be interested in buying my story. He handed me over to Mackenzie who asked certain questions to verify that it was the real Ronald Biggs. Satisfied with my answers, he said that the *Express* was ready to send him to Brazil just as soon as he presented some written evidence. The paper wanted some concrete proof as it had been left with egg on its face over another hunt for a fugitive in South America. The fugitive in question had been, or rather turned out not to be, Hitler's number two, Martin Bormann.

I sent Mackenzie a letter bearing my signature and a copy of my fingerprints. The letter read: 'Hi, Colin. Perhaps not the best set [of fingerprints] that have been taken, but certainly as good as those found on the Monopoly box and the sauce bottle! Convinced?! R.A. Biggs.'

My letter having been received, Mackenzie sounded ecstatic on the phone. It was a great story, he enthused, and there would be no problem with regard to the 'bread'. Everything was being kept top secret, he assured me, as did the *Express* news editor Brian Hitchen, who came on the line. The date was 24 January 1974. Only Colin and Conti would be travelling to Rio, Hitchen assured me, while only the very top brass on the paper were in on the story.

Early on the morning of Wednesday 30 January, there was a phone call from Conti informing me that he and Mackenzie had arrived in Rio and were comfortably installed in room 909 at the Trocadero Hotel [now the Arena] on Copacabana beachfront – a stone's throw from where I was living.

I had made an arrangement with Lucia, with whom I still remained friendly, despite the presence of Raimunda, to meet her at the beach that morning. I picked her up at her flat, told her what was happening and took her with me to meet the man from the *Express*.

When the door opened, I saw that there were two men besides Conti in the hotel room. They were introduced to me as Colin Mackenzie and Bill Lovelace. I reminded Mackenzie that I had been assured that only he and Conti would meet me in Rio, so I wasn't very pleased to see a third person.

'Don't worry about Bill,' Mackenzie said disarmingly, 'you can trust him. We must have photographs for the story.'

Lovelace was already taking pictures, suggesting poses that I should take with Lucia, murmuring the appreciation of her charms all the while. When Lovelace stopped for a breather, I asked Mackenzie how much I was being offered for my story.

'How much do you want?' he asked.

'£50,000,' I suggested.

'My office has only authorised me to go as high as £35,000,' Mackenzie said, looking me straight in the eye. I reached out to shake hands with the representative of the *Daily Express*.

'It's a deal,' I said. 'I'll settle for that.'

I went on to explain to Mackenzie exactly how I wanted the *Express* to handle the money. It was about £325,000 at 2023 rates. Part was to go direct to Charmian and part to Raimunda. I asked if there was any way of avoiding paying tax and Mackenzie assured me that it would all be taken care of.

I had imagined that the *Express* 'team' would want to rest up after their overnight flight from London, but Mackenzie was all for getting started on the story immediately.

Lovelace went off to get some shots of the local scenery and Conti was volunteered to take Lucia to the beach, a chore he jumped at. Mackenzie and I worked on my story for the rest of the day, only taking a short break for lunch.

Early the next morning, Thursday, I was back at the Trocadero with a new round of revelations for Mackenzie. Again we worked through the day and into the evening. I felt like a little light-hearted entertainment after all this work and suggested that we should go out to a nightclub or something of that nature. But Mackenzie made a face and said that he must have eaten something that had disagreed with him; he had an attack of 'tourist tummy' and would prefer to retire for the evening.

The following morning, as I was getting ready for day three with Mackenzie, Raimunda announced that she thought she might be pregnant. She had been pregnant a couple of times before and a friend of hers, who is a nurse, had been called upon to take care of the issue. I saw it as a complication I could do without and suggested that she should visit her friend and take whatever steps were necessary to terminate the pregnancy, should her suspicions be confirmed.

When I arrived that Friday at the Trocadero, Lovelace was already taking photographs of Lucia who was wearing a tiny bikini, the type known in Brazil as *fio dental* (dental floss). Conti and Mackenzie were watching, the latter showing no signs of his malady of the previous evening. Lovelace wanted some shots of me in beachwear and so I changed into a pair of blue-and-white-striped bathing trunks that belonged to Conti.

Not long after the end of the photo session there was a knock at the door which I took to be room service. Conti went to open the door. A much taller person, whom I recognised immediately as the Old Bill, propelled him back into the room. I was sitting on the floor, still wearing Conti's swimming trunks and, regardless of what has been written or reported in the past, I simply said, 'Oh, fuck!'

To give him his full title, it was Detective Chief Superintendent Jack Slipper, head of Scotland Yard's Flying Squad who had stalked into the room.

'Long time, no see,' he said. 'I think you know who I am? I certainly know who you are and I'm arresting you. Where are your clothes?'

In the bathroom, as I was getting into my clothes, there was a conversation between Slipper and me that went something like: 'Look, Ronnie, there's no point in you and I putting questions to each other. As far as I'm concerned, you're going back to London. You've got a prison sentence to finish. The only thing we have to talk about is when you go. You can bugger us about for a time over here by arguing, or you can come quietly now; so if you simplify it for us, we can help you.'

'You're not going to believe this,' I said, 'but I was trying to give myself up. It would mean a lot to me not to go back wearing handcuffs.'

'I don't know about that,' Slipper said doubtfully. 'If I was to go back without you I'd be looking for a new job.'

'I'll go back without giving you any trouble,' I promised Slipper, 'but if I go handcuffed it will look as if I have been nicked and I've already told you that I was going to give myself up. Ask the reporter in the other room if you don't believe me.'

When Slipper had marched into room to 'nick' me (acting without any official power in Brazil whatsoever), he had been accompanied by a fellow policeman from Scotland Yard, Detective Inspector Peter Jones; the British Consul General, Henry Neill; his Brazilian Vice-Consul, Francisco Costa; and the Rio City Police Commissioner, Dr Ivo Raposo, and his assistant.

Back in the bedroom, Slipper gave Jones, who had been taking down the particulars of everyone else, some orders with regard to our exit from the hotel, then he produced his handcuffs.

'If you don't want me to give you any trouble,' I threatened, 'don't even think about putting those on me.'

A short argument followed which was interrupted by the Commissioner, who opened his gabardine jacket to reveal the handle of a gun tucked down the front of his trousers.

Up until that point Raposo had not uttered a single word. I was unaware that he could speak English and certainly had no idea that he was a Commissioner.

Raposo, which appropriately means 'fox' in Portuguese, looked mean and took a step towards me. 'Did you call me a son of a bitch?' he hissed.

'Yeah, I called you a *filho da puta*. I'm unarmed and you might just shoot me. You son of a bitch!'

Slipper stepped into the arena. 'Calm down, Ronnie. No one is going to get shot.' He put his handcuffs away and took a firm hold of my belt. 'All right, we'll go down to the car like this.'

With Slipper hanging on to my belt, we left Mackenzie, Conti and Lucia in the room and departed the hotel in silence. On the way down in the lift I was trying to work out exactly how the police had arrived on the scene. When Slipper had entered the hotel room, Mackenzie had appeared to be as surprised as I was, so I had not suspected foul play as far as he was concerned.

The vice-consul's car, a chocolate-coloured Austin Maxi, was parked in front of the Trocadero and as we approached it Bill Lovelace ran up and began shooting pictures of my 'arrest'. I glared angrily in his direction; the evening before we had been drinking and chatting together like old chums. I was put into the back of the car between Jones and the Commissioner's number two, and Slipper got into the front with the Commissioner and the vice-consul who was acting as the driver. Henry Neill was to follow in his car.

As we pulled away, Slipper turned to face me. 'We're going first to your flat, Ronnie, so that you can pick up some warm clothes,' he said. 'It's bloody cold in England at the moment so you'll need a jacket or a sweater – and you can also collect any personal stuff that you may want to take back with you.'

At that moment I resigned myself to the fact that I had been nicked and there was little point in not co-operating. During the short journey to my apartment the Commissioner apologised for threatening me with his gun and I in turn apologised for calling him a son of a bitch. With Slipper once again holding on to my belt, we went up to my apartment in Avenida Prado Junior. There was no sign of Raimunda.

Keeping a close watch on me, Slipper made small talk while I got together the things I wanted to take back with me to Britain. While there the British Consul General made a surprise entrance. It turned out in all the excitement Peter Jones had gone off with Neill's car keys. With one last look around my Brazilian home, we headed back to the car.

We proceeded from Copacabana to a grand old building known as the Catete Palace in Flamengo. At the time, part of the palace was being used by the federal police in Rio. Between 1896 and 1954 the palace had been used as the official residence of the Brazilian president: that was until President Getúlio Vargas shot himself on 24 August 1954.

The police chief, or *delegado*, was Inspector Carlos Alberto Garcia, a flashy character with a pearl-handled gun showing above the waistband of his pants. Puffing on a cigar, he received Slipper and his party, listening intently to the details of my capture and identity from the British Vice-Consul, Costa. Leaving me in the care of Jones, Slipper, Costa and Garcia retired to the *delegado*'s office to discuss the matter further.

A federal agent, probably acting on Garcia's orders, appeared from nowhere and slapped a pair of handcuffs on my wrists. Moments later Henry Neill arrived in the charge-room puffing and panting. Having witnessed my reaction to handcuffs when Slipper wanted to put them on me, he protested on my behalf. He explained who he was and the handcuffs were removed.

Neill sat down beside me and told me what he thought would be the best way to treat my present situation. 'I'm most anxious,' he said, 'that you should do everything to avoid spending any time in a Brazilian prison. I have visited one and I can assure you that it would horrify me to see you pass even one night in such a place.'

He explained that I would have to make a statement to the Brazilian authorities, but to be certain that I could leave Brazil without a hitch I would have to be careful what I said. If I was asked how I arrived in Brazil, it would be better if I didn't mention that I had entered Brazil on a forged passport; such an admission might result in up to six months in a filthy Brazilian prison before being sent back to England to serve my time there. The best thing, the Consul General advised, was to say that I had entered the country from Paraguay, having crossed the border without a passport. It sounded like good advice, and when I was called to make my statement I explained my arrival in Brazil along those lines and signed my statement.

From that moment on, I was considered by Brazil to be in the country illegally – I was no longer 'on the run' – and, as a result, it was necessary to take my fingerprints 40 times. I asked the cop why he needed to make so many copies and he simply said that it was normal in cases of 'expulsion'. That didn't sound good.

Raised voices came from the *delegado*'s office and a little later a disgusted Slipper came out to say that nothing was going to happen until after lunch. I was left in the care of two Brazilian cops who promptly put me back into handcuffs as soon as Neill was off the premises. The afternoon session was much like the morning: another shouting match. Jones was pacing up and down, glumly looking to his watch as the hours ticked by.

Finally Slipper emerged from the *delegado*'s office looking distinctly miserable. 'We won't be flying back tonight,' he said dejectedly. 'The chief has got to wait for instructions from Brasilia.' I sensed a slender ray of hope. The *delegado* came to speak with me, telling me that I would have to spend the night locked up. He seemed quite friendly and shook hands with me as he was leaving,

I was taken under a heavy armed escort to a tiny prison located in Praça XV, close to the docks. It wasn't really a prison, but a very old police station that had half a dozen cells in its basement. It served as a 'special' prison where, it was said, political prisoners had been taken for interrogation. 'The Presidential Suite', as one cell was called, was under several inches of water. Neill had not exaggerated when he had described a Brazilian prison.

I was put into a cell which already housed three other prisoners, all awaiting trial. One of them, Mario, a middle-aged taxi driver wanted to know how and why a gringo had landed in their midst.

There were no beds or mattresses in the cell and the prisoners were expected to make do with newspaper and cardboard to lie on. Whilst I told them the outline of my story, Mario prepared a place for me to sleep, taking paper and cardboard from the existing makeshift pallets. The Brazilians listened carefully to what I had to say, finding it difficult to believe that anyone involved in the robbery of the *trem pagador* (pay train, as it's known in Brazil) should be sharing their cell. Mario had an immediate answer to my problem.

'You've got to arrange a Brazilian child,' he said emphatically, 'Buy, borrow or steal one if necessary, any colour, any age – the only way to get out of the fix you are in is to get a kid and say it's yours. Do you have a girlfriend? Would she help you?'

I told them about Raimunda and mentioned that only that morning she had told me that she might be pregnant.

'*Que beleza!* (How beautiful!),' said the taxi driver. 'You lucky son of a bitch! If you've got a Brazilian girl who's expecting your child you've got it made! *Puta que pariu!* If you father a child in Brazil you will never be made to leave!'

Mario's words were cheering and the slender ray of hope broadened, but I was still a long way from being 'home and hosed'. It occurred to me that Raimunda might not be pregnant, or might not want to have the child even if she was. Perhaps Slipper would get me on a plane before I could get to see Raimunda.

The following morning, with my predicament in mind, I filched the razor blade I was given to shave with and hid it under the lining of one of my shoes. I had read an article about an American con who had avoided a court appearance by swallowing razor blades wrapped in bread – I, for one, was ready to give it a try if it kept me off the plane and I was rushed to the hospital and not to the airport.

I was far from being the only major news story in Brazil on 1 February 1974. Tragically a huge fire had ripped through the Joelma Building in São Paulo killing at least 179 people and injuring more than 300. It remained the worst skyscraper fire in terms of fatalities, until the September 11 attacks in New York. It dominated the news in Brazil, as few in Brazil knew who I was or had heard of the Great Train Robbery.

By the time I was transferred back to the federal police HQ, Slipper, Neill and the *delegado* were already involved in another heated discussion and it became clear that it would be impossible to get me to the airport in time to catch a morning plane. The session ended with Slipper and Jones being told that as it was Saturday nothing more could be done until the following Monday or Tuesday. Even though I was sitting handcuffed I was delighted with this piece of news.

Not long after they left, Raimunda was escorted into the room where I was being held. When she saw that I was handcuffed she broke into sobs and began protesting. The chief came out of his office, no doubt wanting to know what all the noise was about. He managed to calm Raimunda down, giving her his handkerchief to dry her eyes.

Garcia put his arm around Raimunda and led her into his office, talking to her like some kindly uncle. I could hear some of the conversation between them from where I was sitting and Raimunda was clearly doing her best to let the *delegado* know what a wonderful and kind person I had been to her and her family. Garcia now wanted to hear what I had to say, from the time I had arrived in Brazil until today. I began by telling him that the statement I had made the previous day was not true, mentioning the fact that the British Consul General had advised against telling the true story. After I had told my tale, the *delegado* repeated his desire to help us in any way he could, indicating that he had not exactly fallen in love with his visitors from Scotland Yard.

After a fresh and lengthy statement, I was given time to have a private conversation with Raimunda. She was pregnant and was certain that she wanted to have the baby whether I went back to England or not. At that time, I assessed my chances of staying in Brazil as close to zero but, even so, I also wanted Raimunda to have my child.

All the time our little drama was going on inside the *delegacia*, a horde of reporters and photographers, many of whom had flown in overnight from England when word of my arrest had got out, were struggling to get to see us. But the good Dr Garcia had given strict orders to keep them at bay – he had a special presentation of his own in mind.

At the time of my arrest, the most popular television programme in Brazil was a Sunday evening series called *Fantastico! (It's Fantastic!)* on TV Globo. The programme combined news, current affairs and entertainment with a weird and wonderful mix of events from around the world. Dr Garcia had come up with the idea of putting Raimunda and me on the programme with a view to letting the Brazilian public see us 'in the flesh' – and, at the same time, collecting a few cruzeiros for his trouble. The filming took place in the *delegado*'s office, Raimunda and I sitting side by side on an ancient settee. As the camera rolled, Dr Garcia stood to one side assuming the role of director, making signs for us to snuggle up together, to hold hands and kiss.

Dr Garcia's production was shown on television the following evening and although I didn't get to see it, I heard that the programme created a lot of public sympathy.

On the Monday morning, with the razor blade still in my shoe, I was taken once again to the Catete Palace. A decision was expected with regard to my position and the mob of reporters and photographers were pushing and shoving at the front gate as we drove into the palace grounds. Raimunda was there, now a celebrity after her TV appearance and a weekend of giving interviews to the press. So were Slipper and Jones, neither one of whom was looking particularly cheerful. Mackenzie, I was told, was taking care of Raimunda and had given her some money to buy some clothes.

At that time I was still unaware of the *Daily Express*'s double-cross, believing that Mackenzie and Lovelace had been followed to Brazil. I had not seen the issues of that particular newspaper following my arrest and I was foolish enough to believe that the £35,000 'deal' I had made with Mackenzie was still valid. The Brazilian newspapers that I had managed to get hold of were mainly focused on the Joelma fire and gave no indication that the *Express* had put the Yard on to me. There was, however, much criticism levelled at the British police for the manner in which they had arrived in Brazil unannounced.

Mackenzie swore later that he had no idea that his superiors at the *Daily Express* had contacted the Yard. However, according to Slipper in his biography, *Slipper of the Yard*, the *Express* had tipped off the Yard from the word go, but did not tell Mackenzie at first, in case he took the story to the *Daily Mail*. But Slipper and Jones did meet with Mackenzie in London prior to the trip, along with Hitchen and the *Express*'s legal advisor. Mackenzie subsequently told Slipper that he had planned to tip me off about the Yard, but had expected Slipper to turn up on the Sunday and not the Friday.

At six o'clock on Monday 4 February, Garcia made an announcement. I was to be detained in Brazilian custody for

90 days pending further enquiries. Slipper and Jones, without their man, returned on that night's British Caledonian flight to Gatwick to a cruel reception from the newspapers who had not got the goodies. In Britain an enquiry was already under way as accusations and excuses began to fly between Scotland Yard, the Home and Foreign Office.

It was on the flight back that the famous photo of Slipper sitting next to an empty seat was taken. It was not, however, as the press liked to make out, my empty seat, but was taken when Jones had gone to the toilet. Slipper was learning the hard way about how the press played hard ball.

On 7 February I was on a plane, but with a federal police inspector as my escort and flown to Brasilia where there was a special prison for foreigners. Apart from the inspector and me, the only other people on the flight were a reporter and a photographer from the Brazilian newspaper, *O Globo,* one of the most influential in Brazil. Through *O Globo* and other newspapers, Brazil was slowly learning the truth about 'Michael Haynes', who had been living in Rio for the last four years.

After we had taken off, the *Globo* reporter showed me a copy of the *Daily Express* with screaming headlines of my capture. Reading on, I soon discovered that I had been well and truly shafted and the *Express* was not about to come up with any money for my story. These tidings plunged me into a black mood, but a little later I was cheered up somewhat by a conversation I had with the inspector. Back in 1974, he explained, there was quite a large number of left-wing Brazilians who had sought political asylum in Great Britain, some of whom were wanted for alleged acts of subversion. Even though there was no Treaty of Extradition between Britain and Brazil, the Brazilian authorities had approached the British government, seeking the extradition of certain individuals, but

Britain had steadfastly refused. With that in mind, said the inspector, he found it hard to imagine that Brazil would hand me over to the Brits.

At Brasilia Airport, the inspector and I parted company and I was handed over to another federal policeman, Vivaldo, who was the jailer at the 'special' prison. Still handcuffed, I was put into the back of a closed police truck which must have been standing in the sun for hours before I arrived; it was like getting into an oven. On arrival at the steel and concrete jail where I was to pass the next three months, I was greeted by an educated voice coming from one of the cells.

'Good afternoon, Mr Biggs. How was your flight from Rio?' Before I had time to reply or see who it was that had spoken, Vivaldo had unlocked an empty cell and hustled me inside.

I was relieved of everything except my underpants, with Vivaldo carefully inspecting each item and passing it to a trustee who stood holding a cardboard box. There was a wafer-thin mattress on one of the beds which Vivaldo flung into the corridor with a *'Puta merda!'* A newspaper had been concealed under the mattress and when Vivaldo saw it he started shouting and stuttering at the guard for not having removed 'everything' from the cell, as instructed.

Well, I thought, Mr Vivaldo and I are going to get along just fine. He slammed the gate of the cell and locked it, then shook the gate to make sure it was locked.

'Welcome to Brasilia, Mr Biggs.' said the same refined voice when the jailer had left the area. 'Please don't let Vivaldo disturb you. He's really quite nice when you get to know him.'

There were eight cells all on the same side of the corridor, so it was impossible to see who was speaking to me. He introduced himself as Fernand Legros, a Frenchman and, according to what he told me, a wealthy art dealer unjustly accused of selling paintings that 'turned out to be' forgeries. He was awaiting extradition to face charges in France.

There were five other prisoners there besides myself, most of them also waiting to be 'repatriated'. Every evening, Monsieur Legros had dinner sent in from a nearby French restaurant for everybody. He would go from cell to cell with a menu, taking the orders.

My mattress had been returned and I was given a thin blanket that didn't smell too pleasant. But I stayed in my underpants for the first three days; no clothes, no comb, no toothbrush. And the food was served without knives, forks or spoons, obliging me to eat with my hands.

Late in the afternoon of the seventh day, Vivaldo appeared bearing the cardboard box containing my clothing and other items. He unlocked my cell and handed me the box.

'Get yourself ready quickly,' he ordered. 'Your wife is here to see you.' He went away and returned with a razor holder and blade. 'Here. You need this,' he said. 'You must make yourself look tidy!'

My wife had arrived! I almost felt friendly towards Vivaldo for bringing me such news. I shaved and got myself ready in record time while my jailer waited poker-faced. Then he led me out of the cell block, across a yard where a number of police vehicles were parked, and up a staircase and into another building.

My first meeting with Charmian in four years was limited to little over an hour, and we were not left alone so it was difficult to discuss our situation. Charm's visit was being paid for by a Rupert Murdoch newspaper in Australia. It had taken her two days to fly from Australia via the US to Brazil. She was allowed to show me photos of the children, and to my surprise to have a photo taken of us for her to take back for the boys.

On the Saturday, Charm was back to see me. Without knocking, Vivaldo had opened an office door and nodded for me to enter. I found myself not with Charm, but in a large room full of about 30 seated people with notebooks on their laps. Close to where I had entered the room, there was a desk and a chair. It seemed I had been conned into giving a press conference.

Many of the journalists were Brits, wanting to know how I was being treated and that kind of stuff. I was feeling somewhat hostile about the way I had been tricked, so I wasn't really in the mood to answer questions. I was just thinking how gratifying it would be to see Vivaldo drop dead when another visitor came through the door. It was Charmian.

She was glad to see me, but was very unhappy as she had been given no warning that the press would be in the room for our meeting. With flashes going off and questions being shouted, Charmian burst into tears. 'Can't you leave us alone for a single minute?' she shouted at the press.

I asked the press to give us a minute and they were escorted from the room. Charmian quickly regained her composure and we both realised it would be better to get the press conference out of the way. The only person who would not be happy was Colin Mackenzie who still wanted to keep my story an *Express* exclusive.

After 15 minutes the press were shown back in. Charmian now made it clear that for me to be living with another woman was one thing; but to be having a child with her was something entirely different. But, said Charmian, what was more important than anything was for me to keep my freedom.

I had explained to Charmian at our first meeting that I would need to divorce her so I could marry Raimunda. She was in shock, but said she was prepared to divorce me if it would strengthen my case. If I should be sent back to England at the end of my spell in

Brasilia she said she would also return to England so that we could live again as man and wife when I had 'paid my debt'.

The following day, Legros passed me one of the Brazilian Sunday papers. It reported on the press conference and included a large photo of me kissing Charmian with the caption '*E Agora, Raimunda?*' ('What now, Raimunda?').

I had one more meeting with Charmian before she had to return to Australia. We discussed our future and possible plans. She told me that she had met with Mackenzie and was going to sort out a book deal. We decided it was best for her to cancel the plan to bring the boys out to see me. Mackenzie even got to introduce her briefly to Raimunda before her long flight back.

I was allowed to keep my clothes and other possessions – and was surprised to find that the razor blade was still concealed in my shoe! Life was more pleasant now that I could eat my food with the handle of my toothbrush. I was allowed the 'privilege' of buying certain foodstuffs from my 'private cash' and was permitted to join the rest of the prisoners for an hour or so in the sun each day.

Mackenzie and Raimunda had taken rooms at a hotel in Brasilia and became frequent visitors to the prison. When I had learned that the *Express* had called Scotland Yard to bring about my arrest, I was reluctant to see Mackenzie, believing that he must have known I was being set up. He swore to the contrary and said that he had been 'devastated' when Slipper had entered the scene. Lovelace, he went on, a case-hardened Fleet Street photographer who had captured many a heart-rending moment on film, had 'cried like a baby' when I went off as Slipper's prisoner. Subsequently Slipper clarified that it was Lovelace who signalled to him from the hotel window that I was in the room.

Mackenzie, as Charmian had mentioned, was interested in writing a book with me. He felt that I had been treated unfairly;

he too had been betrayed by his own newspaper. He also said that the proceeds of the book would ensure that Charmian and Raimunda could be taken care of financially if I eventually went back to do my time. In view of the fact that I had already given him a large part of my story before Slipper's arrival, I agreed to work with him in putting a book together. All he wanted for his labour, he said, was 30 per cent of whatever the book might net.

One day he turned up at the prison with a wide smile. Granada Publishing had advanced him £65,000 on his book (about £600,000 today).

'Colin,' I said, when I heard the news, 'I need a lawyer!'

A week later, Dr José Paulo Sepulveda Pertence, a highly respected Brazilian attorney whom Mackenzie had engaged to fight against my possible deportation (for $10,000), visited me. I was not too impressed with him on his initial visit; he looked and acted bored, frequently examining his nails. He drove a red Porsche convertible. But after receiving half his fee he started to shape up and one of his first moves was to get me before a Family Court, where I duly swore that I was the father of Raimunda's expected child.

Raimunda was looking radiant in her pregnancy and was a familiar figure in the Brazilian newspapers. She made a lot of friends and won people over with her smile and her cheeky repartee. Fernand Legros, who met her during visiting hours, admired her, and asked if he could 'have the honour' of becoming the godfather to our child. We accepted. In late March he was deported to France where, although found guilty on some charges, was set free because of the time he had already spent in prison in Brazil awaiting his deportation.

Just as Fernand had departed, Dr Brito, the prison's actual Superintendent, had returned from his holidays and was back in charge. Perhaps upset to have missed all the action, radios and tape-recorders that had been permitted by Brito's stand-in were promptly removed. Visiting time was reduced and cells were searched daily. Vivaldo was reduced to a stuttering mess; such was his fear of his boss.

It was coming to the end of my 90 days and I knew that Dr Pertence, my attorney, was standing by with a writ of habeas corpus to get me out of jail. In the April he had managed to get confirmation of paternity from the Family Court.

On the morning of 6 May, Pertence arrived at the prison to visit me but was not allowed to enter. I wondered if it could mean that my case was before the judges at the Supreme Court. An agent took me from my cell to the adjacent office block where he took five copies of my fingerprints. I asked if he had any idea what was happening in my case, to which he said he knew nothing. I mentioned the fact that when I had been fingerprinted in Rio, 40 sets had been taken.

'Forty sets are taken in the case of expulsion,' the agent told me.

'Well,' I said, 'as you've only taken five sets that must mean that I'm not going to be expelled!' My case had been heard. I could feel it!

During the afternoon, Vivaldo came to my cell and said mysteriously, 'Biggs. Prepare your soul for a journey.'

'What do you mean by that?' I asked.

'Nothing. Just prepare yourself.'

'Vivaldo,' I said, 'you know something! What you mean is, that I am going to be released!' I was almost dancing around the cell by now.

'I don't know anything,' Vivaldo insisted. Then, to my amazement, he put his hand out to shake mine: 'Good luck, Biggs. Go with God.'

A short while later, the second-in-command, Barbosa, paid me a visit. 'Get yourself ready, Biggs. You're being taken to Rio de Janeiro in half an hour.'

'Has my case been heard?' I asked. Barbosa was a decent bloke and had often come down to the cells to shoot the breeze with us, so I knew he would tell me what had transpired.

'It has,' he told me. 'You're going back to Rio tonight. Tomorrow morning you will be released on conditional liberty.'

Even though I was going to Rio to be released, Dr Brito still insisted that I should make the journey in handcuffs. When I protested he said that once we were on the plane he would remove them, but he never did.

The press had got word that I was travelling to Rio and despite Brito's best efforts, a small army of reporters and photographers were already on the plane when I got on with my loony escort. Mackenzie and Lovelace were among them and immediately started talking to me.

'Ron, you're free!' said Mackenzie delightedly, 'Why the handcuffs?'

Before I had a chance to say anything, Brito shouted at the reporters. 'No talking! No pictures!'

The press were as baffled as me by Brito's attitude and I found myself thinking that some kind of trick must be taking place. Perhaps I was being taken to Rio to be deported after all, as that is from where the international flights went.

When we finally touched down in Rio, Brito insisted on waiting until everybody had left the plane before taking me off. We went down the steps of the aircraft with Brito holding the blanket over my head and shoulders.

A car was waiting to take us to the federal police headquarters at the Catete Palace. When I entered the charge-room where the drama had begun to unfold three months earlier, the first person I saw was Inspector Helio.

Helio told me that I was free to go but, he pointed out, there was a large crowd of newsmen waiting at the front gate and it was going to be virtually impossible for me to get away from them. He suggested that I pass the night in the *delegacia*, in a room that had no bars at the window so that I would not feel that I was still being detained. He would instruct an agent to wake me at 5 am, by which time, we hoped, the mob would have dispersed, and I could be driven anywhere I wanted to go. I was given the nightwatchman's room where there was a bed with a comfortable mattress – and the windows were wide open. But I was too excited to sleep. I was a free man!

CHAPTER 12

LIFE IN THE SPOTLIGHT: FAME AND INFAMY

It was the beginning of a beautiful morning as I was driven out of a side gate of the Catete Palace on my way to an address in Copacabana that Raimunda had left with Helio. It was a 'new dawn, a new day, a new life for me, and I was feeling good!'

I was back in Rio, and this time as Ronald Biggs. Michael Haynes had had his day in the Rio sun. The date was 7 May 1974; 3,925 days since the Great Train Robbery; 3,225 days since my escape from Wandsworth; 1,518 days since arriving in Brazil; and 95 days since I was arrested by Slipper.

The *Daily Express*, still interested in getting every last little scrap of news on 'Biggs', had rented an apartment in Rua Gastão Bahiana in Copacabana for their team of reporters, which now consisted of Mackenzie, Lovelace and a friendly Irish fellow by the name of Michael O'Flaherty. Raimunda was also staying in the apartment, but when I got there she was out. The lads from the *Express* had been up late celebrating my release.

It soon became clear that the *Express* was trying to keep the 'copy' I could provide as their exclusive. My attitude was 'fuck the *Express*!' Mackenzie was now saying that he thought I should 'string along' the *Express* for the time being. He was only staying on, he said, because he wanted to be in a position to take care of that 'little matter' of £35,000. I was hoping he could make the 'bastards' cough up.

I ran a bath. I felt like having a long relax in the tub to get the stink of prison and travelling off my body. It was good to be out of that shit-hole.

I was stretched out in the warm sudsy water, probably humming 'The Good Life', when Mackenzie brought the telephone to the bathroom. Charmian was on the line, happy to know that I was a free man but glum at the implications. She supposed it meant that I had gone back to my 'Indian whore'.

I had asked Mackenzie to get tickets for Charmian to come to Rio and she told me that she would be arriving in Rio with Farley and Chris in a week's time. Whilst I was talking on the telephone, Lovelace pushed open the door and snapped a picture; another 'scoop' for the *Express*. The following week the picture appeared as a centrefold in the Brazilian magazine, *Manchete*, and pissed off a lot of people in high places. The Feds advised me to adopt a lower profile.

Raimunda arrived, bringing with her an entourage of reporters and photographers, some of whom managed to push their way into the apartment. Lovelace and O'Flaherty went into action, physically ejecting their uninvited guests. Xuxu looked a picture of health and happiness, laughing delightedly at the wild confusion she had caused. We were pleased to see each other, hugging and posing for Lovelace, who was still breathing heavily after his struggle with his brothers from Fleet Street.

Dr Pertence paid us a visit and outlined the findings of the court. I had gained a victory disguised as a defeat, he explained. An order had been made for my deportation that gave me 30 days to look for a country that would accept me. But, there was a rider to the effect that it had to be a country that did not have an extradition treaty with the United Kingdom. Pertence explained that deportation would mean extradition and the letter of the law – which was also to help me later when in Barbados – clearly stated that the father of a Brazilian child could not be extradited. He advised me to comply with the order and go through the motions to see if I could find another country willing to accept me. The *Daily Mirror* took this chore off my hands. There appeared to be only two countries in Latin America that did not have an extradition treaty with Britain – Venezuela and Costa Rica – and when approached by the *Mirror* they were swift to decline my company. The Venezuelan authorities had by now learnt that I had passed through Caracas Airport on a false passport and would be happy to charge me with that offence should I return.

As the news of my arrival in Copacabana spread, the press started to gather in the street in front of the apartment building. The commotion brought residents to their windows to see what was going on. Some photographers talked their way into the apartments across the road and waited with cameras at the ready. Lovelace told me to keep away from the windows. But I'd had enough. I had just spent three months cooped up in a prison with rats and cockroaches for company and I wanted to feel my freedom. I wanted to walk along the beach, see people, drink a beer at a bar and visit my friends. The *Express* men whined about losing their 'exclusive' story. But I wasn't interested; I wanted out.

Outside was worse than I had imagined. Questions were being thrown from all sides in both Portuguese and English. I tried to reason with the mob, which was a complete waste of time. I managed to get into a nearby bar, but it was immediately packed out with reporters and photographers, all desperate to buy me a drink. By now the *Express* gang had joined me. Mackenzie suggested that we should get in a taxi to get away from the pack. But the pack took taxis too, and followed us in a wild chase down Copacabana. Finally I decided that I would have to talk to the journalists and let them get their precious copy and photographs. Then, mercifully, it would be over – or so I thought.

It was early evening when I got back to the apartment where Raimunda was preparing a meal. We were alone and had a chance to sit down and talk. She had been busy during the three months I had been away. She had knitted and crocheted a lot of baby clothes and had even found time to crochet a beautiful poncho for Mackenzie's wife, Tina. Although Raimunda was only a little over three months pregnant she carried it well and was obviously happy with her 'lump'. Raimunda was now well established in the hearts of the Brazilian people, many seeing her as a heroine who had saved the hapless gringo.

There was a light tap at the front door and I went to investigate. It was another reporter, notebook in hand. His name was Harold Emert, he said, an American reporter for British newspapers resident in Rio, and he would like to ask me a few questions. I turned him away. I couldn't take any more punishment. But I saw Harold many, many times over the decades since that day and, it's funny, he always called on me when all the other reporters had gone home.

It was strange meeting my old friends again, especially the ones who had only known me as 'Mike Haynes'. The Blumer family had said kind things about me to the press while I had been away and received me with open arms, offering me their home if I needed somewhere to stay. Scott Johnson, who I had at one time thought might be a CIA agent, had found it hard to believe that his carefree friend was a famous fugitive.

Shortly before I met up with Constantine, Phyllis had introduced me to one of her best friends, an attractive mother of three young children, named Ursula – or Ulla – Sopher, and she and I had got to know each other. Ulla was also very surprised when she heard that I had been taken into custody for my involvement with the train robbery, but it didn't affect our friendship.

Thankfully, the press interest began to taper off and most of the newsmen disappeared from the vicinity of the flat. Mackenzie and Co. stayed on, awaiting Charmian's arrival.

Charmian and the boys arrived on 16 May, the eve of her 35th birthday, and booked in at the Sol Ipanema on Ipanema Beach. Farley was now seven and Chris a stocky 11-year-old. Seeing my kids and being able to hug them for the first time in four years was a great treat, but there was a certain amount of uncertainty on their part. Farley was gabbling away excitedly, but Chris was much less effusive, answering my questions in monosyllables. Charmian's attitude was friendly enough, but somewhat frosty. During the day, however, the initial stiffness wore off and we began to enjoy ourselves.

Within the terms of my conditional liberty I had to be 'home' no later than 10 pm. My plan was to spend my days with Charmian and the boys, returning to the apartment each night in time to beat the curfew. Raimunda was aware that Charmian had returned to Brazil and was not exactly enthusiastic about me passing the days in my wife's company. I had asked Mackenzie to give Raimunda extra attention during the visit and he bore the brunt of Xuxu's displeasure.

As Charmian would spend at least two weeks in Rio, Mackenzie arranged a two-bedroomed apartment in Copacabana that was within walking distance of the apartment I was sharing with Raimunda. He also hired a maid and these expenses, he explained, would be coming 'off the top' of his book.

Mackenzie also wanted to spend time with Charmian as she had a lot of information about our lives, as well as material for the book, such as family photos.

The weather was still hot and much of the time we spent on the beach where Charmian and I would discuss our complicated situation at length while the kids played and swam. Charmian said again that she would give up everything in Australia and come to live with me in Brazil, but we both knew that this was not a practical solution or even a possibility. The more we talked about the subject, the bitterer Charmian became until one evening when I was preparing to leave to meet my ten o'clock deadline, she put her foot down.

'I've had enough of this,' she declared angrily. 'I'm your wife and I demand my rights! I'm going to that apartment with you and I'm going to sleep with you!'

As good luck would have it, Raimunda was not at the apartment when Charmian entered with her sleeves rolled up, ready for action. In the bedroom that Raimunda and I were using, Charmian noticed a baby-doll nightdress draped over a chair together with the poncho that Raimunda had made for Tina Mackenzie. She picked it up between finger and thumb and dropped it instantly as if it was going to contaminate her.

I could see that Charmian was in an ugly mood and offered to make tea, leaving her in the bedroom to cool down. While I waited for the kettle to boil, I was praying for Raimunda not to return. I was pouring the tea when Charmian appeared in the kitchen doorway, almost snorting with rage.

'I'm not staying here another moment,' she announced

belligerently. 'I can't stand the smell! Please have the decency to take me downstairs and find a taxi.'

Hiding a sigh of relief, I went to the bedroom to get my shirt. As I was about to leave the bedroom I noticed a piece of material on the floor beside the bed, and I stooped down to pick it up. Then I saw more pieces of the same material under the bed. To my horror, I realised that Charmian had cut up Raimunda's nightdress and Tina's poncho. I put everything into a plastic bag and went back into the living room where Charmian stood smiling maliciously.

'Charm,' I said. 'That was an insane thing to do.'

'Perhaps it was,' she said viciously, 'but it's only a small token of what I would like to do to that bitch!' I tried to calm her down as we went down to the street and stood waiting for a taxi. I knew that she was hurt and frustrated and I did everything I could to console her, but she was not to be mollified and left in tears.

Raimunda arrived the next morning having spent the night in a small, first-floor kitchenette that she had rented in one of Rio's busiest thoroughfares, Avenida Nossa Senhora da Copacabana. She had found it a few weeks before I was released from Brasilia and had rented it principally for herself, knowing that we would not be able to afford the high rent of the *Express* apartment when the pressmen left. With Mackenzie's help she had bought some second-hand furniture and a refrigerator. All the kitchenette needed, she said, was a coat of paint.

Later that day, when I went to meet Charmian and the kids, I was pleased to see that Charm had recovered her composure. Her vandalism of the previous evening was not mentioned and we decided to have another afternoon at the beach. There, Charmian told me that she had reluctantly resigned herself to the fact that she would be facing her future without me. It was not what she wanted, but she would divorce me, as she had said, so that I would be free to marry Raimunda and give the child my name. And, she hoped, it would also enable me to keep my freedom. We loved each other but, under the circumstances, we could only be friends.

When Charmian and the boys left Brazil at the beginning of June, I moved into Raimunda's tiny apartment. There was a double and a single bed, a dining-room table and four chairs and the refrigerator in the principal room. There was a minute bathroom and an even smaller kitchen. The rent was $50 per month (about US$270 today).

The front window looked out on to the roaring Copacabana traffic, seemingly within touching distance. There was a bus stop immediately in front where buses would stop with a squealing of brakes and pull away again with high revs, leaving a trail of black smoke. When the window was raised, it was possible to see the smoke and fumes creeping into the room. Worse still, cockroaches outnumbered the tenants in the building by a thousand to one.

I set to with sandpaper, filler and paint and in a week or so I got the place looking bright and cheerful. One of my hippie friends painted a huge blue butterfly on the wall where we planned to install the baby, and one of the Blumer children, Linnie, did a beautiful job of painting a golden lion on a facing wall because she knew that the new arrival would be a Leo. Ulla's young daughter, Carla, also came and painted some animals on the wall of the 'nursery'.

Although Raimunda seemed perfectly happy with the apartment and did her best to keep it clean, I started to look around for somewhere more salubrious. One afternoon, not long before Raimunda's confinement, I found myself in a lazy-paced, picturesque fishing village called Sepetiba. It was about 45 miles west from Rio and could easily be reached by bus in about 90 minutes. I liked the place and made a mental note of the name.

It was around this time that I first met John Stanley Pickston, a fellow Londoner a few years younger than me. Highly entertaining and always ready for a laugh, we soon became firm friends. He was married to a Portuguese lady named Maria Emilia (known as Lia) and lived only a couple of blocks from our apartment. We found we had a lot in common, both having the same working-class background. And, of course, we both liked a pint. We met frequently.

Raimunda and I had already agreed on names for our offspring and Michael Fernand Nascimento de Castro Biggs, to give him his full name, was born at 10 am on 16 August.

Reporters had renewed their interest with the new twist in the Biggs story and were vying for the first picture of the new Baby Biggs with offers of a thousand dollars for an 'exclusive'. But a wily nurse at the hospital beat us all to it and had her palm greased by a Brazilian freelance photographer who was let into Raimunda's room a few short minutes after the baby was delivered.

As we did not have a telephone, an arrangement had been made with a neighbour to receive a call the moment the baby was born. When she knocked at the door to tell me 'It's a boy!' I was as delighted as I had been when my other three sons had been born. Our apartment was full of friends and reporters waiting for the news and, after 'wetting the baby's head' with beer and a bottle of champers, I grabbed a taxi to the hospital to visit Raimunda and our new little Brazilian. Newborn children are rarely up to their fathers' expectations, but Raimunda thought he was *lindo* (beautiful) and I had to agree. The old fortune-teller had been right again; I had had a child with a woman with long black hair.

Back at the flat, the booze was still flowing and the newsmen were waiting for my comments on fatherhood and my future plans. Was I going to marry Raimunda? At that time, the terms of my conditional liberty did not permit me to marry and it was to be 18 years before this restriction was rescinded. It was to take 28 years before I made an honest woman of her, or rather before Raimunda and I made an honest man of our son. We eventually married in July 2002 in the salubrious surroundings of Belmarsh Prison.

As I was not allowed to work in Brazil, it was difficult to say what my plans for the future would be. I could only hope that Mackenzie would come through with enough of the proceeds from his book to keep us going.

A couple of days later I picked up Raimunda and Mike at the hospital and brought them back to the flat. Neighbours and friends soon arrived with presents and congratulations, cooing and baby talking. Mike was a great little kid with lusty lungs and a healthy appetite.

During 1974 I found time to help to write and record *Mailbag Blues*, a jazz-rock-fusion soundtrack to my life. The album was recorded by some of the top session musicians in Rio led by my American friend, bass player Bruce Henri.

By Christmas, at four months, Mike – or 'Mikinho' as we all called him – appeared to be making good progress, but I was not happy about bringing him up in the pollution that surrounded us in Copacabana. I decided to take another trip to sunny Sepetiba to see what I could find by way of alternative accommodation and found exactly what I wanted; a house with a big sandy garden, about 50 yards from the beach. The house had not been lived in for some time and was badly in need of decorating. But the rent was only slightly higher than the shoebox in Copacabana, so I closed a deal with the owner of the property and returned to Rio delighted with my good luck. Raimunda was uncertain about making the change. I had done so much to our flat, she said, and we would be so far away from our friends.

I took Ulla to see the place, driving to Sepetiba in her car. We took cleaning materials and cleaned the house from top to bottom between us. Afterwards we passed a couple of hours relaxing at a bar on the tree-lined seafront and, later, became lovers.

Fernand Legros, the fraudulent Frenchman, had made contact soon after Mike was born. He had read of the event and wanted to keep his word with regard to becoming Mike's godfather. Xuxu had been very impressed with Legros's claims to fabulous wealth and liked the idea of having someone like him to look out for her son's spiritual requirements. Legros suggested that Mike should be baptised in France – at his expense – and so it was agreed.

About the same time, the *News of the World* became interested in Raimunda and Mike and approached her with regard to an exclusive story. A deal was made to take them both to England and Raimunda was to be paid a thousand pounds. So, at the beginning of January 1975, she and Mike flew to London. Shortly afterwards, Xuxu, the little half-Indian girl from the interior of Brazil, showed her beautiful tits in a 'world exclusive' on the front page of the world's biggest selling Sunday newspaper.

It was a picture spread that I later learnt had particularly upset Charmian, as she believed it was a catalyst that had contributed to her father's suicide.

By the start of 1975 I was no longer the only British fugitive to be making headlines as a certain Lord Lucan had gone AWOL after being suspected of murdering the family nanny on 8 November 1974. Over the following decades there would be hundreds of alleged sightings of the missing Lord, even an assumption that I knew where he was!

A few days after Raimunda left for England, I hired a van and took our bits and pieces to Sepetiba. I was glad to be away from the noise and grime of Copacabana and got busy with tools and paint to set about fixing the place up.

I renovated our furniture and shaped up the garden, enjoying the hard work. Twice each week I had to take the bus into Rio to sign a register at the federal police headquarters. And twice a week I spent the night with Ulla whom I was becoming deeply involved with. Although Raimunda and I lived and slept together following my release, we had not resumed an intimate relationship. Furthermore, she knew of my affair with Ulla.

From England, Raimunda moved on to France for the much-publicised baptism of Mikinho on 14 February 1975. Legros spared no expense to turn the event in Piscop, north of Paris, into an unforgettable experience for Raimunda and to introduce her to artists and show-business friends. Actress Nicole Argent acted as the godmother. Champagne! Bright lights! And phoney promises. Xuxu was enchanted.

The godfather bestowed heavenly protection upon his godchild in the form of a diamond-studded gold cross, which turned out to be as snide as the canvases he was dealing in. But Raimunda would not have a bad word said against Monsieur Legros. She saw him and his friends as people who would enable her to become an artiste and open her *caminho* (road) to stardom.

On their return I met Raimunda and Mike at the airport. Raimunda was using French perfume, and elegantly dressed in expensive-looking clothes, while Mike was just beautiful! We went by taxi to Sepetiba. I had hired a friend's sister as a maid and when we got to the house it was clean and polished as well as being freshly painted. Xuxu was pleasantly surprised. Mike's room was ready, with a white mosquito net hanging over the 'dream bed' I had built.

So Raimunda was back and we continued to live together. With the ease with which she made friends, Raimunda was soon mixing with the neighbours, inviting them in for a *cafezinho* and a spot of gossip.

Dona Maria Jose was our immediate neighbour and very *simpatica*. She had a gang of kids of her own to take care of but she was always ready to look after Mike if Raimunda and I had to go out. Her youngest – adopted – daughter, Renata, was about Mike's age and as they grew up they became sweethearts and sparring partners. Raimunda also made friends with a couple named Borges, who ran a small general store around the corner from where we lived.

Borges and his wife were involved in a religion known as Candomblé, often described as *macumba*. Candomblé, which was brought to Brazil by African slaves, is widely followed in Brazil and involves many weird and wonderful rites which, it is said, can bring about good fortune, good health and spiritual fulfilment. It is Brazil's voodoo, if you like, but more established.

Mr Borges said he thought that Raimunda and I should submit to one of these ceremonies and 'seek out our true destinies'. Raimunda was all for it and I – after my experience with the fortune-teller – agreed to go along, more out of curiosity than anything else.

The first part of the ceremony took place in a house close to where we were living. We had been told to arrive wearing old white clothing, bringing with us a clean set of clothes, also white, to change into. After Raimunda and I had been introduced to the *mae-de-santo* (spiritual mother), decked out in her traditional voluminous white clothing, she asked us what it was that we were looking for in our lives. What were we asking of our saints? Raimunda had answered that she was looking for the road that would lead her to a career as a professional entertainer. My request was to receive a 'document' that would enable me to stay in Brazil legally. We were instructed to kneel on two rush mats placed side by side. A *pai-de-santo* (spiritual father), also taking part in the ceremony, and a female acolyte, a form of altar girl, began chanting while the *mae-de-santo* 'sprinkled' Raimunda and I over our heads and shoulders with a mixture of cubed fruit and vegetables which she took from two earthenware dishes. Then, two live black chickens were produced and, with the assistant holding them, the *mae-de-santo* cut their throats, letting the blood flow over the fruit and vegetables in the two dishes. This was an offering to Exu, the devil, and was put into a locked chamber at the side of the room where the ceremony was taking place.

Then, with Mr and Mrs Borges, who were going to be our 'witnesses', plus the *mae* and *pai-de-santo*, we were taken in a van to a secluded, wooded area where there was a waterfall. Here all four of us took off our clothes down to our underwear and threw them into the fast-flowing water which, we were told, would take all our worldly problems out to sea. After 'cleansing our bodies' in the icy water we were instructed to get dressed into our clean, dry clothing. Then we were led to a flat rock where the assistant, who was by now in a trance, was preparing for us plates of sliced apple covered with honey.

On the way back home, Raimunda's eyes were shining. As far as she was concerned it had been a hundred dollars well invested.

A month after Mike's first birthday, Raimunda took off on her second trip to Europe; this time alone. She said she would be away for three months. I was left holding the baby. But I didn't mind in the least; Mike and I got along fine. The only blot on the horizon was that funds were running low and Mackenzie had not responded to an SOS for more cash which I assumed was still forthcoming from our deal and the book, *The Most Wanted Man,* which had been published on 1 September. I started buying goods on credit from Borges's store, running up a hefty bill. Then, when I had a number of bills to pay, I borrowed money from Ulla to get by.

Things were tough from a financial point of view and I reluctantly dismissed the maid. I could no longer afford that luxury. I took on the housework, washing clothes and nappies and doing all those other domestic tasks. Mike got accustomed to seeing me do the housework and started to call me *mae* – almost pronounced 'mine' – meaning mother! After a fall, he would pick himself up bawling, *'Mae-eh!'* Patiently I would wipe the sand out of his mouth and tell him that I was his *pai.*

Living in Sepetiba without a telephone I was somewhat cut off from the outside world, but I was enjoying rural life and my anonymity out of the spotlight. I liked the people in the area, who were simple but friendly. Everybody, it seemed, had a kindly word for 'Biggies' (as I was known) and Mikinho. At weekends, a small group of musicians would gather at a nearby bar and play samba, with everyone singing along and having a good time. There was always someone having a barbecue, or a *feijoada*, and I was frequently invited to these informal parties. Most days I would take Mike to the beach for a couple of hours. Friends often came down for the day. Johnny Pickston was a regular visitor – and so was Ulla. She would sometimes bring her children, Alex, Felipe and Carla, and stay for the weekend, enjoying the relaxed lifestyle that was Sepetiba.

Over the next few years there were many financial ups and downs. There were numerous offers of 'big money'. Merv Goldfinger – for want of his real name – invited me for dinner at the Copacabana Palace Hotel to put to me a deal for the film rights to the story of my life. It looked good: $100,000 at the signing of 'the contract', $100,000 at the beginning of the filming and the rest when the film was in the can. But Merv was only one of a string of people who wanted to make some kind of a deal in the hope of a quick buck.

In 1975 I was facing a fairly bleak Christmas as Roy James, Jim Hussey and Gordon Goody looked forward to their first taste of freedom after 13 Christmases in the nick. I was wondering how I was going to put a turkey on the table when a television crew from Argentina turned up at the front gate wanting to interview me. I told the producer a story of Yuletide hardship and charged $200 (about US$1,000 today) for the interview.

The word must have been passed around that I was tucked away in Sepetiba as I was quickly sought out to give interviews by TV networks from Germany, Japan, Belgium and Australia. Now I had raised my price to $2,000 ($10,000 today) an interview, and was soon able to hire another maid and pay back Ulla the money I had borrowed.

There were other visitors to our house in Sepetiba, besides the newsmen. Total strangers, some from abroad, would manage to find their way to the home of 'Biggies'. Often they would just be looking for a chat and the chance to pose beside me for a photograph, although others had a more professional interest.

During early 1976, most of the rest of the gang were released from prison, and only Bruce and Charlie were still inside. Then, one morning in July, I received a visit from a smooth-tongued South African named Gary van Dyk. He told me that he had been sent over by the gang and had a letter from Bobby Welch. Bob's letter was to introduce van Dyk and went on to say that the gang were in the process of putting a book together with a writer called Piers Paul Read who had done well with a book called *Alive,* about a disaster in the Andes. I had read the book and I knew that Mr Read was a competent author. Bob suggested that I should throw my lot in with the 'boys', as most of them had come out of prison hard up, as their 'minders' had scarpered with the dough. Van Dyk was 'one of us', Bob wrote, and I could put my trust in him. I agreed to join forces with my colleagues, so I found a lawyer and signed the contract which van Dyk had brought with him.

I didn't like van Dyk. He had a dangerous look that didn't go with his glib tongue. He told me that various members of the gang had tried unsuccessfully to get the story of the train robbery published and he, van Dyk, had come up with the idea that had got W.H. Allen, the publishing company, to do business. There was going to be a new angle introduced into the story; the robbery had been financed by a group of Germans, one of them being 'Sigi', who was said to have been with us at Leatherslade Farm.

For their investment the Germans, supposedly led by one Otto Skorzeny, an officer in the Waffen-SS who had rescued Mussolini from the Marshal Badoglio government, had 'creamed off' a million pounds from the haul and the gang had divided the rest. I thought it sounded a pretty stupid idea and said as much to van Dyk, arguing that someone with Piers Paul Read's ability could write a sensational book by simply sticking to the facts. But van Dyk's plan had been approved by the gang and that was the way it was going to be done.

Soon, van Dyk told me, I would be visited by the author with a view to substantiating the German angle and I would have to be 'letter perfect' with what I told him. He would write, he promised, giving me the full details of the plot. He left, leaving me with $1,000 which the gang had 'scraped together' for me. With regard to the proceeds from the book, said the South African, I would be in for a 'full whack' of £14,000, about £90,000 today.

I heard nothing more from van Dyk, Read or the gang for over three months, then I received a call from van Dyk. He hadn't been in touch for various reasons, but now the 'business' was very much on and he would probably be arriving with Read within a couple of weeks.

Another three months went by without further contact from van Dyk. Then in January 1977, I received a telegram from a certain Jeffrey Simmons, representing W.H. Allen, inviting me to telephone him to discuss the book business and the pending visit from Read. I was wondering what I should do when van Dyk contacted me again out of the blue. I told him about the telegram and reminded him that I still didn't know what I was expected to say. He told me not to worry because he would be back in Brazil before Read got there. Under no circumstances should I phone W.H. Allen. But I did phone and I got in touch with Simmons.

During our conversation, Simmons asked me if I had received the £2,000 from van Dyk. I assured him that the only money I had received up until that moment had been $1,000 – and that had been a handout from my old pals. Simmons insisted that I must have received the £2,000. He had personally handed that amount to van Dyk with the instructions to pass it on to me in Brazil.

'Our intention,' Simmons said, 'was to pay you between £4,000 and £10,000, depending on what you are prepared to tell us. We understand that there are certain things that only you and Buster Edwards know about and we will pay you the full £10,000 if you can confirm what he has told us.'

I wasn't surprised to hear of van Dyk's little deceit and I

suddenly lost interest in the whole business and told Simmons that I would be pulling out of the deal. He pleaded with me not to.

'Just meet our author at the airport,' he said. 'Have a few words with him and if you still want to forget the matter, put our man on the next plane back to London. If you will do just that we will pay you a further £2,000. Do we have a deal?'

I reluctantly agreed, and a couple of weeks later Ulla drove me to the airport to meet Read. We went to his hotel, the Castro Alves in Copacabana, where without preamble I told him he was being hoaxed and that there was no truth in the German connection. Up until that moment he had been the essence of self-confidence, chatting away about the 'fine bunch of lads' he was working with.

I could see that he didn't want to believe me and later, when his book, *The Train Robbers*, was published in 1978, he went so far as to say that he thought the 'German connection' had paid me a visit and told me to say that the whole thing was a hoax. Ulla's Germanic looks seemed to have strengthened his suspicions.

Read paid me my £2,000, packed his bag and returned to London. Later he sent me a copy of his book and wrote in it that he hoped it was the better book than we had both talked about. Unfortunately, it wasn't.

The federal police HQ had moved from the Catete Palace and was now in a dockland area of Rio known as Praça Mauá. It was here that a squadron of British warships docked on 15 April 1977. I had been to sign in at the *delegacia*, and was on my way to have a beer when I noticed a couple of uniformed British sailors standing around a newspaper kiosk. They appeared to be buying postcards and were having a bit of a problem with the currency and language. Mr Nice Guy stepped in.

'Can I be of any help to you fellows?' I offered. The sailors looked at me.

The sailors looked harder. 'You wouldn't be Ronnie Biggs by any chance, would you?' one of them asked.

I confirmed that I was.

'Blimey!' We only came off our ship not ten minutes ago and I said to my mate here – joking like – we might run into Ronnie Biggs, and we've done it!'

We got the postcard business out of the way and stepped into one of the bars in the area. The sailors – Harry, a signaller, and George, a cook – told me that they were off a ship named the HMS *Danae*, and that the squadron was in Rio for naval exercises with the Brazilian fleet. George mentioned another cook on the *Danae*, 'Slinger' Woods, who was on duty and unable to get ashore. George described him as a 'great fan' of mine and said that he was going to be pissed off if he didn't get to meet me. Harry suggested that I go aboard the *Danae* with them to 'meet the lads'.

'I can't go on board,' I said. 'I wouldn't be allowed in the dock without an identity document.'

'You don't have to worry about that,' Harry insisted. 'You're dressed in civvies. If you walk in with us, the blokes on the gate will think that you're one of our officers. Come on – me and George will take care of you.'

I allowed myself to be persuaded, even though I realised that I was taking a bit of a risk.

We went through the dock gate without being challenged, then on to the flagship, the HMS *Tiger*, which we had to cross to get aboard the *Danae*. As we boarded the *Danae* a ceremony was in progress, so we stood waiting silently until it was over. The officer in charge of the proceedings then turned to me and said, 'I know you. You're that fellow, Biggs, aren't you?'

'Yes, sir.' I replied.

'Well, welcome aboard, lad, but if anyone should ask you how you got on the ship – I don't know anything!'

I went down a steel companionway, with Harry and George leading the way, until we arrived at a room where a number of sailors were sitting around writing letters, etc. Harry spoke. 'We would like you all to meet our friend – Ronnie Biggs!' The sailors all looked up, registering surprise and pleasure.

I was talking to the lads, drinking the duty-free booze and signing autographs when George reappeared at the cabin door.

'Sorry to have to tell you this, Ron, but the word has gone around that you are on board and the top brass are in a bit of a panic. Perhaps you had better go ashore. Harry and I are coming with you – and if anyone wants to join us I'm sure Ronnie won't mind.'

About a dozen of us invaded one of the clip joints in Praça Mauá, grogging on until it was time for me to meet my curfew. I still hadn't met 'Slinger' Woods so, at Harry's insistence, I agreed to meet them at the same bar the following morning when 'Slinger' would be off duty.

I spent the night with Ulla, and when I got to the bar the next morning, there was a whole mob of sailors waiting to meet me. The beer began to flow. Harry told me that he had been up the best part of the night sending and receiving messages to and from the Admiralty.

'They've gone potty about you being aboard one of our ships,' he told me. 'They want to know why you were not arrested and put in irons!'

I had planned to get back to Sepetiba during the afternoon to spend some time with Mike. Ever the genial host, I invited some of the ratings back to Sepetiba with me and five of them agreed, including 'Slinger'. We went by bus.

Smothered in tattoos, the boys off the *Danae* were a hit in sleepy Sepetiba with their rousing sea shanties. They were having a lot of fun and a lot to drink. It was a great party, but the next morning the sailors had to be at their posts. I called on a local taxi driver to take them back to Praça Mauá. A price had to be agreed. With the driver there would be six of them in the vehicle, the roads were bad, the passengers were drunk – and they had passed the best part of their money over to Mr Borges at the bar.

Predictably, perhaps, the taxi broke down and the HMS *Danae* sailed off without the help of 'Slinger' Woods and his mates. They had to be flown out to their ship by helicopter and were no doubt up before The Old Man.

When the ships returned to port to let the jolly jack tars have one final fling in Rio before heading for calmer waters, they were issued a notice: 'All personnel are advised against making contact with Ronald Biggs.'

The incident was blown up by the press and much talked about. Rumours included one about a rating making a citizen's arrest and the Brazilian Navy threatening to blow the British ships out of the water if they tried to leave Rio with me on board. Pure fantasy, as were stories that the incident caused a major diplomatic incident between Britain and Brazil.

The British Navy is a regular visitor to Brazil and when they were you could normally find a group of ratings and officers enjoying the hospitality of the Biggs household. My snooker table was proudly covered for many years by a Union Jack that was presented to me by members of the crew of the HMS *Campbeltown*.

Raimunda finally returned to Brazil. She had been away for two and a half years rather than three months, thrilling European audiences with her 'exotic dancing', and had plans to return. She now appeared to be worldly-wise and could speak French well, but she was still a country girl and happy to be back in her own country. She had arrived with presents for everyone. Raimunda and I were still 'the best of friends' and she lived with us in Sepetiba until she went back to France to continue her artistic career.

In January 1978 the punk rock group, the Sex Pistols, had fallen out during a tour of the US. Johnny Rotten, the singer, and Sid Vicious, the bassist, decided to pull out of the group. The Pistols' manager, Malcolm McLaren, took their desertion in his stride and on 24 January 1978 landed in Rio with the two remaining members of the group, guitarist Steve Jones and drummer Paul Cook.

McLaren, always one with an eye for publicity, planned to reform the Pistols in Brazil with two of the world's most wanted men: Nazi war criminal Martin Bormann and little ol' me. Realising that it might be difficult to make contact with Herr Bormann, McLaren hired the services of a Hollywood bit-player, Texan James Jeter, dressed in uniform and jackboots, as a stand-in. Once more the gentlefolk of Sepetiba had reason to raise their eyebrows when the punks arrived. Even the poorest locals looked well dressed alongside the tatty lads from London.

Over drinks, McLaren invited me to 'join in the fun' with the boys, outlining what he had in mind. They had been filming their antics during their trip to the US and McLaren's plan was to turn the footage into a film, which was subsequently released under the title *The Great Rock 'n' Roll Swindle*.

If I participated in the film, said McLaren, I would be paid a fee of $2,000 and if I sang on a record with them a further $1,000 would be coming my way. I pointed out to McLaren that although I came from a talented family, I was not much of a singer.

'So much the better,' he declared. 'That's what "punk" is all about!'

Well, $3,000 (about $13,000 today) was an offer that I couldn't refuse and I didn't dilly-dally in signing the contract.

The visit of the Sex Pistols coincided with carnival in early February, so I found myself as their de facto tour guide taking the boys to the parade and various parties. They were not the only stars in town that carnival, with both Elton John and Rod Stewart enjoying the revelries as well as a film crew for James Bond's *Moonraker*, in town to shoot carnival scenes for the film.

After carnival it was time to work. First holding a press conference where some of the press seemed to think Herr Bormann was the real one. Then record the tracks and film the videos to support them with Julien Temple being flown in from London to direct. *The Great Rock 'n' Roll Swindle* would finally be released in the UK on 15 May 1980.

Having listened to the Pistols' *Never Mind the Bollocks, Here's the Sex Pistols*, I felt that I could write something in a similar vein and suggested as much to McLaren. I wrote a piece which I called *A Punk Prayer* and recorded it with Steve and Paul in Rio. The main verse was:

> *Ronnie Biggs was doing time*
> *Until he done a bunk*
> *Now he says he's seen the light*
> *And he's sold his soul for Punk*

The song was released in the UK on 30 June 1978 as the Sex Pistols' fifth single under the title 'No One Is Innocent', and as 'Cosh the Driver' in France, and sold over seven million copies worldwide, reaching number seven in the UK and outselling the group's 'God Save the Queen'. The 12-inch version was released as 'The Biggest Blow – A Punk Prayer'.

I also recorded a track called 'Belsen is a Gas' which had been written by Johnny Rotten. I was not overly happy with the lyrics, which even Rotten would say crossed the line into gratuitous bad taste. I did end up adding an extra verse:

Dentists searched their teeth for gold
Frisk the Jews for banknotes fold
When they found out what they'd got,
Line them up and shoot the lot.

One of the scenes of the video had us performing on top of a boat. As should have been predictable, most of the instruments ended up going over the side to sink into the murky depths. Unfortunately the instruments were rented and not insured, and McLaren did not have the funds to pay for them, and I certainly didn't. So EMI had to cover the damage while Julien was held 'hostage' in Rio until McLaren wired the funds from London back to EMI. Julien also discovered his return air ticket had been issued under the name of John Lydon, Rotten's real name.

The Pistols had barely exited Rio stage left when another of Britain's favourite sons dropped by, arriving in Rio on 8 March 1978. It was HRH the Prince of Wales, whom I decided to give a wide berth to.

CHAPTER 13

KIDNAPPED: SECOND TIME LUCKY

'Ronnie! Long time – no see!'

The cliché came from Clive Wilson, an Englishman to whom I'd taken a dislike the first time I met him. He had lived in Rio for many years working off and on as a tour guide. Until Clive's appearance I had been enjoying an afternoon barbecue in Rio. It was 7 March 1981.

'Ronnie, I've got this journalist chap and he'd like to do an interview with you and perhaps take a few pictures.' Clive had sat himself down at my table and was warming to his subject. 'It's for *National Geographic* and the fellow can pay $200. What do you say, Ronnie – a hundred for you, a hundred for me?'

'You piece of shit,' I wanted to say – but I needed the money so I let it pass. 'Okay,' I told Clive, 'invite your friend over on Monday morning around eleven.'

I have met many reporters and photographers over the years before observing this one at work and I had a feeling, right from the start, that something was wrong. He didn't have a tape recorder or a notepad. Neither did he have the brash line of bullshit particular to some journalists. He was not professional with a camera – and he only had the one. But for the amount of time the 'interview' took, a hundred bucks was money for old rope even if he wasn't a reporter from *National Geographic*.

The reporter, who went by the name of Patrick Richardson King, paid me. Smiling and looking more relaxed than before the interview, he told me that his wife would be joining him in Rio later in the week. He asked for a suggestion for a restaurant and a show he could take her to and then asked if I would care to join them.

I met up with King a couple of times in the week and said I would join him and his wife on Monday 16 March, the eve of St Patrick's Day. As I had nothing else planned, except for my weekly signing on with the federal police, I thought why not?

Sugarloaf Mountain, which I could see from my Botafogo apartment at the time, is one of Rio's best known attractions. The peak is reached by a two-stage cable car trip, a trip made famous by James Bond's struggle with Jaws in *Moonraker*. The first leg of the journey takes visitors to the top of Urca Hill where there is a restaurant and a semi-open air amphitheatre where samba shows were a weekly Monday attraction. This was my suggestion for Patrick and his wife.

I arranged to meet them at around 9 pm at Roda Viva, a barbecue restaurant at the foot of Urca Hill, next to the cable car station. I was also expecting John Pickston and some of his guests in from London to put in an appearance. If not at the restaurant, then at the show.

I arrived ten minutes early, just as a busload of tourists pulled up. I pushed through them and took up a place a few tables away from the entrance so I would be easy to spot when Patrick and his wife arrived. I need not have worried, as apart from one couple at a nearby table, the place was basically deserted. I ordered a beer and then a second. I looked at my watch. It was 9.10 pm.

Without warning, I was grabbed from behind in a 'choking' neck lock. I reacted and struggled for air. A second person ran at me, punching me in the pit of my stomach. I kicked out and managed to break free from the person holding me around the neck.

Instinctively I ran for the exit. As I flew, half falling, through the door of the restaurant I was grabbed by other strong hands, overpowered and forced into a VW Kombi van that was parked close to the entrance. I was pushed, struggling into the van. A hand appeared in front of my face. I bit the person's thumb and bit hard. I tasted blood. They had me pinned face down on the floor of the van, and it was then that I heard a Scottish voice that I would never forget: 'It's us again, Ronnie! This time we got you bang t'rights – an' if you don't do everythin' I tell you to the letter there is every chance that you won't see your wee kid again – so fucking behave.'

The voice belonged to the man who had tried to kidnap me two years earlier, ex-Scots Guardsman John Miller – sometimes known as John McKillop.

The van pulled away from the restaurant under the noses of some armed sentries guarding a nearby naval establishment.

While Miller was talking and giving orders he was taping my hands behind my back. It was obvious that he knew what he was doing. I was then gagged and blindfolded and bundled into a sack which I later discovered had been tailor-made for the operation, equipped with four handles to facilitate carrying and a sticker 'Cobra Viva / Live Snake'. Miller continued talking.

'Now listen up. We are going to drive around for a wee while then we are going to transfer you to another vehicle. Don't try and make any noise – I don't want to have to give you an injection – and let's not forget that we have got wee Michael.'

It had been exactly two years since I had first met Miller. At that time, late March 1979, I was still living in Sepetiba. Miller had arrived in a small yellow Volkswagen with two hefty friends whom he had introduced to me as Fred Prime and Norman ('Norrie') Boyle. Miller was well over six feet tall, powerfully built and sported a small diamond earring in the lobe of his left ear. They were all ex-Scots Guards, he told me, and said they were in Rio as a second unit film crew working for Lewis Gilbert, who earlier in the year had directed *Moonraker*. Gilbert had also directed *Alfie,* a favourite of mine.

Fred presented me with a bottle of Johnnie Walker Black Label telling me as he squeezed the life out of my hand that there was plenty more to come as long as they were around.

Although Fred had been a regular in the Scots Guards like his two mates, he was clearly a Londoner. He said he had been a boxer and a physical training instructor during his years in the army. Norrie, like Miller, was a Scot. He appeared less boisterous than his friends and said little. The quiet type, he enjoyed playing with Mike – who was four at the time.

Miller was clearly the leader of the little band, exhibiting brash self-confidence. Towards the end of his army service, he said, he had been an undercover agent in Northern Ireland, posing as an IRA sympathiser.

Over a lunch of giant prawns, Miller told me that their work on Gilbert's new film would be taking them down to Argentina, but they would be returning to Rio soon. They wanted to be back in Brazil to celebrate Norrie's birthday on 4 April.

Not even a week had gone by and Miller was on the phone to say they were back. 'So when are you coming into town next, Ronnie?' Miller asked. 'We're staying at the Copacabana Palace and we would like to invite you and Michael to come and

have a spot of lunch at the pool. Would Friday at one be okay?'
It was, so I signed off agreeing to meet them at the hotel at the end
of the week.

Something bothered me, however. Miller was being just a bit
too friendly for my comfort. I already had a feeling he was up to
something, but I needed to find out what. I telephoned Armin
Heim, a German friend of mine and a respected photographer.
I outlined recent events to Armin and expressed my suspicions.
Finally I asked him if he would come along and meet the friendly
'film crew'.

When I arrived with Mike at the Cop Palace, Miller and Co.
were already holding a small but somewhat noisy party around
the pool. The group's behaviour was certainly not what would
normally be associated with a place of such old world charm.
Besides my three new friends, there was a young English couple,
a blonde Canadian lady of ample proportions and the tour guide,
Clive. Now it became clear how Miller had got my address in
Sepetiba. The big Scot pumped my hand and put his arm around
my shoulders.

'Glad you could make it, Ronnie. Let me first introduce
you to these fine people. Are you ready for a drink? I've got some
great news for you. I've got you a part in the film. I'll tell you the
details later.'

Over lunch, Miller told me about the film part. When
he had been in Argentina he had told Gilbert that he had had
the 'privilege' of meeting me. He had mentioned that I was on
conditional liberty and not allowed to work so was badly in need
of a 'few bucks'. Apart from being something of a fan of mine,
Gilbert, Miller said, was quite sympathetic with regard to my
situation and had come up with the 'great idea' to give me a small
cameo role in his film: a chase scene.

'Shouldn't be too difficult for you,' Miller said. 'I have also taken the liberty of telling Mr Gilbert that you would require $10,000 (about $40,000 today) for participating in the film. I hope that will be enough?'

Work was to begin on the film soon, but not in Rio, rather in Porto Alegre in the south of Brazil. I pointed out to Miller that under the terms of my conditional liberty I could not leave the State of Rio de Janeiro.

I went back to the Copa the following morning with Mike. He wanted to see the 'crazy men' again. Miller asked me to be at the hotel around ten as he was expecting a call from Gilbert.

On arrival we found the gang in their rooms on the third floor. Drinks were poured by Norrie. The phone rang and Miller picked up the receiver. 'Is that you, Lewis? . . . Aye, Ronnie's sitting right here in front of me . . . Aye, he's quite willing to take part in the film, but there's a wee problem; he's not allowed to leave Rio . . . you can't change the location? Och! That's too bad . . . aye, I understand. I'll talk to him, Lewis, and get back to you later. Bye.'

Miller replaced the receiver. 'Ronnie, there is no way that Lewis can change the location for the shoot. It would cost too much to bring the cast and crew back up to Rio – we've just got to get you down to Porto Alegre.'

'Forget it,' I said. 'There's no way I'm leaving Rio. I'm not willing to take the chance. I can't afford to.'

Miller broke the building tension with a new idea which had nothing to do with the film. Clive had told him about Paradise Island, a boat trip offered to tourists.

'I'd like to take you, wee Mike and your pal Armin to the island tomorrow. Let's have some fun. Fuck the film deal! What do you say?'

Mike said yes!

Above left: The happy couple. Charmian and I on our wedding day, 20 February 1960.

Above right: My prison book from HMP Wandsworth at the time of my escape in July 1965. Last entry records me heading to the exercise yard at 2.30 pm never to return.

Below: D326 (40126) was an unlucky engine, and not just for its part in the Great Train Robbery. It was moved to Cheddington Station before the police got to examine it at the crime scene. It was finally cut up for scrap in 1984.
© *Shutterstock*

Right: Our hide-away, Leatherslade Farm, after being discovered by the police.

© Shutterstock

Middle: The exercise yard I escaped from at HMP Wandsworth. You can see why we had to get the timing just right and I needed to be close to the wall when the rope came over. © Shutterstock

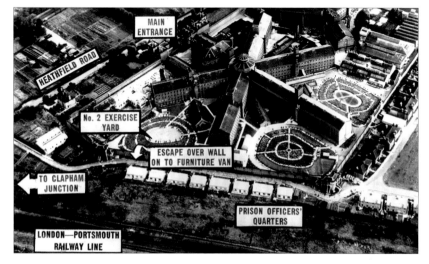

MAIN ENTRANCE

HEATHFIELD ROAD

No. 2 EXERCISE YARD

ESCAPE OVER WALL ON TO FURNITURE VAN

TO CLAPHAM JUNCTION

PRISON OFFICERS' QUARTERS

LONDON—PORTSMOUTH RAILWAY LINE

Below: My escape route from HMP Wandsworth on 8 July 1965.

Below: Reunited with Nick and Chris in Australia in June 1966.

Above: Charmian and I enjoying a dinner date in Australia. Not sure who was baby-sitting.

Below: Mike and I with some of the crew from the HMS Danae in April 1977.

Right: The photo I used as "Michael Haynes" for his passport in January 1970. A short haircut, added weight and glasses did more to change my appearance than any plastic surgery.

Below: With my nemesis, John Miller, in April 1979. The man who tried to kidnap me twice and failed miserably on both occasions. Taken in April 1979, at the Copacabana Palace Hotel.

Above: Early photo of Raimunda and I on a night out in Rio.

Below: My first reunion with Charmian on 16 February 1974 after being 'discovered' in Brazil. Despite the smiles it was a tense and awkward moment. © *Shutterstock*

Above: Newspapers have always played a big part in my life. Over the decades I was never far from the headlines.

Right: With a prop newspaper from the filming of *Prisoner of Rio.* 1987.

Left: Mike holds up a newspaper as I talk to the press on my return to Rio on 25 April 1981, 40 days after I had been kidnapped.

© Shutterstock

That night I took the boys off to the local British pub, the Lord Jim. While John set about hooking up with one of the many young ladies in the bar, Fred and I stood at the bar and talked about London.

Miller, having picked up a cute blonde called Lucia, suggested, at the young girl's instigation, that we move on to Dancin' Days, a popular disco on Urca Hill. As we emerged from the cable car, the lights were flashing, the music was belting out, and young Brazilians were getting it together.

While Miller took Lucia off to the dance floor, I continued my chat with Fred.

Despite the late and boozy night we all met outside the hotel the next morning, Sunday, and took the tour bus to the coastal town of Itacuruçá. The sun was shining and there was a clear blue sky. Everyone was in high spirits. Fred had arranged a case of cold beers and Mike was sitting on Norrie's lap, chatting away.

All in all it was a jolly day, swimming and playing football on the beach, the visiting 'gringos' against the locals. We ate well and drank many a *caipirinha*. Ulla's brother happened to be at the island and he fell in with our group. He shared my opinion that Miller and Co. were 'up to no good' and suggested that I should be on my toes.

During the fun and games in the sea, Miller had grabbed me around the waist and stripped me of my bathing trunks in just a few seconds. His physical strength was obvious. At a later date somebody sent me the front page of a Scottish newspaper with a picture of John Miller in training for my kidnapping. He was photographed jogging in a park while carrying somebody across his shoulders.

That evening, Mike and I returned to the relative peace and calm of Sepetiba. Even though I trusted the gang less and less,

I was now even more curious to find out what they were up to. Miller had told me what 'a great guy' I was. He didn't want to be a nuisance, but could he and the boys see me again before they left Brazil – they would be leaving at the end of the week. I said that I would see them again on Tuesday, two days later.

I arrived at Ulla's apartment in Santa Teresa (about 20 minutes by car from Copacabana) at around seven o'clock that Monday evening.

'Hey!' said Ulla when she saw me. 'Guess what? You are supposed to have been kidnapped and on your way back to England on a chartered boat! I have just had a call from some man called Chris Buckland, who said he was a reporter with the *Daily Mirror*,' Ulla went on to explain. 'He told me that you had been grabbed by a group of ex-Scots Guardsmen and were now on your way back to England. He called from New York and I told him I was expecting you so he said he was going to ring back later.'

I brought Ulla up to date with regard to what had been going on with my Guardsmen 'buddies', the film offer and the conversation Miller had had with 'Lewis Gilbert'. We discussed the whole thing at length. Why would they want to kidnap me? Why the cock-and-bull story about a movie deal? Why Porto Alegre – which was way down south – when Rio had a port and numerous places where a yacht could be moored.

As promised, Buckland, the *Mirror*'s New York bureau chief, returned his call confirming everything that Ulla had told me. The ex-Scots Guardsmen had indeed been highly trained for the job, he told me, and their plan was to get me aboard a yacht and return to England with me as their prisoner. He wanted to know if this information coincided with anything that was going on in Rio at that moment. I gave him a brief account of recent happenings and he said that he was going to speak to his editor in London to see if he could fly down to Rio to cover the story. Sadly he never made it.

A little later, Ulla's 16-year-old son came home. He told me that earlier in the day he had answered the telephone to somebody by the name of Kenny Lynch, who was staying at the Intercontinental and had left his room number so that I could call him. I wondered if it could be the entertainer of that name, so I rang the hotel. Sure enough it was the real Kenny Lynch. He was in Rio with his friend Bobby Moore, the great England footballer and captain of the 1966 World Cup-winning side. This was a pleasant surprise. Lynch explained that he and Bobby were both fans and would like to get together while they were in Rio for a 'meal and a chat'. He suggested the following Saturday as he and Bobby were in Rio for a pro-am golf tournament and had to be on the course every day till then. We agreed to meet at their hotel for lunch.

Ulla thought I was crazy, but I decided to go to Copacabana the next day to meet Miller as arranged. In a strange way I was starting to enjoy our little game of 'cat and mouse'.

When I got to the Cop Palace on the Tuesday the boys were already around the pool, grogging on. Big John told me that he had just got back from Fortaleza, a city in the north of Brazil that is nearly twice the distance from Rio as Porto Alegre is to the south, having flown there the previous day.

Miller had also found time during the past two days of travel to check out Rio's domestic airport, Santos Dumont.

'The film offer is still open, Ronnie,' Miller went on. 'I went down to Santos Dumont. It would be dead easy to get you on a plane and fly you to the shoot. Don't say "no" just yet. Just come down to the airport and see for yourself – would you do that? I would just love to see you score the ten grand.'

Before leaving Ulla's apartment I had phoned Johnny

Pickston. I had not seen him for some time and as he only lived a couple of blocks back from the Cop Palace, I invited him to join me for a drink. I told him about Miller and that I was due to have lunch with Lynch and Bobby Moore at the weekend. John expressed envy as he was a fervent West Ham supporter and a great fan of Bobby. Next I called Armin and filled him in on the developments from the *Mirror* reporter. I asked him to appear at the hotel as well.

Soon after I got to the hotel, John and Armin arrived together. We sat around and had a couple of beers and Norrie suggested going up to his suite on the third floor for 'some serious drinkin''. There were still a couple of bottles of Black Label remaining. Norrie poured generous measures of whisky into six tumblers. I finished my drink, and now feeling quite drunk decided to go and sit by the pool. Armin and John joined me. Suddenly, I made a decision.

'I'm going out to the Intercontinental! I'm going to go and see if we can give Kenny and Bobby a nice surprise.'

By the time we reached the hotel it was close to midnight. As luck would have it we found Moore and Lynch sitting alone in the hotel's nightclub, the Jakui Bar. Most of the lights had been turned down and it was quite gloomy. We all shook hands and then my two friends and I joined them at the table. John soon made it known that he was a football buff and launched into a conversation with Moore while Armin and I talked 'show business' with Lynch.

The visiting VIPs were still a little jet-lagged, but said they looked forward to our lunch on Saturday. It was time to say goodnight as they were expected early at Gavea Golf Club. I got a cab and headed over to Ulla's place in Santa Teresa to spend the night.

Miller phoned early next morning. 'Ronnie, it's fuckin' heartbreaking, but we've only got a day or two left in Rio,' he began. 'Look, come by the hotel for lunch and bring wee Michael as Norrie's got a present for him, the walkie-talkies we've been playing with. We're covered; Norrie will just say they were stolen when we get back.'

I told him that I had to go and sign on with the federal police, but Miller was most insistent that I come over and have lunch first.

'Look, Ronnie. I'll even drop you off after lunch and as we are in the area you might as well get a look at Santos Dumont. See you at noon.'

I had left Mike with my neighbour in Sepetiba, so I went over to the hotel alone. I wasn't really interested in having lunch or seeing the 'boys'. My main interest was to see if I could make Miller part with some money up front. A reward for all the trouble they had put me to.

After lunch we took a taxi down to Praça Mauá where the federal police are located. The gang went into one of the local clip joints to wait and I went into the *delegacia* to sign on. At that time it was a ritual that had to be followed on every Wednesday and Friday. Then I joined them at the clip joint. Again Miller broached the subject of the filming.

'The only place I am going,' I told Miller, 'is back to Sepetiba. There is no point going to the airport because I'm not going to go ahead until I get paid something. At least two grand, because before I start putting my liberty at risk there are a few debts I want to clear up first.'

'Ronnie, old son,' Miller interrupted earnestly, 'I promise I'll ring Lewis as soon as I get back to the Copa and I'll have your bread by Friday. You have my word.'

I rose early the following morning in Sepetiba and took Mike to the beach. While he played in the sand I sat thinking. It was not very likely that Miller would come up with the money – but he just might. If he did I could try and grab the money and run. Soon after we got home from the beach there was a call from Ulla. She had just received a call from an editor on a Manchester newspaper. A Scotsman called McGovern, he had given Ulla much the same information that the *Mirror*'s Buckland had provided, emphasising the fact that I should avoid contact with the Guardsmen at all costs. He described them as 'extremely dangerous' and wanted me to call him just as soon as I could.

I called Manchester, I think it was the *Daily Star*, and got straight through to McGovern. I told him I was calling with regard to some 'dangerous' Guardsmen.

'I'm sorry,' he said to my surprise, 'I'm unable to help you.'

'But didn't you just call and speak to my girlfriend and tell her that I should avoid some ex-Scots Guardsmen at all costs?' I asked.

'I'm sorry,' he repeated, 'I know nothing about the matter.'

To say the least, I was baffled. I decided to ring Ulla back and tell her what had happened.

'Come back to Rio,' she urged. 'In Sepetiba you are a sitting duck.'

I knew she was right so I started to prepare to head for Rio that very night with Mike.

Minutes later, as if he had been listening on the line, John Miller called. 'Ronnie! How are you this morning you old reprobate? Did you get a good night's rest . . .? That's magic, Ronnie. Look, I rang Lewis as I promised and he is sending down the two grand. That okay for you . . .? You'll be coming into Rio tonight for Norrie's birthday party, won't you? . . . Och don't say you can't, you've got to come to Rio tomorrow anyway to sign in, right . . .? If you can't make it for Norrie you'll have to come and have a spot of lunch at the hotel. About one then . . .? And listen, Ronnie, what I'd like to do is for you to come straight up to my room when you arrive . . . See you tomorrow, old son – oh, and by the way it might be as well if you were to leave wee Mike at home, as we do have business to discuss.'

I had a feeling that Mr Miller was preparing to pounce.

I was still far from happy about the conversation I had had with the editor in Manchester so I decided to call him again. The same Scottish voice came on the line. He was glad that I had called back. He explained that when I had called earlier there had been someone in his office and he was unable to speak freely. He endorsed all the things he had told Ulla and went on to say that Miller was being financed by a wealthy jet-setter, an Englishman who spent much of his time abroad. He said he knew the identity of this person but he was afraid to name names. He was not a brave man, he said. He was also unable to tell me why Miller wanted to abduct me.

If I wasn't confused before, I was now. Who was the mysterious Mr Moneybags? What was his interest in having me kidnapped? Why did an editor on a Manchester-based newspaper, and a Scot to boot, want to play Mr Nice Guy to Ronald Biggs? One thing was for certain, it was time to stop putting my head in the lion's mouth.

I phoned my mates, Armin and Pickston, and brought them up to date with the latest twists to the 'plot'. I suggested that they might like to go to the hotel the next day for yet another free lunch – but not to be surprised if I didn't put in an appearance. With that organised I packed my bag, grabbed Mike and headed for Rio.

As 'my gang' gathered poolside at the Cop Palace with Miller's gang, I was having a quiet lunch with Ulla. The pieces were beginning to fall into place. A friend had called from London to say that he had been in touch with Lewis Gilbert's office and they were quite certain they had no film crew operating in South America nor had Gilbert ever heard of John Miller. I had made a decision that was quite foreign to my nature – I was going to call the cops!

Before doing anything I had to go to the police to sign in. If I saw a certain friendly cop – Barradas – I would tell him the story and ask for his advice. As I went into the *delegacia* about an hour later, the very same Barradas was standing in front of me.

'Hello, Biggs! How's the shrimp in Sepetiba?'

'You,' I said pointing at the smiling cop, 'are just the man I'm looking for. Can we step across the road for a *cafezinho* or something stronger?'

I told him about my big 'friend' John Miller, giving him a detailed description which included the diamond earring.

'And now, you – the thief of the century – are asking the Brazilian federal police to protect you? I don't believe it,' laughed Barradas. 'But let's go back to the *delegacia* and you can tell the story to my boss – give him all the details and he'll decide what needs to be done.'

Dr Bizzo, a dapper fellow in a pale blue gabardine suit was the boss or *delegado,* as they are known in Brazil. I told him how Miller had been trying to lure me out of Rio, mentioning an offer of $10,000. Bizzo listened intently to my story, making notes on a pad on his desk and occasionally asking questions for clarification.

'Find these clowns and bring them in,' he instructed as I finished. 'Biggs, you stay here. I might want you to make a statement.'

Barradas left the room and was back within five minutes.

'You're not going to believe it but we've got the big son of a bitch with the earring,' he announced. 'He was standing across the road.'

Bizzo asked me where I was staying and at what number I could be reached. I told him I would be with Ulla.

'Go there now and stay there,' Bizzo said. 'I'm going to ask this fellow some questions and it will be better if he doesn't see you.'

I left the *delegacia* a happier man knowing that Miller was out of circulation. I made contact with John and Armin, who recounted the lunchtime episode at the Cop Palace. Seven of my friends had turned up for lunch at Mr Miller's expense, a host who had been as genial as could be until it became clear that I was not going to appear.

'Where the hell is Ronnie?' he had asked the boozy congregation with obvious agitation. He had then gone into a huddle with Norrie and Fred before excusing himself, saying that he had to make some important phone calls. John, on the pretext of going to the gents, had followed him out of the hotel and saw him hail a taxi.

Ulla also had her own story. Shortly after I had left her flat to head down to the federal police, Norrie had called. He wanted to know if Mike or I were there. When Ulla said I wasn't he was most insistent that he wanted to drop around with Mike's walkie-talkies. Ulla told him to leave them at the desk but he kept wanting to know where Ulla lived. Miller, Norrie and Fred had, in fact, dropped me off at Ulla's, but thankfully they had forgotten to make a note of the address. In Santa Teresa, where Ulla lived and where I would live for many years, if you don't know where you are going you can spend weeks looking for the right road.

Later, after Miller and his friends had left Brazil, we also discovered that the gang had booked out of the Copacabana Palace at midday on that same Friday and booked rooms in the Gloria Hotel, just a stone's throw from the Santos Dumont airfield.

A federal agent – aptly named, Cobra (snake) – worked as a clerk at the same *delegacia* as Dr Bizzo. He spoke English quite well and had been the interpreter when Bizzo interrogated Miller. Cobra was in charge of the file which I had to sign twice weekly and frequently had a number of questions to ask as he was eager to perfect his English. I had recently explained to him what 'piece of cake' signified.

When I went to sign in the following Wednesday, he told me what had happened to Mr Miller and his friends. Fred and Norrie had been tracked down to the Gloria Hotel and had also been brought in for questioning. All three denied all knowledge of a film deal involving me. They went further and said that they had obviously heard a lot about me and their only intention was to meet me and have a good time. They had been due to leave Rio that same evening and had hired a Learjet to take them up to Belem in the far north of Brazil, where they had a yacht waiting for them to sail back to Britain. They had been cleared and released and Cobra had personally escorted them to Santos Dumont to catch their plane.

'Tell me something,' I asked Cobra. 'Would it have been easy for them to get me on that plane?'

'It would have been a "piece of cake", Mr Biggs,' he winked.

Miller and Co. were probably saved by their passports which, because they had only recently left the Scots Guards, still showed their occupation to be 'government service'. Given the manner in which Slipper and Scotland Yard had tried to grab me in 1974, the federal police probably thought it was another bungled attempt by the British government to get me. Rather than start another diplomatic incident they simply sent Miller packing without taking further measures.

I never did get to have my lunch with Kenny and Bobby Moore. When I rang their hotel on the day we had arranged I was told they had gone travelling. Happily, I had not.

As life returned slowly to normal I got news that Brian Field – in theory the link to the 'Ulsterman' – had been killed in a car crash on 27 April. His wife was also killed. At the time we assumed this was Karin. But she had left and divorced Brian after the trial and returned to Germany. Fair to say that without Brian (and Karin) there would have been no Great Train Robbery.

CHAPTER 14

UNWELCOME CARIBBEAN EXCURSION

That first failed kidnap attempt had been two years ago in 1979. Now they seemed to have pulled it off. Inside the bag I was seething. Clive Wilson had obviously set me up for the phoney interview with Patrick King. My guess was that I was being driven to Santos Dumont to take the trip I should have made two years earlier. I tried to control my rage. Miller could well be bluffing about having grabbed Mike, but I could not afford to take that risk.

'You're probably wondering what this is all about, Ronnie,' Miller said breaking into my thoughts. 'Well, I'll explain everything to you in good time. First we're going to transfer you to another vehicle.'

The other vehicle, as I expected, turned out to be a plane. The gang unceremoniously bundled me into the back of the cabin as a piece of luggage.

The jet engines started up and in a very short time we were

airborne. The air pressure rose rapidly, painfully popping my ears in the process. I was in a very uncomfortable position and squirmed around in the bag trying to stretch out and find a more comfortable position. My movements alerted Miller and brought him back to the bag. He spoke in a low voice.

'Take it easy, Ronnie. Keep yourself quiet and still. I don't want to have to inject you, but I will if I have to.' He gave the bag a couple of light taps and moved away.

Exerting all my strength in the confined space I tried to get my hands free. I clenched my fingers, forcing my wrists apart. Suddenly there was a sharp snap. I had managed to break one of the tapes which secured my wrists behind my back. I rested, hoping that the sound had not been heard by anyone above the sound of the engines. I could feel more freedom in my hands now. I made a further mighty effort and the other tape snapped. My hands were free! Now, when we arrived at wherever the gang was taking me, I would tear the gag off and start screaming bloody blue murder.

Unknown to me, somebody had been sitting close enough to hear the sound of the tape snapping. Miller came to the bag and loosened the rope that held the sides together. I could guess what he was going to do so I clasped my hands together. Miller's hand probed into the bag taking no time to discover that I had freed my hands. His face was close to mine, so close I could smell his breath.

'You're being very stupid for someone with a reputation for being so smart,' he said softly. 'Another stunt like this and I'm going to give you a jab of sodium pentothal. If I do, there's every chance you'll vomit into your gag and fuckin' choke to death. Think about it, Ronnie!'

As Miller talked he pulled my hands from behind my back and

roped them to my belt. He gave my bonds a tug. Satisfied, he laced the bag up again.

In all my life I had never ever felt the urge to kill somebody. But with Miller, I decided to make an exception.

After several hours the plane landed and taxied across an airfield before coming to a stop. I could hear Miller giving orders, then talking to someone whom I assumed must have been our pilot. Then, with Miller supervising, the canvas bag and its contents were dragged and heaved from the plane. I was being carried again and as I was, I heard someone speaking Portuguese. At least I was still in Brazil, perhaps in Fortaleza.

From what I could tell from within the confines of my bag, the gang met with little or no resistance in getting me out of the airport and into a waiting car. I was lying on my back, stretched out along the back seat. As the driver started the car, the radio came to life.

'Rádio Belém. Uma hora da manhã . . .'

The radio was turned off abruptly, I imagine by one of the gang, but at least I knew I was in Brazil, but it was Belém, Brazil's northernmost seaport which is just south of the equator, 975 miles north-west of Fortaleza and over 2,000 miles north of Rio. I calculated I was already a third of the way back to Blighty.

There was no conversation made by the gang between the airport and what I later learnt to be the Belém Yacht Club. On arrival at the club I was dragged from the vehicle in my bag and put on the ground. I heard the car drive off. I later discovered that the gang had left a car at the airport but could not find it and had to use a taxi instead. I also learnt that when the gang arrived in Rio, they went looking for me in Sepetiba, not knowing I had long since moved to Rio. These boys were a class act!

Miller and another voice started bawling the name, Greg.

They shouted several times before I heard any response. After a short time I heard the unmistakable splash of oars and I was dragged into what I imagine must have been a dinghy. Miller, still giving the orders, was telling everyone to take care not to overturn the boat. When we reached the yacht, Miller unlaced the bag.

'From here on in, Ronnie,' said Miller as he stood over me, 'you can have it hard or you can have it easy. It's up to you. We're going aboard the boat now and then I'm going to tell you all about our little operation.'

The boat, a 62-foot schooner, the *Nowcani II* (Now Can I Too), had been hired by Miller in Antigua in the Caribbean at a cost of US$16,000, about US$50,000 today. Owned by Dallas businessman Robert Sabinski, it was roomy, comfortable and fully equipped with up-to-date seagoing devices. There was a saloon, with a U-shaped seating arrangement around a dining table.

I was sitting at this table facing my kidnappers. Besides Miller and Fred Prime, there was a fair-haired guy called Thorfinn Maciver, another Scot, this time from Hawick – and he was the skipper of the yacht. There were two other men in the team, both in their mid-twenties: Anthony 'Tony' Marriage, of medium but wiry build, and Mark Algate, a tough-looking character who was obviously into body building.

Miller was the essence of good humour thanks to the apparent success of his operation. He was standing drinking from a can of beer. He offered me one.

'You look as if you could do with a wee dram, Ronnie.'

I ignored him. 'Where's Mike?' I asked sharply.

'Wee Michael? Och, as far as I know, he's with your babysitter where you left him. That was all cobblers about having grabbed him. I knew you wouldn't call my bluff. But don't worry about the kid, we haven't laid a finger on him. However, I expect you are still a little pissed off with me, Ronnie, and I have to tell you, you have every right to be. But let me tell you what this business is all about and hopefully you'll see I'm not the total asshole you think I am.

'It is not our intention to hand you over to the cops. There wouldn't be any point in that as there is no longer any reward for your capture. Simply, we're going to sell this story to the highest bidder – after all we did the job that Scotland Yard failed to do. We're going to make a shitload of bread, Ronnie, and if you play your part and co-operate then you're in for a share of the proceeds. Fred only came along this time on that understanding.'

Fred nodded. 'That's the Gospel truth, Ronnie. I promise.' There was no mention of Norrie Boyle and why he had decided to forgo the pleasure of coming back to get me.

Miller ran through his plan. Unfortunately, he said, he wouldn't be making the trip with us, but Fred would be taking care of my every need. He was not able to tell me where our next port of call would be, but I figured that his plans included as my final destination a branch of HM Prisons.

Before he left he promised that we would not land anywhere for the present. 'Any deal that's made will be on this boat,' he said, 'and outside territorial waters.' He elaborated, talking of flying a film crew out to the yacht to prove to the world that he really did have me. 'One thing is for certain, Ronnie, you're going to come out of this little drama as the hero. We're going to be seen as the villains.'

Years later some journalist told me that Miller had been asking £500,000 for the story. About £7 million today.

Miller got some more beers from the refrigerator and passed them around. I waved him away. Then, almost casually, Thorfinn, the skipper, tossed a clear plastic bag on to the table in front of me.

'Perhaps you would prefer to roll a joint?' he suggested. 'It's pretty good weed.'

Well this was a different matter; if ever I had needed a joint it was now.

Just as Popeye can take on overwhelming odds with a can of spinach, I felt that I could better face my situation after a few puffs of the proven panacea. I rolled a fat one and lit up. The gang sat quietly as I silently dragged away on my joint. The captain was not wrong, it was good. The doors of my mind, with a little help from the weed, were beginning to open. We were still in Brazil and while I was in Brazil there was hope.

'I'll tell you something, Ronnie,' Miller went on. 'Before we came to Brazil I·had a good heart-to-heart chat with your old friend, Jack Slipper. I wanted to find out what our position might be in the event of getting caught during this operation.'

Since the kidnapping, I had been involved in several interviews with Slipper. I tried to approach him about Miller's statement but he was always evasive, although never denied knowing Miller who thanked him for his help in his book.

'The most I will ever tell you, Ronnie,' Slipper said on one occasion, 'is that shortly before you were kidnapped, I did meet a group of likely lads – more than that I'm not prepared to say.'

Obviously, the 'likely lads' were Miller and Co. and I feel certain that Mr Slipper had knowledge of my kidnapping before it took place. And if Slipper knew I was going to be kidnapped, who else did? That is a question that over the years the authorities and the media have chosen to ignore.

In fairness to Slipper, when my autobiography was first published he tried to clarify his position. He said that he had met Miller two years prior to the kidnapping and was told of a plan involving fast planes and boats. Slipper asked him what it would cost and who was going to pay? Slipper was convinced that Miller was a Walter Mitty dreamer, yet still reported the meeting to the Flying Squad.

'It wasn't until I heard Biggs had been kidnapped,' Slipper wrote, 'that I thought of Miller again. If I chased up every nutter I talked to I'd have done nothing else.'

Miller was leaving the yacht, shaking hands with the rest of the gang. He whispered a few words to Fred then, in a louder voice said, 'Show Ronnie to his quarters – and don't take your eyes off him!' To me he said, 'Use your head, Ronnie, don't try anything heroic – and before you think of jumping over the side, remember you'll be in shark-infested waters!'

My cabin was equipped with two bunks, small but comfortable. Fred fastened the door open and stood 'at ease' on the threshold, very guardsman-like, with his hands behind his back.

With the knowledge that Mike was not in any danger I started to calm down and with the gentle rocking movement of the boat plus the soporific effect of the grass, I finally fell asleep.

At breakfast I saw a slim, blond youth whom I hadn't noticed the previous evening. He was the 'Greg' the gang had been calling to pick them up. Greg Nelson explained that he was not one of the kidnappers, but a deckhand from North Carolina who had been hired with the yacht.

Later in the voyage I found myself alone with Greg, who was also fond of a smoke. As he was rolling one he said, 'Mr Biggs, the other night when I saw you smoke a joint in front of your kidnappers, I just knew that you were a cool dude, and,' he lowered his voice, 'if I can help you in any way, I will.' Sadly he never could. I also learnt that the cook, Veronica, a young girl from Scotland, had jumped ship on arrival in Brazil as she was far from happy about the company she was having to keep on the yacht.

Preparations were made to sail on the afternoon tide. There was some speculation that Brazilian customs and immigration officials might come aboard and Muscles informed me that if that happened I would be tied up and gagged again.

Soon we were chugging towards the mouth of the Amazon and the open sea. If I had any ideas about jumping over the side of the boat once we were sailing it would have been difficult. Fred had returned to duty and stayed close to me at all times.

'Once we are out of Brazilian waters,' he said, 'you'll have the run of the boat – until then you won't be allowed to show your face on deck.'

I thought it was best to try to give the impression that I had resigned myself to the situation. I conversed with my captors in a civilised manner, drank a few beers and smoked a joint or two.

Whatever thoughts I was having on the second morning out of Belém were broken by the noise of a Brazilian Air Force spotter plane as it flew low over the *Nowcani II* several times. The gang rushed on deck, waving and pretending to take photographs. Fred stationed his bulky frame in front of the companionway, warning me not to 'try anything'. I had got a glimpse of the plane from a porthole in the galley and felt a sudden surge of hope. Perhaps the game was up for my kidnappers and the Brazilian cavalry was on the way.

'What do you think the penalty would be in Brazil for kidnapping?' Muscles enquired.

'Anything from 30 to 50 years,' I said sincerely.

My kidnappers were most certainly in a panic and the order was given for 'full speed ahead' to get out of Brazilian territorial waters as fast as possible. Maciver, the skipper, calculated that we could be out of Brazilian waters as early as the following morning if the engine was kept at full throttle.

The following morning was sunny and there was a stiff breeze, favouring the course of the *Nowcani II*. The gang were all smiles as it became clear we would soon be out of the reach of the Brazilian authorities. A few hours later Maciver calculated we were out of Brazilian waters and I was allowed on deck. As promised, I had the complete 'freedom' of the boat. I could make my own meals and do my own thing.

Ripping across the water, with Brazil far behind us, my shipmates were becoming more liberal in their behaviour and attitude, especially with their intake of booze. The party livened up, with the usual horseplay among young men.

Now that I was beyond help from Brazil, I thought it was only a matter of time before I ended up in England. I would probably never see Brazil again. I worried about Mike, hoping that Raimunda would be able to get to Rio to take care of him. For myself I was not worried; I was trying to work out a way to sink the yacht. That evening the refrigerator packed up. The crew tried to fix it, but without success. A lot of beer was going to get warm and a lot of foodstuff was going to spoil, so the order went up to eat, drink and be merry!

On the fourth morning I woke early and immediately noticed that the boat was strangely silent. The engine was not running and we were becalmed. Suddenly, the skipper shouted, 'All hands on deck. We're sinking!' I was probably the only person on board who was pleased to hear Maciver's cry. And we really were sinking. My only regret was that Miller was not with us to go down with his mates.

Overnight water had flooded into the *Nowcani II* and I went on deck to watch the crew feverishly bailing out with saucepans. Fred looked up from his labours at one point and said: 'I reckon you're doing a bloody Uri Geller on us, Ronnie!'

'I'm working at it!' I replied.

By late afternoon, the 'engineers' had made the necessary repairs and got the engine going again. The voyage continued. By now the beer in the refrigerator was warm and eventually all the meat and poultry had to be thrown to the sharks. During a relaxed moment on the fifth day, Thorfinn offered to read the Tarot cards for me and I agreed. While I was shuffling and cutting the cards as he instructed, he repeated his conviction that the Tarot cards did not lie.

I had no idea what Maciver was seeing in the cards as he turned them over but whatever it was, he was obviously puzzled.

'It's amazing,' he said incredulously. 'Here we are but one day from our destination and already with one foot in Great Britain, yet the cards show that you are going to come out of this as the winner.' He sat looking at the cards shaking his head. I don't know if he knew it, but his prophecies gave my flagging morale a much-needed boost. It was also useful to learn that we were only a day away from our destination – wherever that might be.

There was excitement in the air on the morning of our last day at sea, 23 March, and everyone seemed extra friendly even though the engine was playing up again and what headway we did manage was made mainly under sail. The skipper had radio contact with someone, somewhere, but I was not permitted to hear what was said. I assume the conversation was with Miller who was planning to rendezvous with us.

As it could be my last meal aboard the *Nowcani II*, I decided to prepare my own lunch. While I was searching in a cupboard for some condiments I came across a full bottle of Grand Marnier, a liqueur that I am particularly partial to. I opened the bottle and started pouring myself healthy nips. After lunch, without being told why, I was confined to my cabin so I took with me a book, the grass and the Grand Marnier. I could see no reason why I shouldn't enjoy my last hours aboard as they might also be my last hours of 'freedom' for some time.

Fred came to my cabin for a chat, perhaps to offload his conscience as we were going to be parting company soon. I was rather drunk by this time and I only vaguely remember what was said and the events that followed. I fell asleep but awoke to hear raised voices and shouting. Marriage was shaking me.

'Biggsy! You're needed on deck! Right now!'

As I lurched up on deck I saw, to my surprise, a huge grey gunboat close by, bristling with armaments and people.

'Who's the man in the red cap?' called someone from the gunboat with a loudhailer.

'It's Ronald Biggs!' shouted Algate. 'A fugitive from Great Britain.'

The voice from the gunboat announced that we were going to be towed into port. The coastguard vessel put the *Nowcani II* under tow.

The next thing that I remember clearly was being in the middle of a sea of perspiring faces all gabbling away excitedly. A tall man wearing a light-coloured uniform and a cap with a lot of 'scrambled egg' on the peak, was holding me firmly by the arm saying, 'This way, Mr Biggs.' Later I discovered it was a gentleman by the name of Kenrick Hutson, who was the Chief of Immigration. The rest of the events of that evening are far from clear, but I remember being fingerprinted and examined by a doctor who announced that I was in a 'state of shock'.

I woke up in a single bed in a small room. There was a table and a chair, where a middle-aged black man sat reading a newspaper, and a window with six vertical bars. It brought back memories.

I was in a cell of some kind. The man put down his newspaper and we exchanged polite morning pleasantries. I discovered that I was in Barbados and the Bridgetown police station. I was feeling a little hung-over and asked my guard if there was any chance of a wash and brush-up. There was 'no problem'.

Breakfast of coffee and croissants was brought to me and this was followed by a visit from Mr Hutson, who politely asked how I had passed the night and was there anything I needed. Hutson was a very pleasant individual with impeccable manners. He explained that, for the time being, I was his responsibility, having landed on the island without a passport. But every effort would be made to ensure a pleasurable stay on the island. He promised to have me removed to more comfortable quarters as soon as I was officially handed into his care.

I was taken to the office of the Assistant Commissioner, a Barbadian by the name of Whittaker, which he pronounced 'Widdiger'. He was more business-like than the affable Hutson and very much a policeman. Early on in the piece, it was evident that Whittaker wanted to see me returned to Great Britain. He made some enquiries about the kidnappers and explained that in due course I would be appearing before a magistrate who would decide my fate.

My kidnappers, who had been held in the same police station, had already been released to take the yacht on to Antigua, Whittaker told me. It was not considered necessary for them to be in town for the hearing with the magistrate.

Miller's original plan, I was told, had been to rendezvous with the yacht off Barbados so that he could have his moment of glory by sailing into English Harbour in Antigua with me on board. The *Nowcani II* sailed into English Harbour all right, only Miller and I were not on board. Before leaving, however,

Fred had thoughtfully left a hundred-dollar bill with Whittaker to take care of whatever needs I might have.

As soon as I was back in my room after seeing Whittaker, another visitor was announced. It was a certain Mr Ezra Alleyne, a lawyer, bespectacled and very dark-skinned. He presented his credentials, adding that on the island he was known as the 'Perry Mason of Barbados' having never lost a case. The *Jornal do Brasil* was to describe him as a mixture of Sidney Poitier and Gilberto Gil.

'You sound just like the man I need,' I said, not really interested in the services of a lawyer at that time. 'But I have to tell you that I have arrived on the island penniless.'

'Let us not think about money,' said Mr Alleyne in a most un-lawyerlike manner. 'Let us just think about getting you back to Brazil!' He saw my smile. 'You don't know me from Adam,' he went on, 'but I know you very well. When the train robbery trial was in progress I was in London, studying law with Mr Ellis Lincoln – does that name ring a bell?'

I knew the name well. Lincoln was the solicitor who had handled the defences of Wisbey, Welch and Hussey. 'Sunshine', as I had called Mr Alleyne back in 1964, had been a regular presence at the original trial as part of the Lincoln & Lincoln legal team.

'Mr Lincoln taught me something that I will never forget,' continued Alleyne. 'It doesn't matter how difficult a case may appear – there is always a loophole. And, if you will allow me, I would like to find the loophole that will enable you to return to Brazil.' I shook hands with 'Sunshine' for the second time and happily accepted his offer.

While I was still talking to Alleyne, yet another visitor was announced. A David Neufeld was waiting to see me. Neufeld turned out to be a smartly attired lawyer from New York.

David Levy, a writer who had collaborated with me on the book *Ronnie Biggs: His Own Story* had retained him after speaking with Charmian. The book was being serialised in *The Sun* and, at the time I was grabbed, many people, including the Brazilian authorities, thought my disappearance was all part of an elaborate plan to hype the launch. It was not.

Neufeld explained that he was in Barbados to secure the services of Frederick Smith QC, a former Barbados Attorney General, who would take care of my case. He showed little interest in the fact that I had just engaged Barbados's Perry Mason. He had his 'instructions' from Mr Levy and he wasn't about to settle for anyone other than Frederick Smith. We were facing something of an impasse until I made the suggestion that Alleyne and Smith might possibly like to work together. Alleyne was instantly agreeable. Smith, he said, was an extremely competent counsel.

So Alleyne and Smith it was – with the very able assistance of Alleyne's partner, Alan Shepherd. The hearing before the magistrate was set for 5 April giving my team just a few days to prepare a defence. In the meantime, the immigration chief had me moved into the middle of a dormitory that housed about 20 of his agents, all nice lads who stood in line for autographs!

There was a PA system in the dormitory and during the day, music and Bajan comedy programmes were played. One afternoon, I found myself listening to the country and western tune 'Lucille' and remembered my German friend in Rio, Armin, who played and sang that particular piece often and well. I was singing along in my mind, 'You picked a fine time to leave me, Lucille . . .' when one of the cops came into the dormitory holding a piece of paper.

'Do you know a person by the name of Armin Heim?' he asked. 'He's here to visit you.'

Armin had convinced a German newspaper that he could

get a photograph of me in custody in return for his expenses to Barbados plus a few Deutschmarks on top. He also convinced Whittaker that as my close friend he was on a 'mercy mission' in Barbados, to get 'just one' photograph of me for my son, Mike, who was asking for a picture of his daddy. The same excuse used by Charmian back in Brasilia.

It was a tonic to see the big Kraut. The great news was that Mike was safe and had been delivered into the tender care of my friends, John and Lia Pickston. Mike was missing me, said Armin, but the Pickstons were doing a top job of keeping him happy. John had sent me a kind, humorous letter allaying my worries.

As we talked, Armin casually got his Nikon out of his camera bag and shot half a dozen frames before Whittaker could get a protest together. A true pro.

On the day of my first appearance before Mr James King, the magistrate, a great crowd assembled around the courthouse and a cheer went up as I stepped handcuffed out of a police car. My 'hand-picked' escort hustled me towards the court, one of them stumbling in the process, losing his gun from a shoulder holster.

The confusion was much like it had been on the evening of my arrival in Barbados. It seemed to be the same sea of black faces around me. A fat lady with few teeth and a hat full of imitation fruit was calling to me in a loud voice: 'Mr Biggs! I'm praying for you! I'm praying for you to go back to Brazil and your son! You're going back because it's God's will!' At every subsequent court appearance, that lady was there to tell me that she was still praying for me.

An aisle divided the courtroom with rows of benches on either side. To the left, facing the magistrate, sat the prosecution and the big noises of the Royal Barbados Police Force and the immigration department. To the right the goodies, plus two of Whittaker's armed cops who sat a bit too close to me for comfort. My legal team sat at a table behind me with a fine array of law books. The prosecution brought one.

Every day the courtroom was crowded to capacity. The international press pack, enjoying this winter break in Barbados, were standing by, notebooks at the ready. Many of them had already been in the West Indies to cover the England cricket tour, and were still in Barbados following the third Test.

Shortly after my arrival in the courtroom on the second morning, I heard someone behind me making hissing noises, trying to get my attention. I turned around to look straight into the smiling face of one Ronnie Leslie. There was no mistaking those pissholes in the snow! It was the same Ronnie who had helped Paul Seabourne to spring me from Wandsworth!

In town at the expense of the *News of the World*, Ronnie was allowed to exchange a few words before the cops stepped in and put the block on further conversation. Needless to say, the *News of the World* was hoping that Leslie would be allowed to visit me so that they could put together some kind of 'exclusive'. I would have been only too happy to help my good friend – God knows he had helped me and served a three-year prison sentence for taking part in my escape. But the headline in the local newspaper the following morning ruined whatever chance he might have had. 'What is Ronald Leslie Doing in Barbados?' it screamed.

The prosecution, led by Elliott Belgrave QC, an ex-student of Frederick Smith, opposed my application for bail, stating: 'If Mr Biggs is released on bail, I'm quite certain that he will make a beeline for the Brazilian Diplomatic Mission and then we'll never be able to get him out.' Once again I called upon my ability with regard to 'specious and facile lying', and swore that the idea had never entered my head. But to no avail. I had to remain locked up.

Whittaker, the police chief, gave evidence describing my arrival on the island and pertinent facts relating to my story. He made it quite clear to the magistrate that the police were seeking my return to Great Britain.

'Brazil!' boomed Frederick Smith, for the defence, 'This poor man must be returned to Brazil! He was kidnapped from that country! Taken forcibly, against his will!' How sweet it sounded – especially in Bajan, 'Mr Biggs should be put on a plane and sent back to Brazil today!'

The court adjourned. Mr James King, the magistrate, wanted time to think.

During the hearing, Alleyne and his partner discovered a certain omission on the part of the police. A document, relative to my presence on and possible exit from the island, should have been prepared by the police and handed to a certain parliamentary official. The official was then responsible for passing the document on to whatever department of the government required it. The police, however, had neglected this small chore. Alleyne tracked down the parliamentary official and brought the fellow to the hearing. The official went on the stand and took the oath, going on to describe his job and duties. With regard to a document concerning me he said that he had received nothing. Yes, he was quite sure. And yes, it was customary to receive such a document.

The next day the police prepared and submitted the missing document. I asked 'Smithy' why so much importance had been given to the oversight on the part of the police if they had been able to prepare the document and hand it in a day later.

'The police are wasting their time,' Smith reassured me. 'It's not retroactive!'

Towards the end of the hearing, Scotland Yard sent a couple of beefy coppers over to Barbados in the hope that they would soon be returning to England with me.

It looked as if they would get their way. The magistrate's findings were that I should be handed over to the British authorities and returned to prison in Great Britain. I was given time to appeal against his decision. Without loss of time, the cops took me off to the cells at the back of the courtroom. Whittaker paid me a brief visit while I sat waiting for a car to take me to the police station. He was all but smiling when he asked: 'Well, Ron, and how are you feeling?'

I was in a mental slump but I was not about to let Whittaker see it. 'I'm okay, Mr Whittaker,' I replied. 'It's only the end of the first round.'

Hutson was at the police station when I got there, looking more serious than usual.

'Mr Biggs,' he said, 'I am sorry to say that you are no longer in my care. As far as I'm concerned you are free to go but I don't think Mr Whittaker is going to let you go very far.' We shook hands. It was nice knowing you, Mr Hutson.

Hutson was right. Glendairy Prison was not very far at all. From the clang of the front gate to the stink of 'receptions' I was thinking, I've seen this film before. The same old screws with the same old bull. Wandsworth all over again.

I was shown to my new address: 'Cell 10, Death Row'. The cells were tiny and dirty, with precious little space to move around. There was a bed with the traditional lumpy mattress, and a foul-smelling wooden commode in a corner. The door was a stout wooden frame, faced on the inside with heavy gauge iron mesh that was fixed with staples. I could see across a narrow corridor to the cell immediately in front of me, occupied on my arrival by a young burglar named Pedro Weekes. Pedro introduced himself and the other tenants of Death Row whom I couldn't see, telling me their sentences and why they were segregated from the rest of the prison. Four of our number were 'waiting for de rope', Pedro told me, while the others were considered to be 'security risks'.

I asked my neighbour where the black door at the end of the corridor led. He grinned.

'Oh, man! That door leads to Paradise Island! And you don't need a passport to get there! The only problem with going to Paradise Island is, you never come back!' It was, of course, the 'topping shed'.

Many would argue that the man who should have been heading for the topping shed was John Miller, but instead he was being tipped off by a man from the British High Commission to get as far away from Barbados as possible. Funny that!

My time on Death Row gave me ample time to think about my kidnapping, yet it was only in my later years that missing pieces of the puzzle came my way which formed a picture that suggests that the plot to kidnap me was known by some of the very highest people in the UK, including at least one member of the British Cabinet. Whether these gentlemen backed and supported my kidnapping because they believed they were righting a wrong, or for other motives, I don't know.

Miller, himself, has said that the first kidnap attempt was paid for by a German business colleague based in London, a nephew to a German steel millionaire, Baron Heine Thyssen, who put up the necessary £50,000. The *Sunday Times* Insight Team would, however, have me believe that Miller's benefactor for the first kidnapping was one Baron Steven Bentinck, the wealthy son of a Dutch ambassador.

The second, more expensive attempt, Miller credits to Sir Hugh Fraser, a fellow Scot whose family at one time owned Harrods, and who was said to be holidaying in Barbados at the exclusive Sandy Lane resort at the time of my arrival. He conveniently died on 5 May 1987 and with his death I would never get to know who else was behind or knew of my kidnapping and if indeed Fraser was involved or got the official approval of his many political friends. What is certain is that while Miller shopped the first attempt around the newspapers, something he lived to regret, for the second kidnapping he was more discreet, making far better use of his Scottish connections and those of the Scots Guards.

Another name that kept cropping up was Patrick Anderson, at the time the heir to the Carpets International fortune. Anderson had visited Brazil on a couple of occasions and, I am told, even had a few problems with the Old Bill at Heathrow Airport for trying to carry certain substances into England that he shouldn't. Anderson, it is said, played the role of the mysterious reporter, Patrick Richardson King, whom I was set to meet at the Roda Viva the night of my kidnapping. Miller would have us believe that 'King' got cold feet and hurried off to Miami. Others have told me that it was 'Anderson' who hotfooted it to England to try and sell the story to the press.

In a further twist in 2005, after Miller had milked my kidnapping for all it was worth, King emerged from the shadows to claim in an ill-thought-out and untruthful TV documentary that he, and not Miller, was the brain behind my kidnapping. King's documentary and book should be filed firmly under fiction. King claims all sorts of links to the 'security services', and the murky world of MI5 and MI6, but I think in his and Miller's case, it is more about the M25, and going around in circles!

Whatever was going on behind the scenes, the other cons in Glendairy Prison showed me much sympathy and friendliness. Everyone was convinced that, despite what Miller might have planned, I was going to be sent back to Brazil. With a few exceptions, the screws were friendly too, and agreed that I shouldn't have to return to England. One morning, when the shifts changed, a screw told me that he had heard on the radio that the Brazilian government had asked for me to be returned to Brazil. I couldn't believe it! I was sure the screw had got it wrong, but later Smithy confirmed the good news.

In a dank but spacious dungeon beneath the court, I paced back and forth contemplating my fate. A jailer came and unlocked my cell. 'Okay, Mr Biggs. You're on next!'

The courtroom was packed. The appeal was going to be heard by two judges from the High Court, Barbados Chief Justice Sir William Randolph Douglas and Deputy Chief Justice Denys Williams, who had not yet taken their places on the bench. Smithy came over to the dock with a warm greeting and some words of comfort. He was confident that we would win. Whittaker, bristling with self-importance, was standing to my left, no more than a yard away from the dock. He also looked confident.

'All stand!' The two black judges, looking somewhat incongruous in their white wigs, entered the court and took their places. When everyone was settled, the Clerk of the Court rose to say his piece and the hearing began. Smith got to his feet and ran smoothly through the story of my arrival in Barbados.

My appeal had been carefully prepared and focused on 12 different points. The judges listened attentively, interrupting from time to time with a question. As Smithy warmed to his work, outlining the points of the appeal, one of the judges stopped him. They were interested in hearing details of point number eight: the one about the document that the police had failed to deliver. Smith was quick to provide the details, indicating that the witness was in court again should he be needed.

The judges also focused on the 1979 Barbados Extradition Act and if it was in fact legally valid; another potential loophole that had been spotted and raised by Alleyne. Sunshine had spent days researching the records of the House of Assembly to unearth the constitutional point of law relating to the Extradition Act. He was asked by Smithy to present the argument to the judges that although The Act was valid, due to significant legal reasons of interpretation, The Designation Countries Order was invalid and that included for Great Britain.

After a short conversation with their heads together, the judges withdrew from the court to discuss the matter between themselves. There was a small hubbub when they left, everyone wondering what this signified. Smithy knew. He hurried over to the dock.

'Look, Ron,' he said with conviction, 'if those boys are out of the court for more than ten minutes, you're going back to Brazil.'

The 'boys' were absent for 25 minutes and when they returned I could see by their faces that Smith was right. One of them addressed the court, speaking at length about the laws existing on the island and the necessity to observe those laws to the letter. It was quite clear that the procedure with regard to the document in question was imperative. The procedure had been neglected – and Mr Biggs was free to step down from the dock and leave the court. The court even awarded me $500 in costs!

The Barbados Supreme Court also ruled that the Barbados Parliament had not yet ratified an extradition treaty with the United Kingdom so the 1979 Barbados Extradition Act had not become law. It looked as if Miller had taken me to the only island in the whole of the Caribbean that lacked a valid extradition agreement with Britain!

The decision set off a commotion in the court, with people coming from all sides to congratulate me and shake my hand.

I stood rooted to the spot in the dock, almost disbelieving the verdict, uncertain what to do next. A smiling David Levy appeared in front of me.

'Come on, Ron!' he exclaimed, 'Let's get you out of here! You're a free man again!' Whittaker, who was standing within touching distance, didn't look at all happy. I offered him my hand in the time-honoured gesture of gentlemen.

'End of round two, Mr Whittaker!' I said. But the police chief declined to shake my hand.

A crowd had gathered outside the court and were milling around, patting me on the back and shaking my hand. Levy was trying to get me through the multitude to a taxi, wanting to get me to the house of the Brazilian Consul. Suddenly I found myself in the embrace of the lady with the missing teeth.

'I knew you would be freed!' she cried between rum-flavoured kisses. 'I knew because I've been praying for you day and night!' Tears of happiness were running down her cheeks – and mine!

At the Brazilian Consul's house there was the same degree of euphoria, everybody pleased that I had been able to make the 'beeline' that had previously been denied to me. From the moment I arrived, the telephone did not stop ringing. Levy monitored the calls, anxious that I did not speak to any journalists. He had hopes that a major deal could be made with a newspaper and he did not want me to leak any part of the story. In my elation, and with a beer in my hand, I was ready to tell everybody who was willing to listen – quite free of charge!

By late afternoon, a televised telephone call to Mike was organised, but when the time came to speak I was so overwhelmed with emotion that it was almost impossible. I could hear Mike on the line saying excitedly in Portuguese, 'Dad! Is that you? Are you coming back? Dad! Are you coming back today?' but I could only blubber a few words to confirm that I really was going back to Brazil.

Arrangements were made to charter a Learjet to pick me up in Barbados and fly me on to Brazil. All we needed was $16,000 but we had received two offers from television companies interested in covering my return to Brazil – ITN from London and TV Globo from Rio de Janeiro – and they were each happy to contribute $7,500 towards the flight. Levy covered the remainder. A temporary passport – a *laisser passez* – valid for 23 April to 2 May 1981 was prepared by the Brazilian Consul to enable me to make the trip. I would be entering Brazil legally this time, and as a Brazilian!

My old friend Whittaker turned up at the house with my bits and pieces of 'property' which he had had picked up at the prison. He had regained his composure and went so far as to shake hands and congratulate me on my good luck.

The Learjet arrived in Barbados stocked with champagne and caviar – this was not going to be an ordinary trip! Then, still unable to believe that it was all happening, I was driven to the airport in the car of a friendly Brazilian diplomat.

It was a bit like *Casablanca* updated. It was dark, the tarmac was slick from a recent thunderstorm and the sleek jet plane stood waiting. Come on, I thought, let's get out of here before someone issues an order to cancel the flight! I could imagine Whittaker and a couple of his heavies turning up at the airfield with a warrant for my arrest. But we took our places in the plane and my fears dispersed as we sped down the runway and rose into the sky.

In Glendairy Prison I had fantasised more than once about the possibility of a miracle happening that would permit me to return to Brazil and Mike. I made a promise to myself that if that happened I would kiss the ground on my arrival! A few hours later, as I looked out of the window of the plane, I could see the Brazilian coast below, red in the first light of dawn. The miracle I had prayed for was happening! Minutes later we touched down at Belém Airport. It was the morning of 24 April 1981, 40 days since I had been grabbed in Rio.

As soon as I stepped from the plane I kept my promise, dropping to my knees like Pope John Paul II to kiss the ground. I wanted to embrace it! My trusty photographer friend, Armin, was waiting on the observation deck, camera in hand, but he had missed the shot.

'Do it again, Ron!' he bawled out. I was only too happy to oblige!

CHAPTER 15

A STAR IS BORN: MIKE BIGGS

For most of the flight from Belém to Rio – on a commercial jet – I was pinned down in my seat by journalists clamouring for the details of the kidnapping. All I wanted to do was to look out of the window and appreciate beautiful, bountiful Brazil that was passing below, but it was not to be!

David Levy, who had accompanied me from Barbados, was doing his best to hold back the reporters but he was not as successful as Dr Brito had been on my flight from Brasilia to Rio in 1974. Levy, like Brito, had his reasons.

'Every word you tell them, Ronnie,' he warned, 'it's another grand off the value of your story!'

Later in the flight, once the journalists were satisfied that they had got their pound of flesh in advance of their colleagues awaiting my arrival in Rio, I was finally able to gaze out and reflect upon the miracle that had allowed me to be on my way back to Rio – and with the blessing of the Brazilian government.

Writing in a British paper in 1994, Jack Slipper wrote: 'My personal view is that Biggs was rightly returned to Brazil after the kidnap, as it was illegal and our use of that illegal act would have condoned it.'

Cruzeiro flight 251 from Belém arrived a few minutes early at Rio's international airport, touching down just before 10 am. A few minutes later, as I passed into the baggage claim area, I saw Mike on the other side of the sliding glass doors that separate passengers from the people awaiting their arrival.

Mike was with John and Lia, waving his arms excitedly. They were not alone. There was a huge crowd of journalists and photographers who were jostling around them. A kindly federal agent, seeing Mike's predicament, opened the glass door and pushed him through into the baggage area. Mike came running.

'*Pai!*'

As I picked him up and hugged him to me, he asked me through our tears, 'Dad, why do people cry when they're happy?'

As I had no luggage and had already legally entered Brazil on arrival in Belém, I passed quickly through the airport formalities. Then, with Mike sitting on my shoulders, I went through the sliding doors and faced the army of newsmen. John and Lia were there, pushing through the crowd in an effort to get us to their car.

As we scrambled into the Pickstons' Opala, the press rushed to follow us into Copacabana. A similar scene of confusion greeted us at the entrance to the building where they lived. Lia went in first, wielding her handbag and laid open a path through the crowd of newsmen and curious onlookers. Finally we arrived at the apartment on the ninth floor and could start to celebrate my return with a nice cup of tea.

My friends had done a wonderful job of looking after Mike while I had been taken off to Barbados. At first, when it was known that I had been kidnapped, John and Lia had tried to keep the news from Mike but it was an impossible task given the media attention. Once Mike discovered the truth it must have been very difficult to reassure him and keep his mind occupied. But John, who had not doubted for one moment that I would get back to Brazil, is a born funnyman and, among other things, he could make kids stop crying. Nor was he the British community's favourite pantomime dame for nothing, so during his time with Mike he taught him a number of song and dance routines from England which included 'Knees Up Mother Brown'.

My thoughts were broken by the noise of the frustrated press corps who were now banging on the door demanding an audience. Finally – much to Levy's despair – I agreed to hold a press conference in the play area on the first floor of the building. Once that was over, I wanted to enjoy my freedom and went with Mike and John to the beach. But the reporters were not about to lose interest in a story that had dominated their pages over the last 40 days and they followed us at close quarters, asking more questions and taking endless photographs. Finally, we decided to take refuge in the Copacabana Palace, the hotel where so long ago, as it now seemed, I had begun the drama with Miller and his men two years earlier. The same kindly and attentive waiters were around ready, as always, to make a fuss over 'their little prince', Mike.

The next day I met up with Levy who declared that I had 'thrown away' whatever chance we might have had of writing a story about my kidnapping. He was returning to England that same evening. He had been staying at Le Meridién, one of Rio's better hotels, and there was one night remaining on the booking that he had made and paid for. He suggested I make use of it.

Thinking that there might be some cash forthcoming from our book that had recently been published and sold well, no doubt helped by the publicity of the kidnapping, I asked Levy if he could leave me with some money. He laughed without mirth and told me the bad news: the expenses that I had incurred during my adventure in Barbados were in excess of $50,000 which more than took care of my earnings. He was kind enough, however, to leave me with $200 and the keys to his room before catching a taxi to the airport.

I had already spoken to Ulla; now I called her again and asked her to meet me at the Meridién hotel for a get-together. A week or so before Miller had grabbed me, Ulla and I had had a bit of a row and we were not exactly on speaking terms when I left the scene unexpectedly. Now seemed like a good time to forget our little squabble.

A few days later, Charmian turned up in Rio with Farley. To help Levy (and I) with the legal bills, Charmian had managed to raise $10,000 by agreeing to do an exclusive story for Rupert Murdoch's Melbourne *Herald Sun*, and that included a reunion with me in either Rio or the UK, depending on the outcome of the court case. Happily it was in Rio, but unhappily my mind was all over the place and after just four days Charmian returned to Australia. Not my finest hour.

*

About a year before my kidnapping, Mike (aged nearly six) and I had moved into a rather luxurious apartment on the 18th floor of a building that overlooked the bay of Guanabara and Sugarloaf Mountain. I was looking after it for an American friend who had gone back to the US on business. It offered the same picture postcard view that had first attracted me to Rio when I was in hiding in Australia.

When I got back from Barbados, I found myself facing school, electricity, gas and telephone bills, plus $1,000 in rent for the nearly two months that I had been away. Things were tough and I had to borrow money from friends to make ends meet. Little did I realise that certain things that had happened while I had been away would be the solution to our current financial crisis.

TV Globo, who had shown a great interest in my kidnapping from the start, had visited Mike at the Pickstons while I was in Barbados with a view to interviewing him for their Sunday evening prime-time show *Fantastico!*, the same programme that his mother and I had appeared on seven years earlier when I had first been arrested. Given the opportunity, Pickston prompted his protégé to go through his 'Knees Up Mother Brown' routine for the TV camera. Mike ended his performance with a heartfelt plea to the Brazilian authorities to do something about getting me back to Brazil. He knew that the Queen of England wanted me, he said, but he needed me more.

By a happy coincidence, the then Minister of Justice, Ibrahim Abi-Ackel, was in the Globo studio waiting to be interviewed and saw Mike's section of the programme. When he appeared on the screen he was smiling and said words to the effect that an effort must be made to bring about my return. With the minister's words the great wheels of state and diplomacy were put in motion, all of which helped my speedy return.

Another gentleman who caught Mike's performance, and who was equally impressed, was a Spaniard by the name of Tomas Muñoz, at the time president of CBS Records in Brazil.

The day Muñoz knocked on my door I was just thinking about moving to somewhere less expensive. Muñoz saw Mike as an 'extremely talented child'. If I had no objection, he said, he was interested in making a record with Mike and two other youngsters. He had come up with an idea to create a children's vocal group. Auditions were already taking place, but he knew he wanted Mike. We asked Mike what he thought of the idea and he agreed without hesitation!

I had nothing against Mike participating in a musical group, providing, I said, that it didn't interfere with his education. At the beginning, I suppose, I thought it might be fun for him, but not for a moment did I think it would develop into anything serious or financially rewarding.

Until Muñoz's arrival on the scene, I had only ever heard Mike sing snatches of my best-seller 'No One Is Innocent' and the first few notes of 'Oh! Susanna' when playing 'cowboys and Indians'. I mentioned this fact to Mr Muñoz, but there seemed to be no problem; in fact he liked the idea of 'Oh! Susanna' as a piece for Mike to start rehearsing and it was to be included on the band's first album. The following day I went down to the CBS office in Praia do Flamengo and signed the contract.

When the group was formed it was given the name A Turma do Balão Magico, or The Magic Balloon Gang. Besides Mike, two other talented kids were chosen from the auditions: Simony, a six-year-old, and Toby who was eight. With the release of their first long playing record the group was an overnight success with the kids; the record's sales rocketed, a fat cheque was deposited in my bank account and Balão Magico were presented with their first gold record!

Tracks from their first album were heard every day on the radio, even on programmes not aimed at a normal children's audience. It did not take long until the group was invited to participate in shows on all the major Brazilian television networks.

CBS Records appointed a capable young Brazilian lady, Monica Neves, to manage the group and soon after the first record was released the kids began to travel around Brazil, doing live shows as well as making promotional visits to shopping centres and record shops. The terms of the contract allowed for one parent to accompany each child and, after the federal police had given me permission, I travelled with Mike on most of the journeys.

At first the audiences at the live shows were small, but before long the fans of Balão Magico were filling football stadiums from one end of Brazil to the other. At Christmas time, the Globo network took over the gigantic Maracanã Stadium in Rio to stage a free show which was televised live to millions and millions of homes throughout Brazil. The show featured acrobats, clowns and other traditional circus acts alongside show-business personalities and singers who entertained the crowd. The arrival of Father Christmas in a helicopter is the delirious finale.

As the audience is largely made up of children, the Balão Magico was a natural choice for these shows as one of the headline acts. Each Christmas from 1982 to 1985, Mike, Toby and Simony sang and danced, without any show of nerves, in front of a live audience of close to 200,000 people.

The Balão Magico became a household name and in 1983 TV Globo gave the kids their own daily breakfast-time programme. The recordings for the shows were made at the Globo studio in São Paulo, which meant that Mike had to fly down there four or five times a week. I would pick him up at his school at midday, take him home for a quick shower and something to eat then rush off to get the two o'clock flight to São Paulo. The recording sessions often ran into late evening and we would return to Rio on the last flight, getting home after midnight. Homework was neglected and Mike started getting poor marks at school. The programme was very popular, however, and thousands of fan letters poured into the studio.

The group's second album in 1983 was an even bigger hit than the first. On the track 'Superfantastico' the kids were joined by one of Brazil's top artists, Djavan. This catchy tune became a big favourite with the public and was used as the encore to wind up the group's shows.

The album earned Balão Magico a second gold record and their first platinum disc, as well as an even fatter cheque. The shows continued, with the kids giving as many as three performances over a weekend.

Simony was from a large family who had spent most of their lives in the circus. They were rough and ready folk and the girl's mother, Maria, was tough. From the moment that the Balão Magico was formed, she tried to get a larger cut of the proceeds from the record sales and the shows for her daughter. She argued that Simony was the most talented in the group and should receive half the total amount, with the two boys left to split the remaining half. Toby's mother, Dona Rosa, and I did not agree. Monica Neves, who was managing the group, also sided with us.

It was during one of our weekend tours that a row flared up between Monica and Maria over the issue of Simony's pay. It resulted in Maria threatening CBS that she would take her daughter out of the group unless Monica was dismissed. Not to upset the apple cart, or the goose that laid the golden egg, CBS Records sadly bowed to Maria's wishes and gave Monica the boot. An impresario from São Paulo took her place; a slick fellow by the name of Paulo Ricardo.

Paulo was on very close terms with Simony's mother and soon they were calling the shots and banking the shows, paying the expenses and splitting the profits down the middle.

Each parent was, in theory, free to bank at least one show each month. But Dona Rosa and I waived the concession so Paulo and Maria were raking it in.

Flying back to Rio after another show, Paulo dropped into the empty seat beside me and started buttering me up with a load of old cobblers about his interest in Mike's career. He felt like a brother towards me, he said. Then he came up with an offer that common sense should have made me turn down.

'Senhor Ronald,' he said. 'We've got three shows lined up for next weekend. One in Santa Catarina, one in Joinville and one in Blumenau. Now, I know that you've never banked a show before, but I would like you to bank these three shows with me. Do you fancy taking a gamble?'

There was one obvious snag in banking a show: in the event of the show being rained off or not taking place for whatever reason, all the expenses – including the $500 for each child for each show – fell upon the shoulders of the person doing the banking.

Even though I knew that there had to be some sinister motive behind the offer, I decided to have a little flutter even though the area where the shows were scheduled was in the far south of Brazil and it was the rainy time of the year.

It was a cold, grey and rainy Friday that greeted the Balão Magico as we flew into Santa Caterina. It was raining when we landed and it was still raining when we got up the next morning – with the first show scheduled to take place at 11 am. Yet miraculously the weather cleared up and the sun appeared. The show was on!

I went to the stadium to look at my 'investment' and, in no time, the stadium dried out and the public began to come in through the turnstiles. Thank heavens you can always rely on a Brazilian audience to leave everything until the last minute!

It turned out to be a good crowd and a good show. Maria and the members of her family, who had commiserated with me when we had arrived, were now grudgingly congratulating me on having 'backed a winner'.

The next two shows, in Joinville and Blumenau, were also put on under ideal weather conditions before thousands of happy, cheering children – and I was in there cheering with them! Altogether it was a very pleasant and profitable weekend.

About this time a Japanese team from NTV came to Rio to make a drama documentary with me called *Long Time No See, Ronnie*, a reference to what Slipper said when we met in Rio. The film was to include Mike and 'my old adversary', who were both flown to Tokyo to participate in the production. Ulla was invited to go along as Mike's chaperone and jumped at the chance.

The Japanese producers were very anxious to have Mike's recording fame known to their viewers and a special record sleeve for the Balão Magico album was produced for the Japanese market, with a portrait of Mike filling the back cover in place of a group shot. Meanwhile I was called upon to act out my own part in Rio with Brazilian actresses playing the roles of Charmian and Raimunda.

Mike and I also appeared on the BBC's famous *Top of the Pops* live from Copacabana, and I did a lengthy interview with the legendary Merv Griffin at the then Rio Palace Hotel (now Fairmont).

The money was flowing in from Mike's work with the Balão Magico, so I made an investment with a couple of friends. The investment resulted in a nightclub in Copacabana called Crepúsculo de Cubatão which became one of the hot night spots in Rio, especially with the locals. Crepúsculo eventually ran its course and became rebranded as Kitschnet which had a similarly successful run before finally calling it a day in 1993.

At the height of Balão Magico's popularity, CBS Records decided to add another child to the group to keep the momentum going. He was a handsome and highly talented little black kid named Jairzinho. A little younger than Mike, Jairzinho seemed to me to be an asset to the group. His father, Jair Rodrigues, was a well-known samba vocalist and Jairzinho had inherited his father's talent. Jairzinho joined the group in 1984 in time to record the band's third album.

The kids couldn't have cared less about another child entering the group as it gave them someone else to play with during the tedious flights to and from the shows. Mike palled up with Jairzinho immediately and they worked well together on the television programme.

*

After John Miller had tried to grab me the first time in April 1979, Ulla had suggested that Mike and I should move in with her and her children in Rio; she said I was a 'sitting duck' in Sepetiba and I tended to agree. So I sold off my bits and pieces in Sepetiba, paid the rent and moved to Santa Teresa, one of Rio's most historic, bohemian and beautiful neighbourhoods. Ulla's apartment, which her father had bought for her, was situated on the middle floor of a fine old house that had been built in 1943 and converted into three apartments. An elderly tailor and his family, who were the only tenants in the building with access to a large but run-down and overgrown back garden, occupied the ground floor. I used to look down with a certain amount of envy at the abandoned area and imagine what I could do with it if it were mine. I reminded myself that it didn't cost anything to dream.

Sometime later, in early 1980, Ulla moved from Santa Teresa and let her apartment to a young Brazilian couple, while I moved out to the Botafogo apartment.

In February 1984, I heard that the apartment beneath Ulla's was up for sale. I took a taxi over to the house. The place was shabbier than I had thought and it was obviously going to take a lot of time and money to fix. But at $16,000 (about $50,000 today) the price was very attractive. Without haggling, I gave the owner a cheque for half the amount by way of a deposit and arranged to pay the remainder within 28 days. I bought the apartment in Mike's name but said nothing to him about the deal. I wanted to refurbish the place and present it to him as a surprise.

It was exactly a year later, January 1985, when we finally moved into the apartment in Santa Teresa at Rua Monte Alegre, 470. The work wasn't finished but it was nearing completion and I, the ex-foreman, wanted to be around to supervise the final touches. The worm-eaten flooring had been ripped out and replaced with white marble; all the old woodwork, cupboards and door frames had been burned and replaced with dark, polished hardwood, a 7-metre by 4-metre slate-lined swimming pool had been installed and Mike had his own suite, decorated with the colours of his favourite football team, Botafogo. We bought a beautiful Rottweiler puppy that we named Blitz and, a little later, Lua, a Miniature Pinscher bitch. As well as the dogs we also had a number of birds, including a magnificent blue and yellow macaw named Fred.

Finally, thanks to Mike – and, indirectly, to John Miller, without whose 'help' Mike's talent might never have been discovered – we had our own home and castle. Biggsy's bolthole in Brazil that many members of the public (and media) would continue to believe had been bought by the train robbery money.

The popularity of the Balão Magico continued, with Jairzinho now being tagged, for the right reasons, as 'Brazil's Michael Jackson'. Two more albums were produced, one of which sold half a million copies and earned the group a double platinum disc. The group were called upon to advertise various products and contracted by one of Rio's best-known entrepreneurs, Chico

Recarey, to put on a series of weekend shows at his 'emporiums of entertainment'. Every Saturday and Sunday afternoon saw the kids on stage singing the Balão Magico's hits to capacity audiences of young fans.

After five action-packed years, the Magic Balloon Gang's gravy train started to slow down and finally came to a stop. It had been a long and lucrative journey, but now it was time for the kids to rest on their laurels and enjoy the sweet smell of their success as they planned what to do with the rest of their young lives.

Thirty-five years on, Balão Mágico continues to sell well. Mike has a cupboard full of gold and platinum discs to look at as a reminder of his time as a genuine star when he sold over 10 million albums and was part of the 20th most successful Brazilian act of all time in terms of sales. For many Brazilians, Mike was by far the most famous Biggs and I was happy for it to stay that way.

*

There was another quiet retirement in April 1984. Diesel Engine D326 – the one involved in the Great Train Robbery, and an unlucky engine throughout its career – was withdrawn from service and cut up for scrap to avoid souvenir hunters.

CHAPTER 16

AN ENGLISHMAN ABROAD

After five hectic years of travelling around Brazil with the Balão Magico, it felt good to return to a more 'normal' life. Mike had missed a lot of school and had fallen asleep over his homework once too often. He had a lot of catching up to do. Although we were sitting on a fairly healthy bank balance it wasn't going to last forever and I thought I had better look at ways to protect our capital and make it grow.

Shortly before the Balão Magico folded, Raimunda had returned to Brazil pregnant and married to a Swiss gentleman called Gerard. At first they went to live with Raimunda's parents in the north of Brazil then, when their child was born, a boy they named Andre, they came back to Rio. Gerard was a good cook and interested in opening a restaurant in Rio – all he needed was the cash. Not wishing to look a gift horse in the mouth, I put up the money and Mike and I became fifty-fifty partners with Gerard and Raimunda in a small restaurant in Búzios, a sophisticated weekend getaway up the coast for Rio's 'beautiful people' who arrived to take advantage of the peninsula's many beaches during the day and in the evening, the village's many great bars, restaurants and nightclubs.

I hired a team of builders to give our place a facelift and stocked the cellar with a good selection of wines. A barman and a waitress were engaged and 'Mr Big' opened to the public with great expectations.

But the customers were few and far between and Gerard, as chef, found himself with little to do except tipple our best wine and 'fall' asleep behind the bar. The competition was just too strong and like so many would be restaurateurs who have been lured to Búzios before and since, we failed.

Fortunately, I was still considered good copy and regularly sought out to give interviews for newspapers, magazines and television. Journalists came from all corners of the globe, but it was still mainly the boys and girls from London's Fleet Street who knew that 'Ronnie' could be relied upon for a good quote, whatever the topic.

I had also been invited over the years to take part in a number of advertising campaigns that have included coffee, locks and security systems. The attention these campaigns received earned me a sharp reminder from the federal police that I was still not permitted to work in Brazil. I was never sure how they thought I could survive without working.

Ironically I never received a penny for one of the most successful advertising campaigns to use my name. It was a campaign for the British Leyland Mini that, according to the advert and billboards, *Nips In and Out Like Ronald Biggs*.

Tour operators, who had discovered that in certain countries I was as much a symbol of Rio as Corcovado or Sugarloaf, began to approach me with a view to entertaining groups of tourists who were interested in meeting up. 'The Biggs Experience' was the way one journalist neatly described it. For 50 US dollars, tourists could visit me in my bolthole and enjoy my hospitality, eat, drink and splash around in the pool or sit fascinated whilst I held forth about the train robbery. Photos were taken and autographs given. I often think I enjoyed these meetings as much as my guests.

One of my first 'experiences' with visitors was a chance encounter in Copacabana. I was sitting at a seafront bar sipping a cold beer. It was quite early and there were only a few people around.

Four people were walking slowly towards me along the pavement, looking directly at me as they drew near. There were two men and two women. The younger woman came up to my table smiling.

'Are you really 'im'?' she asked.

'Yes,' I said, 'I think so.' Assuming she thought I was who I was.

'Ooh! I can't believe this! – Mum! Dad! It is Ronnie!'

The four were from Fulham; Mum and Dad, Brenda and Ted, all gor blimey Londoners. They were on a cruise and their ship had docked in Rio, giving the passengers a day ashore.

Dad called for a round of beers and Brenda, still smiling, opened up with a string of questions.

'One fing's for certain,' said Ted. 'When we get back, no one's ever going to believe us when we tell 'em that we met Ronnie Biggs!'

On my way home I saw a T-shirt in a shop window that had printed on the front the old tourist favourite: 'I know someone who went to Brazil and all I got was a lousy T-shirt.' It got me thinking and a couple of weeks later I took delivery of a thousand T-shirts similarly printed, but the lettering said: 'I know someone who went to Brazil and met Ronnie Biggs – honest!'

Since Slipper's historic first trip to Brazil in 1974 to arrest me, I was fortunate to have met many more equally illustrious figures, including lots of musicians, actors and other celebrities who passed through to give shows or promote something in Brazil. One of these was Sting who, during our first encounter, was still with the appropriately named The Police, and another was Rod Stewart.

From the rockers to the punks, I have met them all and on many occasions joined them on stage or in the studio. One visitor was reggae star Maxi Priest whom – I discovered – I had a lot in common with. Not only were we both Brixton boys, but we were also at one time both carpenters!

I had a great time with Rick Wakeman, and Mick Jones and Don Letts, who were in Rio with Big Audio Dynamite. Wattie Buchan and Exploited were also great company.

Another visitor was the record producer Gus Dudgeon and his wife Sheila. Any fan of Elton John should recognise Gus's name as having been responsible for most of Elton's classic albums as well as David Bowie's *Space Oddity* and many others. Gus and Sheila visited when they were sailing through Rio on the *QEII*. They promised to come back for the party to mark the 30th anniversary of the robbery and were as good as their word, falling in love with Rio in the process. Gus also got to meet up with Bruce Reynolds in London and learn more about the train robbery than most. Tragically Gus and Sheila were killed in a car crash in July 2002. They were good, good people and Gus even came to visit me in Belmarsh.

Lord Snowden came by to take my photo, while I was also proud to host one of my sporting heroes, Sir Stanley Matthews, arguably the greatest English winger of all time. John Simpson, the BBC's famous world affairs editor, came to meet and interview me, while the now globally famous Piers Morgan spent an afternoon at the flat in January 1991 with the Happy Mondays. Happy days indeed, and great company.

A certain George Harrison put a note under my door when he was in Brazil for the Formula One Grand Prix to say he had dropped by. Sadly I was not at home or I might have recorded with a Beatle.

Another fascinating visitor was Albert Spaggiari, the brilliant thief who tunnelled under the main road to rob the Société Générale bank in Nice in 1976. Spaggiari popped down to Rio for a chat in February 1981. A very nice fellow, but looking quite ridiculous in an obviously false moustache and large Afro wig. Spaggiari's crime, you may remember, was carried out *'sans haine, sans violence et sans arme'* ('without hatred, without violence and without weapons'), a message that he left written on the wall of the vault. He was caught, but managed to escape by jumping out of the window of the court during his trial and made his way to South America, in the process becoming France's 'Ronnie Biggs'.

When the initial cloak-and-dagger style approach was made, there was no mention of who it was that wanted to meet me. I had to meet a French lady named Alice at an old-fashioned tearoom in Copacabana. Once more into the lion's den I went. Alice, who turned out to be a handsome lady in her mid-thirties, came straight to the point.

'How much do you want to be paid to meet Albert Spaggiari?'

The name sounded as if he might be some Mafioso so I was cautious, especially after what had gone on with Miller.

'Who's Spaggiari?' I asked.

This was pre-internet and Wikipedia days, so Alice gave me the facts. *Paris Match* was in Brazil and decided it would be a major scoop to film Albert and me. I did not ask how *Paris Match* came to know that France's most wanted man was in Rio, but I hoped he would have better luck with them than I had had with the *Express*.

I asked Alice for $5,000 in cash, about $15,000 today, to meet with Spaggiari who was to pretend to interview me for French TV. *Paris Match* agreed my terms.

Albert and I were introduced to each other in an apartment in Copacabana. We got on famously but for the fact that he couldn't speak a word of English and I only had a smattering of French guidebook phrases. Without the false moustache and large wig, Spaggiari could probably have walked the streets of Copacabana quite unnoticed, but when we did go out everyone stared.

Our meeting was recorded for television, and the director swore to me that the encounter was exclusively for screening in France. I can't say that I was altogether surprised, however, when our little get-together was shown by TV Globo.

For the recording I was to pretend that I did not know who was interviewing me.

'What would you do, Mr Biggs,' Spaggiari asked me, 'if you came face to face with Albert Spaggiari?'

'Who is Albert Spaggiari?' I replied with a straight face.

'He, Mr Biggs, is the most famous fugitive in the world.'

'Sorry, pal,' I said with a grin. 'You're looking at the world's most famous fugitive.' Spaggiari was in no position to argue.

There were some more pertinent questions awaiting me when I went to sign in with the federal police the following week. Interpol would have liked to have sat in on our little chat and I was warned that I was skating on very thin ice.

Interpol and the French authorities never did get their man. Albert, who had been sentenced to life in prison *in absentia*, died of throat cancer in June 1989. His mother found his body deposited in front of her house in France for burial.

By 1986 I was hoping that my hustling days were over when Freddie Foreman introduced me to Polish film director Lech Majewski. Majewski had read all about me and decided that he was the person who had to make the film of my life. He had a couple of films to his credit, including one called *Flight of the Spruce Goose* which was about as commercially successful as Howard Hughes's plane of the same name.

Lech visualised *Prisoner of Rio* as a masterpiece in the making. A Swiss-based sales-distribution company, Multi Media, had arranged finance for the film but, like many of the deals I found myself involved in, the movie was to be made on a budget that was unrealistic for its pretensions.

Initially, Lech said his intention was to make a true film of my life, a good film, a film that he and I would both be proud of.

As we were in Rio, Lech saw my kidnapping as a good base for the film and I was invited to join him and his American girlfriend, Julia Frankel, in writing the screenplay. We began work immediately. Every day I would go to the hotel where Lech and Julia were staying to work on the project. We seemed to be making good progress when, after nearly two weeks of work on the 'true story', Lech changed his mind and announced we were going to turn to fiction and write yet another kidnap plot, this time to be carried out by an outraged Scotland Yard Inspector, 'Jock' McFarland, who was obsessed with the idea of getting 'that bastard' out of Brazil. Up until that moment I had given the work my best shot, but all my interest dried up when I heard Lech's decision. The stuff Lech and Julia wrote was wishy-washy at best, and at times downright corny.

Paul Freeman was chosen to play 'Biggs', walking into a kidnap set-up for the third time, and Steven Berkoff was to play the role of the avenging Glasgow-born Inspector McFarland. Other actors involved included Peter Firth and the Brazilians José Wilker, Florinda Bolkan and Zezé Motta.

Production finally got under way in July 1987 and I had a cameo role as a guest at my own party. During the following months of bickering and back-biting, *Prisoner of Rio* struggled through to the end, going way over budget and deadlines with filming finally wrapping in the September.

Everybody hated Lech, especially Berkoff, but Lech took this in his stride; it was customary for everyone to dislike the director, he told me. I discovered a certain affinity with Steven and it turned out that we shared a common experience; we had both been to Stamford House Remand Home and both remembered the perverted old director of that disgraceful establishment. Steve lamented the fact that he had not thought of making a film with me. He said he would have written the screenplay, directed the film and played the leading role, instead of getting involved with 'this megalomaniac' Majewski.

'I myself fail to understand why people can change a perfectly good yarn for some hokum,' Steve told *Time Out* on his return to London. 'But that is the nature of people who film the people who live . . . If someone like Biggs expresses doubts about some elements of the script, then a producer who fails to listen does so at his own peril. After all, it comes from the horse's mouth. He was there.'

Prisoner of Rio was unveiled for the first time to expectant buyers at the Cannes Film Festival on 12 May 1988. Now if ever there is an event that is fuelled by hype, it is the Cannes Film Festival with more than 3,000 journalists packing into the French Riviera town.

A publicity scam was concocted for *Prisoner of Rio*. 'Mr Biggs would be putting in a personal appearance at the festival,' the producers announced. Speculation and rumour suggested that they had me hidden away on one of the luxury yachts that were anchored off the beach. When the pressmen – and the cops – gathered to take advantage of what could be the biggest single media event of the 1988 festival, they were not to be disappointed. Mr Biggs was in Cannes, only it was Mr Michael Biggs!

While the press on the whole took the scam well, the same could not be said for the film that got a critical mauling. By coincidence or mismanagement, the film was released in Britain around the same time as a film about Buster Edwards. *Buster* starred everyone's favourite rock star of the time, Phil Collins, alongside the equally popular Julie Walters; predictably, *Prisoner of Rio* did not receive the kudos that Lech had forecast.

My share of the proceeds from *Prisoner of Rio* came to a paltry $13,000 (about $40,000 today), falling well short of the vast sums that had been mentioned at the beginning. But it was enough to keep the wolf from the door.

What Majewski may not have been aware of was just how much of a film buff I was. I was a familiar and regular face at film industry screenings in Rio, thanks largely to my good friend Fred Sill, a senior executive with Paramount.

Fred had a very dry sense of humour and was always great fun to be with, as well as being a very generous host and friend. Generosity that continued even after my return to Britain, and when a Fortnum & Mason hamper turned up at my bedside, it was invariably from Fred.

Over the years I lived in Rio I met hundreds of tourists. A few became good friends and made return trips to Rio to maintain our friendship. Richard Keaney came for the first time in 1987. His friends 'back home' had told him that he couldn't return without a picture of him and me together. So one Saturday,

Richard – a wacky Gene Wilder lookalike – found his way to Santa Teresa. He turned up carrying an airline bag which contained a bottle of whisky and a cheap camera. Drinks were poured and Richard shot off the roll of film that was in his camera. It was evening when he left. Early the next morning he telephoned with a tale of woe; he had been held up by a brace of street kids and they had taken off with his watch, his cash and his camera – with the 'precious' film inside it. He had bought another camera, he told me, and he wanted to know if I would let him return to take another set of photographs? I agreed and arranged a friend for life. Richard returned to Rio many times, always arriving with a ten-pound slab of Cheddar cheese and other goodies.

Richard was in Rio when I received a most illustrious guest; my friend and hero, Paul Seabourne. At the time, 1989, I was working on a documentary with an Australian, Bob Starkie. He was going to cover a party that I was giving to celebrate my 60th birthday and had asked who I thought should 'star' in his production. Without hesitation I suggested Paul – I was having the celebration thanks entirely to him. Bob agreed and contact was made with Paul in London. Miraculously he wasn't inside!

Paul was ready for a trip to Rio and a flight was arranged. Bob wanted to get our first meeting in 24 years on film so set up his camera at the airport where the passengers disembark. First-class travel had provided Paul with a fine selection of alcoholic beverages to choose from over 11 hours and my old pal arrived very obviously drink-lagged. But it was fantastic to see the little bugger again.

Our re-encounter was shot by a drinks stand where we were to toast each other with double whiskies. This scene was repeated several times, as were the doubles. We laughed and joked and took the piss out of each other's old looks. Wet though he was, his wit was as dry as ever. It was the same old Paul and it was great to have him in Rio.

Back at the 'Biggs mansion', I introduced Paul to Richard who had crashed out on a settee the previous evening. A bottle of vodka was produced and my two guests were soon chatting away, both smoking like chimneys. Richard, who knew who Paul was and why he was in Rio, was 'honoured to meet the man who got Ronnie out of prison'. He was loving every minute in Paul's company. During the afternoon they both passed out.

Seeing that Paul was *hors de combat*, Bob proposed that we should forget filming for the day and get off to an early start in the morning. With this in mind I went to bed, leaving the guests to sleep it off.

No one knows what hour it was when Paul woke up and found that he and Richard had smoked all their fags, but it was certainly after midnight. Driven by the craving only cigarette smokers understand, Paul went off to look for a tobacconist or perhaps a slot machine, as he would have back in London. It was late and dark: only a fool would be abroad on a night like this. Thinking he only had to 'pop up the road', he had gone out wearing a pair of thin-soled airline slippers. Santa Teresa is not the easiest area to find your way around in, but Paul followed the tramlines that he presumed would lead him back to the house. He kept walking and finally came to an area where he found bars and nightclubs that were open. With £500 in his pocket and not a word of Portuguese, Paul had wandered into Lapa, then a tough neighbourhood where transvestites swung their handbags and muggings were commonplace.

We were on the point of organising a search party when Paul turned up in a taxi just after seven o'clock. The taxi driver, who claimed that he had been driving my house guest around for the last four hours in the hope that he recognised the road, was demanding $300 from the *gringo louco* (mad foreigner).

We got on 'location', Paradise Island, by two that afternoon and Paul promptly fell face down in the sand. Bob loved the footage that he was getting of the two old jailbirds 'havin' a fuckin' ball'.

By the evening, Paul had made a remarkable recovery and looked quite reasonable. We were off to do some more filming: this time, the two old lags across a dinner table in a swanky waterfront restaurant, with Sugarloaf looming in the background. The strains of 'You and the Night and the Music' reached us. We were rolling!

Sadly that visit was the last time I was to see Paul. His passing in 1994 was a sad day. Hopefully he was standing by the Pearly Gates when I got there, only this time to break me in.

My dear friend Bruce Reynolds was another welcome and distinguished guest. Bruce came to Brazil for a short spell in April 1991 with a tough-looking customer named Tony Thake, the boss of a transport business. The last time I had seen Bruce was on that fateful day way back in August 1963 when I had moved into the 'big time'. Although we had spoken on the phone, it was still an enormous pleasure to meet my old friend again. Bruce, who had served ten years out of a 25-year sentence for his part in planning and executing the train robbery, was marked by the long period of incarceration, which had left him emaciated and looking older than he should have. Nevertheless, we had a great get-together and a lot of laughs. Tony, a gentleman, if not a scholar, filmed our reunion and the fun and games, in the hope of finding someone interested in buying the unusual footage. Tony had financed the trip to Brazil for both of them as Bruce was living on the dole.

A day or so after Bruce arrived, we were joined by his son, Nick, who is every bit as likeable and irreverent as his old man.

Their stay in Rio was all too short, but in my waters I was certain that we would all get together again, only I had not foreseen that one of Bruce and Nick's future visits to Rio would be to accompany me back to Britain.

Nick was back in Rio in 1995 to make a plaster cast of my head and feet that were eventually cast in bronze for his 'Heroes and Villains' exhibition. I had to sit still for him for well over an hour with a couple of straws stuck up my nose.

Visitors came from far and wide and while I would expect to be known in Britain and Australia, I found I had a stream of visitors from Scandinavia, South Africa, Canada, Japan, Poland and Germany. I even had a growing following in the US from where a visitor, Steve Koschal, discovered that there was a market for 'Ronnie Biggs' autographs. Steve, an autograph expert, was surprised by the interest the collectors had in my scrawl. Appropriately Steve had me classified under 'undesirables' on his website.

At the time of his visit to Rio, Steve was a near neighbour of my nephew Terry in Florida. Terry was another regular visitor and had taken after his 'Uncle Ron' in liking to dabble in the kitchen, only he did it on a professional scale with his own catering company. When Terry came to town all hell broke loose in the kitchen as he, Rosa and I fought for space on the stove.

Besides Charmian and the boys, Terry and his brothers, Jack and Chris, plus Terry's own son, Steve, were my closest relatives. Terry's father was my older brother, Jack, who died on the eve of the Great Train Robbery.

Shortly after the visit of Bruce I received a visit from the German punk rock band Die Toten Hosen ('The Dead Trousers'). Formed in Düsseldorf in 1982 they have been one of Germany's biggest bands over the decades, with a huge following in South America, Australia and Eastern Europe.

I enjoyed the company of the band members and a strong and long friendship was forged. The band were amongst the first to be in contact when I was released from prison in 2009, sending a magnificent box set of their CDs. Not sure it was to the taste of the others in the nursing home, but I loved it.

During the band's visit to Rio in mid-1991 I did a 'Sex Pistols' with them and wrote and recorded a couple of tracks and videos. They included the hit 'Carnival in Rio (Punk Was)', the appropriately titled 'Police on My Back' and a new, and I think better, recording of 'No One Is Innocent'.

I also recorded with one of Argentina's top punk bands, Pilsen, who had worked with Die Toten Hosen and had an album produced by the Pistols' Steve Jones. Our hits included 'Pilsen' and 'Dearest Madonna'.

A visitor I had never expected to see again in Rio was ex-sleuth Jack Slipper. Hearing that I was about to stage a party in August 1993 to commemorate the 30th anniversary of the train robbery, the *Sunday Express* telephoned to see if I would be willing to meet Slipper. There had been rumours in the press that I was planning to invite Slipper to the party. The BBC had also shown a lot of interest in the bash and were talking about turning up in Rio with as many of the train gang as wished to come along and talk about old times.

Anxious not to miss out on a story of an encounter between the ex-cop and me, the *Sunday Express* was ready to 'do the dirty' on the rest of Fleet Street and the BBC.

I was not expecting to see Slipper turn up, so I was pleasantly surprised when Oonagh Blackman, the *Sunday Express* reporter, phoned to say that Slipper had agreed to come to the mountain, although not to the party.

Our meeting, in June 1993, was much ado about nothing

and the *Sunday Express* had nothing specific in mind when they planned it. They were hoping that something 'newsworthy' might come from Slipper and me being face to face after all these years.

We met in a quiet corner of the pool area at the back of the Intercontinental Hotel in São Conrado; the same hotel where I had gone to meet Bobby Moore and Kenny Lynch.

We left the hotel and went for a stroll along the beach chit-chatting, while the newspaper's photographer snapped away. I told Slipper that I was surprised that he had accepted the paper's invitation, knowing that his gesture was sure to meet with disapproval in certain quarters. But he was no longer a serving officer and was able to come and go as he saw fit. He was just anxious to keep his visit a secret so that it didn't turn into a 'circus'.

He asked after Mike and Ulla, whom he had met in Tokyo. I politely asked after his wife. Nobody would have guessed – or believed – that the two white-haired old gents ambling along the beach in the winter sunshine were the ex-guv'nor of the Sweeney and the one-time world's most wanted man.

It had been thirsty work and Jack and I were in need of a drink. Jack suggested that we go to a bar where we would be unrecognised, so I took them to a shopping mall close by where there was then a comfortable bar-restaurant called Guimas. A female acquaintance, Beatriz, whom I had not seen for several years, was working as a waitress and immediately came to our table to greet me. Moments later an American musician friend walked through the door. So far Slipper and I had not had a chance to exchange a word. As the musician moved away, Slipper commented, 'I'm glad I didn't suggest going to a place where you are well known!'

Over drinks we found ourselves talking about 'the man who had coshed the train driver'. Slipper assured me that the 'Yard' knew the identity of this person, who was never taken into custody.

The next morning, when I was due to meet Slipper in Copacabana, I took Johnny Pickston along. John used to play 'golf' on Copacabana beach, hitting a tennis ball from one litter bin to the next. He had become quite a dab hand at it and, knowing of Jack Slipper's passion for golf, was anxious to challenge him.

It was a fun day, with beers on the beach. Later the photographer suggested that Jack and I should stand with our arms around each other's shoulders in front of the Trocadero Hotel where he had 'nicked' me nearly 20 years earlier. But that, said Slipper, was a step too far.

Pickston offered to take the group to the airport when it was time for them to return to England. Over a drink at the airport we talked about the 'flak' he was certain to receive when he got back to England. But Jack was an old campaigner and well accustomed to the shit that's thrown in the press. When there's a few quid to be earned he'd have been a fool not to go for it. And the readers loved it, so why not?

As he was leaving we shook hands firmly.

We saw each other sooner than we had expected as just over a month later, but this time over a satellite hook-up, we again came face to face. Jack was in Hamburg to have a chinwag with his favourite fugitive.

I did a number of other satellite links with him over the years. We both appreciated each other's points of view on crime and punishment and the Great Train Robbery. Jack was generous with his comments on my return to England in 2001. He was a class act. I was genuinely very sorry to hear of his passing in August 2005. It would have been nice to meet him one last time, and on his patch.

The family also came calling. Chris and a group of his school friends spent almost a year in Rio in 1986, giving Chris and Mike a chance to get to know one another. Chris returned to Rio in 1988 with Charmian and Farley. We all went to carnival together before Charmian went off to explore Peru and Bolivia before returning in time to celebrate Farley's 21st in Rio. Chris then managed to drop by in August 1992 with his then fiancée, and now his wife, to help Mike celebrate his 18th.

By the end of 1992 I was back to hustling my T-shirts. Despite a radio spot during the Rio Earth Summit, it was tough financially. Tourists had thinned out and the pickings were meagre. Pickston and I were 'working' together. He was the funnyman who would get the punters interested and so four nights a week John and I would sit in the bar of the Leme Palace Hotel waiting for the tourists that never came. Then our luck changed; one night the bar filled up with a crowd of people who were participating in the British Steel Global Challenge, a round-the-world yacht race organised by Sir Chay Blyth.

While I was signing autographs, accepting numerous drinks, posing for photographs and answering questions, John was exposing the merchandise.

Most of them were pleasant, friendly people looking for a little adventure in their lives. One was an ex-prison officer who spoke fondly of 'Gordon' (Goody) whom he said he had got to know well over the years.

On 15 November 1992 I went to see the boats sail out of Rio on their 9,000 mile leg to Australia and noticed that a lot of the sailors were wearing their recently acquired 'Ronnie Biggs' T-shirts. A few people, writers and newsmen who had been covering the yacht race, were still in Rio and I received a phone call from one of them who was interested in taking some of my T-shirts back to the UK. I threw a dozen in a bag and met my 'customer' in a bar close to his hotel in Copacabana. He was with several other people who turned out to be buyers as well, and within a few minutes I had autographed and sold all my shirts.

While I was answering their questions, the 'evergreens' as I call them, one of the group, an enthusiastic Scot, Jock, listened in silence as I related the time-worn facts. Finally he asked: 'Have you ever thought of writing your story?'

'It's funny that you should say that,' I told him, 'because I'm working on it right at this moment!'

'If you need an agent or any help in London,' he said, handing me his business card, 'get in touch.'

Some years before the encounter with Jock, I had become friends with a fellow Englishman and almost equally long-time Rio resident, Christopher Pickard. Chris was a writer and journalist and we had started kicking ideas around with a view to producing a light-hearted guidebook, tentatively entitled 'Ronnie's Rio'. We made a number of enquiries regarding the feasibility of our project, but always got the same answer: there was far more interest in my actual life story.

We got a first chapter, the story of my escape from Wandsworth, knocked up in no time, and a few weeks later, when Chris had business in London, he took the first chapter to present to the friendly Scot. He was to take this to publishers, but suggested we got on with writing the book as these things took time and they may want to see more of my masterpiece.

One very good reason to write a proper autobiography is that over the years there had been many misleading comments and gross exaggerations in the press with regard to my person, and it is a way to put the record straight for those that care about the truth.

When members of the Royal Family visited Rio, certain newspapers would be sure to report that I was doing my best to get an audience with them to plead for a pardon, or some similar crap. When Princess Diana was visiting Rio in April 1991, the news pack who follow the royals paid me a visit. They had organised a whip-round and offered £500 (about £1,000 today) to pose in a Princess Di T-shirt and to say a few words about the dear lady's visit.

During the session, a couple of reporters drew me aside with an offer they thought I couldn't refuse. They knew the Princess's itinerary for the following day and at a certain hour she would be in downtown Rio, bestowing smiles upon the barefoot street urchins. For a further 500 quid, one of the conspirators said, all we want you to do is reach through the crowd and lay your hand on Lady Di's arm . . . I declined the offer.

I shouldn't be too hard on the press, as it is the media that brought me the cock-eyed fame that I enjoyed over the years in Rio. The only thing that ever bothered me is when I told a reporter the truth and they then chose to ignore it. Most of the media still can't get the number of people at the train robbery right. It is 16 at the track, if you need to ask.

When Eric and I went over the wall from Wandsworth, the papers warned that we were probably armed and ready to shoot. The public was advised not to 'have a go'. Gradually the image changed as it became obvious that I was not the vicious desperado I was first painted to be and eventually I found myself on first name terms with Fleet Street and the press in general. When a crime of any magnitude occurred in Britain or involved Brits, the press invariably telephoned me for my comments.

It was just after Slipper's visit to Rio in 1993 that Chris got the call from Jock in London. We had a publishing deal and it was with Bloomsbury no less. At the time, Bloomsbury was considered very highbrow, and known for publishing very serious authors. At this point in time, a certain Mr Harry Potter was not even a glint in Bloomsbury's eye, but they knew they needed some popular best sellers if the company was to go public.

We were too late for a Christmas launch, so Bloomsbury set a 21 January 1994 release date. I declined the kind invitation to the London launch, but agreed to send Mike to represent the family.

The rest of 1993 was spent planning for the book launch. Photos were taken and promotional videos were shot. If I could not physically be in London for the launch, it was decided that we would do a satellite link between the press in London and me in Rio.

Mike, accompanied by Gus Dudgeon and his wife, made their way to the Groucho Club in London that January morning where they met up with Jack Slipper and a crowd of Fleet Street's finest.

Due to the time difference between London and Rio, Chris and I, plus his girlfriend at the time, Ana Claudia, along with Johnny Pickston, were up at the crack of dawn and made our way to a studio in downtown Rio where we met another old Rio friend, Bob Nadkarni, a film-maker who was going to produce the Rio end of the show. Bob had filmed and recorded with me many times over the decades, during which time we had had many a bevy or two.

The Brazilian press, many of whom I also knew well, were up early and invited to the studio for breakfast and to watch the transatlantic conference. I promised to talk to all the Brazilian media, including TV Globo, just as soon as the British press had got their pound of flesh via the costly satellite link.

Knowing that I was not always at my best in the early morning, Chris thoughtfully supplied a bottle of brandy to loosen my tongue. The brandy, along with some strong black coffee, did the trick and despite not being able to see who was asking the questions from London, and trying to remember to look straight into the camera, it all went as well as we could have hoped for and the resulting coverage was generally positive. Even my critics, including Slipper, seemed to like the book. He was also able to assure those in London that they were indeed talking to the real Ronnie Biggs.

'Though it pains me to say it, I enjoyed the book, and I think a lot of other people will too,' wrote Jack who had got hold of an early copy to review for the *Express*. 'So Ronnie, if you are reading this, there's only one thing left to say: it's nice to see you earning money legitimately at last!'

With our work done for the day, except for a couple of scheduled telephone interviews with British radio stations, we decided it was time to celebrate. Still only mid-morning, it was a gloriously sunny day and we headed for the Rio Palace Hotel, now the Fairmont Rio, to sit by the pool area. We could relax and enjoy the view down the length of Copacabana as well as partaking of a few beers and *caipirinhas*, and a spot of lunch.

As morning moved into afternoon, a small crowd started to build up in front of the hotel. Modestly I thought this might be for me as news of the book launch spread, but it was Pickston who pointed out that from their shouts and banners it looked as if they were more interested in the stars of the Hollywood Rock festival who were staying at the hotel.

Now well and truly refreshed, we decided to call it a day and that is when I spotted Whitney Houston sunning herself by the pool. In my state it seemed the most natural thing was to go and say hello and welcome her to Rio. I was a big fan and hoped to get to the show. I had not considered that being one of the biggest stars of the day she might have a bunch of minders looking out for her, so as I approached and Whitney looked up from her book, a number of large gentlemen hove into view.

'Ronnie Biggs! It is Ronnie Biggs, isn't it?' I heard a voice say off to the right. 'Whitney, it is Ronnie. You do know Ronnie Biggs?'

The voice belonged to Steven Tyler, who was also headlining at Hollywood Rock with Aerosmith. The heavies melted away as quickly as they had appeared and Steve was shaking my hand while trying to explain to a somewhat startled Whitney who the strange man was standing in front of her.

Initial reports from Bloomsbury were very encouraging. There were good displays of the book in many stores and it was selling well. In fact it would have been the number one best seller at the time but was kept off the top of the sales charts because of the bookshops that refused to report sales when some of the staff objected to a 'criminal' benefitting from his crime. They had not read the book.

A few years later Guy Ritchie's *Lock, Stock and Two Smoking Barrels* would make gangsters 'chic' and fashionable, and the shelves and sales charts would be full of criminal autobiographies, biographies and other tales. I was clearly well ahead of the curve!

I was pleased that my autobiography had been well received. But not everyone was a fan. A certain lady in Australia had taken umbrage and was not happy by what she had read.

The lady was Charmian, and for what seemed liked months, she avoided my calls. When I did get to speak to her she let me have it with both barrels. 'Did I really need to list all of my conquests?' she asked. She was clearly hurt so I took the only course open to me and blamed Chris. I told her he had been a cunning journalist who had got me to reveal all. Charm was far too smart to fall for that one, plus she knew me too well. She knew there was only one person to blame, and it wasn't Chris.

In my defence, the reaction I got from people who had read the book was that they all wanted to meet Charm, and said she came across as a very special lady. A lot said they could not work out what a nice girl like her had ever seen in a man like me.

During April 1994, the British Foreign Secretary Douglas Hurd made a visit to Brazil. In Rio, Hurd was staying at the Copacabana Palace. I had received a call from a lady travelling with the Foreign Secretary's party who was the daughter of a Lord who had met me on a previous visit. He had asked his daughter to deliver a little present to me and I agreed to meet her in the new bar at the Copa. Little did she or I know that we were sitting exactly in the path of where Hurd was scheduled to pass on his way to dinner with the Governor of Rio. Hurd's handlers were convinced I was sitting there to confront and embarrass the Foreign Secretary. Nothing could have been further from my mind as I did not even know at the time that he was in Rio. It is how rumours about me start and take on a life of their own.

As 1994 came to a close, things overall were looking good. I was a best-selling author and enjoying life in Rio where lots seemed to be going on. I even got a call from my Scottish agent to ask 'what's next?'

Sales were good enough for Bloomsbury to want a follow-up and they were looking at ways to develop their budding author. I still had my plan for a Rio guide, but they didn't fancy that. I also liked the idea of doing a cookbook, *Ronnie Biggs' C(r)ook Book For the Single Man on the Run*. I was going to open with porridge, which can be deceptively difficult to make. Again I was ahead of the curve for celebrity cookbooks.

Bloomsbury thought I should try my hand at crime fiction, and if possible a crime that had links to the Great Train Robbery, my 'calling card', as they politely put it.

I retired with Chris to one of our favourite Rio watering holes, the Casa da Suiça in Gloria, for an extended lunch. Later over a glass or two or three of schnapps with the owner, Volkmar Wendlinger, we came up with the plan to tell the fictional story of the three robbers who got away. The three for whom the train robbery was the perfect crime.

Chris and I had a lot of fun coming up with the storyline and the plot twists, and there were a few outrageous ones we had to bin. At times I had to rein in Chris when some of his fiction came a little too close to the facts for comfort. I always believed it was up to the three involved to tell their story if they wanted to. I was once offered close to a million dollars to name names, but despite what some people might like to think, I don't always have a price.

The new book was published as *Keep on Running* on 31 October 1995. Despite being billed clearly as a work of fiction, it did not stop some of the media going over the text with a fine-toothed comb looking for leads. Even the *Sunday Times* ran with a sizeable story under the title of 'Did great train robber flee with fortune in diamonds?'

Michael Argyle QC, who had defended me at the trial in 1964, and who went on to become an Old Bailey judge, told the paper that a prosecution witness had told him about the diamonds. Well Michael, I have one thing to say: Bollocks! If there were any diamonds on the train I certainly did not see any of them, or get my hands on them, and neither did anyone I knew.

At the end of November 1994 I received a number of calls from the media in London. They called after Buster Edwards had been found hanged in his lock-up. I did not have much to say, but promised to have a couple of beers for him and remember him as a jolly fella who was not too serious about life. In truth I had never spent much time with Buster, other than at the farm. Many of the gang I only got to know when we were being held in Bedford and

Aylesbury in the run-up to the trial. Buster was on the run, and by the time he was caught I was long gone and had been living in Australia for nearly a year. But Buster's death, along with that of Paul Seabourne, was a reminder that we couldn't all live forever and that Old Father Time was catching up with us all, however fast or far we chose to run.

CHAPTER 17

LONG DARK TUNNEL

At the beginning of 1995 you would have found me hunkered down putting the finishing touches to *Keep on Running*. Chris and I were giving the manuscript one final polish before getting our latest masterpiece off to the publisher.

Anyone who has spent time in Rio will know that at the start of the year there is a certain anticipation and excitement in the city as it turns its attention to carnival. In 1995 the city seemed extra excited as it was going to get an early bonus in the shape of the Rolling Stones. The band was coming to Rio at the start of February to perform its Voodoo Lounge tour for two nights at the Maracanã Stadium.

As a great believer that all work and no play might make Ron a dull boy, I was looking forward to taking a break from my literary endeavours and getting the chance to finally see the Stones who had their first release, 'Come On', on 7 June 1963, just two months before the Great Train Robbery. A lot of water had passed under the bridge for both the band and me since then.

This would be the band's first performance in Brazil, although Charlie Watts had brought his quintet on tour in 1992, and in 1984 Mick Jagger was in Rio to shoot a series of videos for his solo album *She's the Boss*. Among the cast were Dennis Hopper, Rae Dawn Chong and Jerry Hall, while behind the camera was to be found a certain Julien Temple, the man responsible for the Sex Pistols' documentary, *The Great Rock 'n' Roll Swindle*.

In these celebrity and media-driven times, the Stones's people should have contacted my people to set up our meeting. The only problem is I didn't have any 'people', so it was Rosa, my cook and housekeeper, who answered the phone. The outcome was that the Stones were inviting me and Mike to the second show and that I should come to the Intercontinental Hotel where the band were staying and from where they would take us across to the stadium. Keith Richards was Mike's idol, so there was no way he was going to miss this.

As so often seemed to happen, Mike and I were running a little late when we set out on the Saturday from home for the hotel in Mike's rather beaten-up car. A car, I assured Mike that nobody would want to beg, steal or borrow, even in Rio.

Traffic was bad as people headed for the beach and when we got to the hotel the Stones had already left. There was only one thing to do, and that was to turn around and drive back across town to the Maracanã, although with a crowd of more than 150,000 expected, parking was never going to be easy. There was also the little problem of not having any tickets or passes in our hand and no such thing as a mobile phone.

Fame and notoriety can have its benefits, so we drove to the back gate of the stadium that Mike and I had often used when the Balão Magico had played at the Maracanã. Luckily the man on the gate recognised us and we were waved into the stadium and shown where to park. Word was passed through to the Stones that 'Mr Biggs and party had arrived'.

We were collected and taken backstage, but I had never seen the Maracaná kitted out like this. It was a fantasy world. Mike and I were placed in the Voodoo Lounge, a room where we were plied with food and drink; by chance many of the serving staff were from one of my favourite restaurants so knew my tastes only too well. Not only was there food and drink, but also a full-size snooker table and video games. Mike and I were in seventh heaven.

We were then taken further into the inner sanctum where we found Keith slumped on a couch looking every inch the rock 'n' roller he is. When he saw me he jumped up and we hugged.

Shortly after, Ronnie Wood came and joined us along with Keith's dad, Bert, who turned out to be a fan. Charlie Watts was now introduced to us. The only one who kept his distance was Jagger who was more content to watch and video everything on a little camera he was holding. Mike was now talking music with Keith who was showing him his guitars. He asked Mike to play a few Brazilian numbers and joined in.

The band were incredibly relaxed considering they were about to step on stage and play to one of the biggest crowds in their long and illustrious career, and although it may sound like a cliché, it was as simple as one of the stage crew coming into the lounge and announcing: 'Gentlemen, it's show time.' The band bade us a fond farewell, and exited out on to the stage.

Minders were sent to take us to the side of the stage from where we could watch the show. I stood with Bert Richards and we had a great time necking back the Guinness and cheering the boys on. It may only have been rock 'n' roll, but we loved it.

In the end I wasn't in great form to enjoy carnival 1995 as after the departure of the Stones I managed to break the bottom of my left leg. I was looking up and admiring the carnival decorations going up around the Teatro Municipal and failed to notice an ornate chain they had hung across the pavement to stop cars parking next to the theatre. It caught me totally on the wrong spot and on the hop; as a result I went arse over tit and broke my leg.

*

On 18 July 1995, during an official visit to London, the Brazilian Foreign Secretary, Luiz Felipe Lampreia, signed a new Extradition Treaty with his opposite number, Malcolm Rifkind. The press naturally put two and two together and came to five, and assumed the treaty was all about getting Biggs back to Blighty. But a treaty, as my lawyer pointed out, is not a law and so I put it to the back of my mind.

Despite the shadow of extradition, life in Rio was busy and fun, and on 31 October 1995 my fictional literary efforts were served up to an unsuspecting public. *Keep on Running* was in the British bookshops and sold well. Again I was called on to do a number of media interviews, but most were trying to second-guess what was true and what was fiction, and I wasn't letting on.

Whatever dreams I may have had, dark clouds were building on the horizon. Buster was not the only one to call it time. Great friends Paul Seabourne and Armin Heim had passed on, two people without whom I would not have been enjoying my liberty. In August 1997 it was Roy James, the brilliant racing driver and London's best getaway driver, who died of heart disease aged just 62. He had been good company during the time we spent together in prison.

In late 1995 it was the turn of my 'best friend', our pet Rottweiler, Blitz, who died without warning. Blitz was a good companion and, despite being a softy if you knew him, he had a presence that made him an outstanding guard dog. I never doubted that he would fight to the death to protect me. If he had been with me when Miller and his gang jumped me, he would have made short work of them and it would not have been the dog's bollocks that Miller would have had to worry about.

We had other pets, including an ageing Miniature Pinscher, Lua, who was going blind. Lua was lost without Blitz, so Mike persuaded me to go to the vet and pick out another baby Rottweiler, which we did. In honour of his noble predecessor he was also christened Blitz.

The death that hit me the hardest was that of my long-time companion in Rio, Ulla Sopher. Ulla had been part of my life in Rio for over 20 years. She was a very special lady who had helped keep me sane and on track on more than one occasion. She was gracious and generous. She was my real best friend in Rio.

When I met her, Ulla was already the divorced mother of three young children, Carla, Felipe and Alex. Over the years we lived together off and on, but realised that the best formula for us was to have our own places – a form of 'marriage' I would recommend. The arrangement seemed to work for us, as we both liked to be free to follow our individual interests and hobbies. Ulla was into art and loved to paint, while I liked to spend hours pottering around my small garden.

Ulla always said she loved Ronnie Biggs the man, but she hated the circus that sometimes became part of my life by necessity, when I often had to become the clown. Ulla preferred to stay in the shadows and would be there to support me when I needed her. She was always there with a wise word, but stepped back into the shadows when I had to 'perform'.

It was from Ulla's apartment in Santa Teresa that I first set eyes and my heart on the apartment below, the flat that I eventually bought for Mike with his Balão Magico earnings. Ulla, meanwhile, had moved to an apartment in the back streets of Copacabana. She and I spent most weekends together. We played cards, Scrabble and snooker, went to the cinema. Everything that a normal couple of our vintage might do.

Ulla's death on 12 January 1996 was not a death foretold. She had been having problems with her stomach, but nothing to raise any concern other than she was having difficulty sleeping. Because of it, we had not seen each other for a couple of days and I offered to go around to her flat and be with her, even fix some food if she felt like it. Being there I might even be able to take her mind off the pain.

When I got to Ulla's flat that afternoon I let myself in. I had keys to her flat and she had keys to mine. I saw Ulla sprawled out on her bed asleep. She was in a T-shirt with a towel wrapped around her waist. I decided to let her sleep on, as lack of it was what she had been complaining about the most. I unpacked the food and wine, and the video I had picked out for us to watch. I put the television on at a low volume and settled down with the paper.

A couple of hours passed and I thought I should think of waking Ulla or she would not be able to sleep later. To start with I started to make a little more noise. I turned up the volume on the TV, and when there was still no sign of Ulla I decided to make her a cup of tea and wake her up. I took it into her and sat next to her on the bed. I noticed that she was bruised on her pale legs. I touched her leg to wake her and as soon as I did I knew something was wrong. I sensed she was dead.

It was a terrible, terrible experience. In Brazil the repercussions of death move very quickly and most people are buried within 24 hours. I had to call Ulla's doctor to confirm my worst fears, as well as her family, including her children and brother. I also called my flat and left a message for Mike to call me.

I was in shock. At the funeral the following day all I could muster was 'Goodbye Ulla' as she was being lowered into the ground. I tried to force back the tears, but Mike could see my torment. He held me tight. 'Cry, Dad,' he whispered in my ear. 'Do it. Don't hold back. Cry.'

I broke down in tears and wept and wept and wept. I had not felt like this since the day I got news of Nicky's death 25 years earlier. I knew for Mike's sake that I would have to gather up the pieces of my life and take this blow on the chin. Ulla's death left a big hole in my life. It left me broken. Normally in Rio I would have turned to Ulla at such a moment, but she was no longer around to help me.

My humour and state of mind was not improved when a few weeks later I put the food down for the dogs and Lua did not appear. I called for her, but she did not come. I found her floating in the pool. She had been going blind and I don't know if she simply lost her directions and walked into the pool or if the playful Rottweiler puppy gave her a push.

In the weeks that followed I moped around not discussing Ulla's death and how I felt. But a good friend came to my rescue. It was Volkmar from the Casa Suiça who invited me for lunch in an attempt to shake me out of my lethargy. I drank far, far too much that day, even by my standards, but it is what I needed. Volkmar knew I should not be left alone so took me back to his flat where I poured out my heart to him about Ulla and life in general.

Eventually I blacked out and Volkmar put me to bed. I woke up around 4 am, but in my state I hadn't got a fucking clue where I was. I called Mike who had been worried sick by the fact I had gone missing, which was very unlike me. I told Mike I was in a dark room, but did not know exactly where. Eventually enough started coming back to me and through my drunken haze I worked out where I had to be and asked Mike to come and get me. I sneaked out of Volkmar's house without waking him. Thanks for the shoulder to cry on, Volkmar. I really needed it.

What I didn't need was the raging hangover, but I think it was a first warning that I needed to start taking more care of my body. I decided I would drink less and eat healthier. Which in Rio is often easier said than done.

Prior to Ulla's death I had accepted an invitation to address the Young Presidents' Organisation's annual summit that was going to take place in Manaus. They wanted me to talk to the young CEOs on the topic of crime and rehabilitation, something they could all probably put to good use later in their careers. I was not sure if I was in the right frame of mind, but I knew that Mike and I could do with the money as well as the break.

In Manaus, Mike made the discovery that his dad had been a porn star when he spotted a magazine in a shop with my name across the cover. When he picked it up he found it was a porn mag with lots of photos of me frolicking in a pool with scantily clad young ladies. He took great delight in bringing it back to the hotel to show me and I had to explain that Armin had taken the photos back in 1989 during a shoot for the *Electric Blue* video series. Sadly I no longer had a copy to show him.

Most of the rest of 1996 and 1997 was something of a blur, but just as I was starting to pick myself up and get back to some form of normality came the hammer blow that the new extradition treaty between the British and Brazilian governments was about to become law. The details of how the new treaty might affect me were not at first clear, but on 14 August 1997 both governments ratified the treaty. Two months later, on 29 October, the British

Foreign Secretary, a certain Mr Jack Straw, officially asked Brazil to send me back to Britain.

The newspapers, of course, were straight on the phone wanting to know my thoughts on the extradition treaty. I told them that I had no plans to fight extradition if that was what the Brazilian government agreed to, but by choice I wanted to stay on in Brazil.

Happily for me, Brazil's Supreme Court did not take long to rule, and on 12 November my lawyers, Luiz Fernando Gevaerd and Edson Abdalla, called me to say the court had rejected the request as it had ruled that the statute of limitations had run out on the robbery as the crime had been committed more than 20 years earlier.

For the second time in my life a court in Brasilia had granted me my freedom, and this time they had closed the book once and for all. I now knew if I was ever to return to Britain it would be on my terms and because of my decision and nobody else's.

While I had tried to remain calm on the outside, the ruling was a huge relief. There was now a very small chink of light at the end of what had been become a very long and dark tunnel.

I had also tried to remain calm when in 1996 news reached me that Charmian had been diagnosed with two primary cancers. She was operated on and spent over a week in intensive care before undergoing over six months of chemotherapy. Always the fighter, Charmian fought the cancer and won, but as had so often been the case, I could not be at her side to help and it was Charm who came to visit me, dropping in on Rio on her way back to Australia after a visit to the UK to see her family.

*

Not long after the Supreme Court's decision that allowed me to stay in Brazil I was approached by one of Rio's major samba schools, Unidos do Porto da Pedra, that had decided it wanted to give me the ultimate accolade and make me part of the theme of the school's carnival presentation for 1998.

To a non-Brazilian audience it is difficult to explain just how big a deal it is to be honoured in such a way. This was like a knighthood in Britain, but bigger. Very few foreigners have ever been honoured, and even fewer have been alive to actually enjoy it. Given my love of samba and carnival I was hugely flattered. The samba was *Samba no pé e mãos ao alto, isto é um assalto,* which roughly translates as *Stick 'em up, put your hands in the air and samba on your feet.*

I am not sure why, but I was then struck down by a rare dose of common sense. Something was making me uneasy and I realised that after the kind and considerate way the Brazilian government, its courts and its people had treated me, I might just be overstepping the mark to become a focal point of carnival, an event that was so important to so many. I had no wish to offend or embarrass my hosts and when I heard the samba school planned for me to stand in front of a replica of the train from the robbery, I decided it was a step too far and declined the offer to appear with the school on the night of the parade.

My decision was not to deter Mauro Quintaes, the *carnavalesco* of Porto da Pedra, so he put the word out that he needed a Biggs lookalike. It was not very flattering to hear he was looking for a 'large old man with white skin and slicked back hair'. Fair to say that the man who stood in for me looked more like the bloke from *The Sopranos* than me.

Sadly for Unidos do Porto da Pedra, the presentation did not go down well with the judges that year and the school ended up coming 14th out of the 15 schools parading, and was relegated to a lower division.

Unidos do Porto da Pedra wasn't the first honour bestowed on me by Brazilian musicians. In the early 1990s I was approached by a group calling themselves Os Intocáveis (The Untouchables), who asked me to appear in a video for their single 'Ronald Biggs prá presidente', or 'Ronald Biggs for President'. The song was a catchy, light-hearted protest song about what had been going on with the Brazilian government and made the point that if you were going to have a bunch of crooks running the country, you might as well elect a professional crook, a crook such as 'Ronnie Biggs'. I'm not sure of the message, but we had a lot of fun making the video.

In early March 1998, about a month after the carnival parade, I was sitting at home chatting with my friend Lou, the wife of Kevin Rawlings, as well as Ian, an Aussie pal up to visit from São Paulo. As per usual we were having a cold beer or two and sitting around shooting the breeze. What happened next I can only describe as an out-of-body experience. I found myself observing the other people in the room, but it was as if I was looking at them from behind a window. There was no sound, just vision. I could see mouths moving and people looking at me, even touching me. Then nothing. I had had a stroke.

According to those in the room I even managed to keep a grip on my beer, and they had to prise it out of my hand. When I did come around I apparently decided for no good reason that a bath would make me feel better. Thankfully I did not pass out again in the bath, but I wasn't feeling any better so Lou drove me across to the São Silvestre Hospital.

The next thing I remember is coming around in hospital. I say remember, but it was all a bit of a blur and my speech was a slur. John Pickston and Lia were there, as was Mike's good friend, Eric.

Mike had been away but was tracked down and he rushed to the hospital. He found me confused and in tears. Not only was I having problems speaking, but I could not remember the most basic facts such as the names of my mother and father, or even when I was born. But the doctors assured me that it was quite normal and that in a week or so I would be as right as rain, or as right as a 68-year-old man living my lifestyle in Rio could be.

I was released from hospital to recover at home. Mike took time off from his studio to look after me, along with Rosa who seemed to show me little or no sympathy, which was probably exactly what I needed.

The stroke was a warning and the doctors told me I would now have to watch what I ate and drank. The memory thankfully started to return and so did my speech.

Once I could look after myself, Mike went back to work in the studio as well as touring Brazil with his band. Mike's stock musically was rising and he got an invitation to play percussion at the Montreux Jazz Festival behind Roberta do Recife. A visit to Switzerland would also allow him to catch up with his mother.

Mike was now more committed than ever to his girlfriend, Veronica, and had moved in with her, living in a small bedsit but still coming home for food and to get Rosa to wash his clothes. In early 1999, Veronica discovered that she was pregnant and Mike broke the news to me that I was going to be a doting grandfather; he also suggested that given the news he and Veronica should both move back into the house. I was delighted and it would be good to have them around.

I was now feeling well enough to receive paying visitors again, and to enjoy the odd glass of wine or two with them. My doctor, however, had other ideas and decided it was time to curtail one of life's little pleasures. He told me that it was not a

good idea for a man of my age who had suffered a stroke to still
be smoking dope.

*

With my seventieth birthday looming in August 1999, I was
coming under pressure to throw one last big party. A last big
bash until I retired to a quieter life as at the time I was seriously
considering moving out of Rio to free up the house for Mike and
his family, and go and live on a friend's farm and breed carp. Not
rock 'n' roll, but I would cope. I also learnt that I had become a
grandfather with the birth of a daughter to Chris and his wife, so
I was starting to feel my age!

Word spread about the party and I was pleased to hear that a
few old mates and some new ones were going to cross the pond to
celebrate. Bruce and Nick Reynolds said they would be there. Roy
'Pretty Boy' Shaw, who had shared mailbag-sewing duties with
me in Wandsworth, and who had visited me for a lively Christmas
in 1998, was another. As was Tony Hoare, one of the writers of
Z Cars and *Minder*. Dave Courtney, whom I had never met, also
jumped on the bandwagon thanks to a media deal he had done to
help get the others out to Rio.

Gus and Sheila Dudgeon confirmed they would be coming,
as did Breiti from Die Toten Hosen, and Chris Pickard, who had
been up in Los Angeles trying to get interest from the Hollywood
studios for a film of my life.

In total I was expecting about 150 friends to descend on the
house in Santa Teresa, and not just to celebrate my 70th, but
also the 36th anniversary of the train robbery and my improving
health. The invitations to the party were printed on the back of a
£5 Monopoly note and said 'Advance to GO, collect £2,631,784
and scarper'.

The planning was something of a military campaign as Mike and I worked out the food, the drink, the entertainment and where to house the overseas guests. I was also coming to the realisation that this was going to be more than a one-night stand, and I would have to entertain and wine and dine my British guests for at least a week or so.

Through a Scottish friend, Billy, who had a bar in Botafogo, thousands of bottles of beer and soft drinks were delivered to the house, along with crates of champagne and wine, and over 50 kilos of meat for the barbecue. I did not know at the time as Mike was sworn to secrecy, but it was another good and very generous Scottish friend, Brian Running, whom I had enjoyed many a long drinking session with over the years, who covered the cost of the beers. That was one hell of a round!

The main group of overseas guests made quite a splash as they strode through Gatwick Airport to catch the flight to Rio. The *Sunday Telegraph* referred to them as 'a charabanc load of sixties villains'. It included Bruce, Nick, Roy, Tony and Dave, and thanks to a generous media benefactor they would all be flying in business class.

It was a great party, even by my standards, with guests from every walk of life. There were politicians, judges, lawyers, doctors, musicians, all rubbing shoulders with a good mix of what the *Guardian* classified as 'rogues'. Lovable rogues, I would like to think.

The media were out in force. Five TV crews mingled with the guests, as did photographers and journalists, many of whom had become close friends during my time in Rio. If they could make some money off me, I was happy for them. Brand 'Biggs' was still alive and well.

At one point I cut the cake and thanked the guests. Somebody had put a plastic bobby's helmet on my head and I wore a special

T-shirt that said 'Happy Birthday Ronald Biggs' and had a picture of my head on a £5 note. To give the press the picture that they really wanted, Bruce and Roy flanked me.

That photo came back to haunt me when I was waiting for my parole in 2009 as the Ministry of Justice used it as an example that I been consorting with 'criminal elements', even if they were retired. It had to be pointed out to them that just off camera were a High Court judge, a member of the House of Lords, several senior police officers, and I could go on.

In the early hours, as the party was in full flow, I was talking with my lawyer and good friend, Wellington Mousinho, when we saw that the people standing at the bottom of the stairs that led down to the apartment from the street were getting a little agitated. I looked up to see a full SWAT team from the federal police descending on the apartment and armed to the teeth. The leader of the team came in, opened his arms and gave me a big hug. He was an old, old friend from my time of having to sign on each week with the police, since when he had risen up through the ranks. He was on his way to raid a nearby favela for drugs, but was not going to miss the chance to drop in and wish me a happy birthday. And people ask me what I love about Brazil and the Brazilians?

As the night wore on I started to wilt, but put on a brave face for my guests. Mike voiced his concern that I should sneak off to bed, as did Gus and Breiti, but I stayed put.

The next week passed in a blur, and for all the wrong reasons. This was serious party time as we all burnt the candle at both ends and then some. When my band of merry men headed back to dear old Blighty, I was sorry to see them go, but glad of the chance to catch up on much-needed sleep and get back to my diet. There would be no wine, beer or red meat for a time.

It's all too easy to be wise after the event, but the party did contribute to my later health problems. I would be a fool to think otherwise.

With the expense of the party, I needed to think of ways to restock the coffers. Luckily I had been contacted by an Australian outfit called Advanced Hair Studio, a hair loss treatment that was being touted by the likes of England cricketer Graham Gooch and Wimbledon striker John Hartson, and by their poster boys, cricketer Shane Warne and rugby player Austin Healey. I was to shoot a print and TV ad for them and the make-up people would be brought in to give me a before and after look. One of my lines was to be: 'I have been involved in the greatest robbery of all time – the one off the top of my head!'

What I have always liked about the Aussies is that they have never been afraid to use controversial figures and humour in their ad campaigns, and the Advanced Hair Studio was certainly not making any excuses for using me.

I was coming to the realisation that I had not fully recovered from the party. I was feeling tired and drawn. Mike was telling me to take it easy, and he could sense that the photo and TV shoot was troubling me, something I would normally do in my sleep.

On the eve of the TV shoot I found myself having problems remembering my script. I wanted to call the treatment a 'wig' rather than an extension or graft. 'Wig' was strictly not in the Advanced Hair Studio vocabulary.

My mind was taken off the task by a call from Chris who was now in London. He had an update on our film project, although not the news I was expecting.

Chris had been talking with a couple of the big Hollywood studios and somehow the book and the project had found its way over to the television division of one of the studios in New York.

They called Chris and told him how much they loved the story of Ronnie Biggs, but they had a couple of questions. The first was if it would be okay to relocate the train robbery from England to the US, as this would play better with their viewers. Chris was slightly bemused, but said we could think about it. There were other questions and clarifications until it reached the point of casting when the studio executive told Chris that they were thinking of approaching Wesley Snipes to 'play the part of Ronnie Biggs'. It was at this point that the penny dropped and Chris realised the studio thought my story was fiction and not fact. We did not hear from them again, although I did like the idea of Wesley Snipes playing me. Again we would have been ahead of the curve!

I never did get to shoot the ad or finish my hair treatment as that evening, 15 September 1999, I had another and much stronger stroke. Luckily Veronica spotted it and called Mike who was at the studio. He rushed back and decided to get me to a hospital. I thought I was making total sense and everything was okay, but he could not understand what I was saying. As I did not qualify for free treatment under the Brazilian health service, Mike had to scrape some cash together and get me to a private clinic.

I had not been long at the clinic when my condition deteriorated and they had to stabilise me. Mike was not about to give up on me and kept talking, even though I appeared to be asleep. He asked me a number of questions and said if I could understand him to give the thumbs up. Which I apparently did. He even checked where I had stashed some money for a rainy day, as he would need it to pay for the hospital. He gave me various options until he hit on the lampshade, and I gave him the thumbs up. It just shows how ill I must have been to tell Mike where my secret stash was!

Fortunately I was still in hospital when a week later I was hit by a third, even stronger stroke. This was the stroke, I have been told, that did most of the damage as far as my speech was concerned.

I was in hospital, an expensive hospital, for over three and a half weeks before they said it was safe for me to return home. Even then I needed round the clock nursing, as although the stroke had not done too much damage to my movements and mobility, I still could not dress myself, or shave, or even feed myself. The nursing was costing £40 a day, which for Mike and me was a lot of money. Money we did not have.

However bad I looked from the outside, at least my brain was still functioning and it was becoming clear to me that the damage done by the recent strokes was far greater than the first stroke. I sensed I was facing another sentence; only I had no idea for how long. Was this a life sentence, a couple of years, or would I recover, including my voice, quickly?

The tunnel was darker than it had ever been and without the smallest chink of light. What made it worse was that I could scream in my head; but nobody could hear me.

CHAPTER 18

SAUDADES FOR RIO: TIME FOR HOME

Recuperation was long, boring and frustrating. Perhaps because I had recovered so quickly from my first stroke, I was finding it difficult to accept my current state, especially not being able to talk. I was a prisoner in my own body.

One of the first people to drop by and visit was quite unexpected. It was Steven Berkoff who was back in Rio to perform his one-man show. He had heard about my stroke and made a point of coming to see me.

The nurse did her best to make me look respectable for Steve and I shuffled through to the sitting room to meet him. Steve was on great form and did everything in his power to cheer me up. He talked and reminded me of fun events from the past when he was filming *Prisoner of Rio*, and I clapped my hands in glee.

Steve later wrote an article in *The Times* about our meeting. He ended it: 'We leave and climb the stairs, accompanied by a friendly black cat that walks us to the corner as if it was standing in for its master. Yet one cannot help but feel that this is a hint to show us that Biggs still has one more life left.'

I did not know how many lives I did have, but seeing Steve made me feel a bit more normal, yet it also made me realise how difficult it was going to be to communicate with people. I was tiring easily. I had real concerns for the future. In my state there was little chance that I could or would be a breadwinner. Ironically, however, the print versions of the Advanced Hair Studio ads were starting to appear in Britain. Complaints to the Advertising Standards Authority followed, including one that suggested the campaign would encourage crime!

Thankfully just before the second stroke I had been contacted by Jane Cavanagh, the MD of a British computer games company called SCi Entertainment. SCi was famous for having developed the controversial hit 'Carmageddon'. Jane had the idea of developing a game based around the Great Train Robbery, but I told her that if the game was more 'robbery' than 'Biggs', then Bruce needed to be involved.

Even with my stroke, Jane was happy to go ahead with the contract and Mike flew to London to pick up a much-needed advance payment and to sign the contract alongside Bruce. If we were careful the money would just about keep us going through the year.

With the contracts signed and sealed, SCi could start planning how they would announce the game to the world. Jane realised they would need some promotional shots and as I could not go to them, they would have to come to me, and that included bringing Bruce out to Rio. It was a real tonic to see my old friend, but he could not hide the fact that he was concerned at my appearance and state of health. I think we both thought this would be the last time we saw one another.

It was certainly the last time I saw SCi. After all the talk and payments, nothing ever did become of the game, but it did generate a lot of positive coverage for the company.

Charmian also came to see me in 1998. She tried to help me with my speech therapy and to cheer me up, but I know I was not a very good patient or fun to be with.

Towards the end of 1999, an ever-darkening cloud was settling over my head. I had no quality of life and I was only causing problems for Mike and Veronica. I could not see how it would get any better. At that point I decided it was best to put an end to it.

One morning I went into my bathroom with a sharp knife and slit both my wrists. I was sorry for how I might be found, but in my mental state I did not care. I could not go on. It took a surprisingly short time until I blacked out.

Luckily, and I do say luckily, Mike woke early that day. He had come into my room to give me my medication. When he did not find me in bed he assumed that I was either in the lounge or the garden. When he could not find me he decided to check the bathroom. The sight that greeted him was not a pleasant one for any son. There was blood on the walls, blood on the ceiling and on the floor. I was passed out face down in a growing pool of my own blood.

My timing, looking back, could have been better, as poor Veronica was nearly eight months pregnant, and when you are in that state you really don't need to deal with what I had served up. The sight of her father-in-law on the floor started her contractions, so Mike had to try and calm Veronica while attempting to save my life.

Mike grabbed a couple of towels and tied them around my wrists to try and stop the immediate bleeding. I tried to kiss Mike goodbye, but fell back on the floor. I was passing out and coming to, occasionally trying to say how sorry I was. In my mind I could hear Mike singing. Mike lifted me up and got me to the bed, but I was still losing a lot of blood. He called a friend who was a doctor and he rushed straight round to see what could be done. He managed to stop the worst of the bleeding and then called for another doctor to come and stitch me up. My right wrist was not too bad, but I had cut through the vein in my left. The doctor told Mike that in another 20 minutes I would have been a goner.

Despite all the excitement, Veronica had managed to stop her contractions by doing some deep, slow breathing. It was not an easy time for her because I was not the best of patients and often made things very difficult for her.

A ray of light came into our lives on 22 January. Just before 6 am Veronica woke Mike to tell him the time had come. It was a Caesarean birth and Mike stayed in the room to watch. He felt sure that after dealing with all my blood he would be fine.

At 8.52 am Ingrid arrived. Mike was a father and I was a grandfather again. And son like father, just as had been the case when Mike was born, the father was not yet married to the mother. And just as when Mike was born, the media were lining up for a first photo of grandad and granddaughter. Mike sold the photos to the *News of the World*, which was very fitting as that had been his first UK cover story.

I was still not well enough either physically or mentally, so Mike launched a new 'Biggs Experience' where he had to entertain the visitors. He put videos on, told stories and did everything he could to keep the punters happy. At a suitable time I would then make my entry, shake a few hands and have my photo taken before retiring.

It was depressing, and not what Mike and I would want, but

we had no choice as we needed the money. Veronica gave us both a much-needed kick up the backside, pointing out that we were selling the T-shirts far too cheap. We had priced them at $10, but Veronica said that anyone who was coming to meet me would happily pay $20. She was right.

One of the other reasons I needed to raise money was to pay Rosa back. Rosa had scraped together all her life savings and given them to Mike to pay for the medical help and medication. I was very lucky with the people around me, but I knew I could not go on abusing or taking these friendships for granted.

In Rio it was now my turn to start to worry about Mike. Because of the strain I put him under he was drinking, putting on weight and even losing his hair. He admitted to his friends he was a psychological wreck. I knew I was putting him under unimaginable pressure, but I did not know that our debts had ballooned to over £30,000.

I did get another small payday in January 2001. I was contacted by Duloren, Brazil's biggest lingerie company, who wanted to use me as part of a promotion for a lingerie range. Would I object, they asked, to posing alongside a couple of underwear models and get paid? Even in my weakened mental state I could not see a downside to accepting the offer. That is how Milene Zaro and Francine Mello from the Elite Agency came to turn up on my doorstep and lap.

They stripped for action and then wrapped in a Union Jack I was flanked by the two truncheon-wielding lingerie models for the shoot. I was never sure what exactly was in the advertising agency's mind, but it was a clever play on the Portuguese word for lace (*renda*) and surrender (render-se), and so in their lacy finery the campaign slogan was '*Sr. Ronald Biggs, Renda-se.*'

Little did Duloren, the agency, or the models know, but the

pictures from that shoot were going to go all round the world, and are still a favourite with the media and editors to this day.

In search of financial salvation, Mike headed off to London in late February to see what might be available for us back in the UK. During the trip, Mike was introduced to Kevin Crace, an old friend of Bruce and Nick Reynolds. Nick thought Kevin might be able to help in a campaign to get me an 'amnesty' in the UK in case I needed it. It was Kevin who introduced Mike to people at *The Sun*. Not that *The Sun* had much interest in my amnesty, but they did like the idea of bringing me back to Blighty.

Kevin first made contact on 8 March with *The Sun*'s assistant news editor, Graham Dudman, who was to end up with the glamorous byline of 'Head of *The Sun*'s Biggs Team'.

'I've got a bloke here who wants to talk about Ronnie Biggs. Can you have a word with him?' the editor's secretary asked Dudman. On the basis that it was always worth listening, if just for a minute, Dudman told the secretary to put the caller on.

'Ronnie Biggs wants to come home – and he wants *The Sun* to help him,' Kevin told a not unsurprisingly suspicious Dudman. However Dudman had heard enough and set up a meeting with Kevin and Mike for the following week.

Just after 2 pm on Friday 16 March, Kevin took Mike and Nick Reynolds through the newsroom at *The Sun*'s Wapping headquarters to meet with Dudman. Crime editor Mike Sullivan, who was to be part of the meeting, looked up. 'Bloody hell,' he exclaimed, 'that is Michael Biggs!'

Negotiations started, and as always happens both parties were far apart on what we wanted and *The Sun* would offer. I'm not sure if I was the prostitute and *The Sun* was the john or the other way around. But we knew we were simply haggling over the price. Both parties were consenting adults and we weren't going to hurt anyone.

Back in 1993 I said that the thought that I might be returned to prison one day did not worry me. It still did not. 'It's a bridge I'll cross if and when I have to,' I wrote then. 'Pretty soon I'll be entering into the last scene of all and, if I'm to become a dribbling nuisance, one of Her Majesty's hostelries might be just the place to spend my twilight years.'

I had become that dribbling nuisance and felt that if I was to give Mike a chance with his life and new family I had to unburden him and take my chances. I had not gone soft though, and my decision was based on Mike being able to negotiate a suitable payday from *The Sun* that would set him up and clear our debts. What was clear was that with my failing health and lack of any health insurance or pension plan, I would only drag the family down more if I were to stay on in Rio to die. However quick that might be.

To be honest, I quietly liked the idea of one last great adventure, even if it did end up with them slamming the prison door behind me. But if I was going to return to Britain, it was going to be on my terms. I would go there because I chose to, not because anyone told me to go.

After a week of talks, *The Sun* camp came up with a plan and offer worth considering, which included being flown back in a private jet. It did mean, however, that we would have to announce to the world that I was coming back so that I could apply for a British passport on which to travel. For all my travelling it would be my first genuine British passport.

Once everything was agreed, and Kevin and my UK lawyer, Jane Wearing, were happy, we set the time of my return for mid-May. Time enough, I hoped, to get my things in order in Rio and say a proper goodbye to the people that mattered most.

Sod's law came to play shortly after when on 1 May *The Sun* got wind that its exclusive had been compromised and a freelance journalist was shopping the story around London that I was about to return. The proverbial was about to hit the fan, and we should be ready for all hell to break loose. The problem for Mike was that I was not at home, but having much needed speech and body therapy. Mike rushed to pick me up and by the time we got to the house, *The Sun* had a simple message, and that was that it was now or never if we wanted the deal.

The Sun's John Askill and photographer Harry Page rushed to Heathrow to catch the first flight to Rio. Mike Sullivan, not wanting to make the mistakes the *Express* had all those years earlier, went to Scotland Yard to brief the head of the Flying Squad, Detective Chief Superintendent John Coles, who was in overall charge of the Serious and Organised Crime group.

To confirm what Sullivan was telling Coles, *The Sun* asked me to drop a note to Scotland Yard. The note addressed to Coles said:

'I would like to give myself up to you.

What I need is passport documentation to travel back to Britain.

I am prepared to be arrested at the gate when I arrive at Heathrow Airport and submit myself to the due process of the law.'

Ronald Arthur Biggs, Rio de Janeiro, May 2nd 2001.'

Just as I had done with my letter to the *Express* back in 1974, I added my thumbprint for good measure. I thought Slipper would appreciate the gesture.

Dudman and Sullivan's first decision was that they would publish two spoof front pages on its early editions of Thursday 3 May, giving Askill and Page one day in Rio to pull stuff together, then break the 'world exclusive' of my return in the main edition that would circulate in London.

As *The Sun* came to realise that the international correspondents based in Brazil, as well as the Brazilian media, would be on the lookout for me, and knew where I lived, it was clear that I had to be moved from the apartment or I would end up a prisoner in my own home. There was only the one way in and out of the flat, and that was up the narrow stairs to the street.

The Sun first had the idea to take me to one of the main hotels and hide me away in a room. With Mike's help, I explained that I was actually quite well known in Rio and if I did enter a hotel they could kiss goodbye to any idea of keeping the location a secret.

Mike made a few calls, one to our American friend, Diamond Dayne Henry, who was something of the American 'Ronnie Biggs' having escaped the clutches of the US tax authorities. Dayne had a very big and secluded house at the end of Barra in a small-gated community that used to belong to one of the samba school bosses.

Everything moved very quickly and I had no real time to say goodbye to the house that had been mostly a very happy home to Mike and me for 17 years. There was no time for reflections or to feel sorry for myself. We had to move fast.

In a scene from a spy thriller we made our way across Rio, doubling back on ourselves and checking we had not been followed. We stopped to take a few photos with Corcovado and other Rio landmarks as a backdrop. When we got to Barra my American friend was pleased to see us, and from the open mouth of the *Sun* team I could see they were suitably impressed by the safe house.

As the news of my imminent return broke on 3 May, the world's media started to play 'Where's Ronnie?' Little did they know that I was sitting comfortably by a pool enjoying my last days of freedom and the Rio sun. Mike had put a message on the answerphone directing callers to contact Kevin in London. He got his first call at 4.15 am on that Thursday morning.

Behind the scenes, *The Sun* had been exploring options with the Foreign Office, the Home Office and Scotland Yard. Just because I said I wanted to come back did not mean they had to accept me. While *The Sun* fretted, I had no doubts that the authorities would like to see my head served up for them on a silver platter, even if the platter belonged to Rupert Murdoch.

With my departure date brought forward, *The Sun* had to get the passport. The British Consul in Rio was put on standby to issue one. But first, the then Foreign Secretary, Robin Cook, had to give his approval. Not wishing to take any chances with what was now a sizeable investment, editor David Yelland put in a personal call to Cook.

The splash on the cover of *The Sun* was 'Biggs on Way Back', which was accompanied by a rather glum photo of me signing the note to Scotland Yard. I was quoted as saying, 'I'll face whatever punishment the authorities give me. I hope they will show me mercy.'

It was in this issue of *The Sun* that my famous wish to walk into a pub in Margate to buy a pint of bitter came out, as well as my apparent craving for a curry. As *The Sun* had a monopoly on the news and access to me, the story and quotes were printed verbatim in most of the other papers. It did not seem to matter that I had not touched booze or solid food for months.

The Friday issue of *The Sun* milked the exclusive for all it was worth. The cover was me with my arms outstretched with the Christ statue behind and the headline of 'CheeRio'. A *Sun* poll had 57 per cent of its readers in favour of letting me go free, and

43 per cent saying I should rot behind bars. Sadly one of that latter group was the Home Secretary, Jack Straw.

Given I was not a very good interviewee, not being able to speak, and the journalists not having the patience or time to follow my spelling board, they decided it was easier to track down other people in my life to speak on my behalf.

Charmian, as always, was a class act, and when asked by *The Sun* if she knew of my plans her reply was a sharp, 'not exactly, no'. She was telling the truth.

I was also happy to give Jack Slipper another payday. He was pictured with a copy of *The Sun* and gave them a suitably appropriate quote. 'I never thought I'd live to see the day when Biggs would be brought to justice. But I bear him no grudges.' Jack even admitted that when he met me I came across as 'a likeable bloke'.

Timing was now everything as there was no way *The Sun* was going to hand the initiative, and its 'Biggs exclusive', to other papers, even its stablemate, the late *News of the World*. It meant my return had to be staged not to benefit the Sunday papers. I would have to fly out of Rio on Sunday afternoon, 6 May, in time to be the cover of the Monday paper, and landing on Monday would give the paper further exclusive coverage of my return in the Tuesday's and Wednesday's editions. I would be *The Sun*'s cover boy for an entire week, and not many people can say that.

The Sun's Saturday coverage was taken up with their 'Flying Squad' coming to Rio on the 14-seater Dassault Falcon 900EX. At the time it was rumoured to be Rupert Murdoch's own private plane, but I was later told it had been leased from TAG Aviation.

On board the flight were *The Sun*'s crime editor, Mike Sullivan, along with reporter Simon Hughes. Also on board in a gesture of solidarity to me were Bruce and Nick Reynolds, Bruce resplendent in the same blue discharge blazer he wore when he left Maidstone Prison in 1978.

'I'm going to get my mate and bring him back before he dies,' Bruce told Sullivan. 'I got him into it all those years ago when I persuaded him to join the gang and now I feel responsibility to be there for him now. Ronnie is a gambler and this is the final adventure for him. This is the final chapter in his life and it is the right way for it to end. We are locked together by our past and it's only right that I bring Ron home. It's what the Americans would call closure.'

The plane took to the sky at 3.07 pm that Friday, at the start of its 6,000-mile journey to Rio. It would stop to refuel at Ilha do Sal in the Cape Verde Islands. On the plane's arrival *The Sun* had to play another elaborate game of cat and mouse to avoid the attentions of the growing media pack that was building up in Rio. Bruce and Nick only had time for a quick wash and brush-up at the then Meridién Hotel (now Hilton) before being brought to the house for an emotional reunion. We all knew it was going to be a very emotional few days.

Also arriving that Saturday was Chris Pickard who had flown in from London. Chris had been tracked down by BBC Breakfast who were looking for a talking head for its Friday coverage of my return. The BBC just assumed that Chris was an acquaintance and never thought to ask him if he was going to Rio or when he had last spoken to me, or even if he knew where I was. Chris was bringing all the UK papers with him, the *Sun* team only having brought *The Sun*!

We went through the papers seeing who was pro and against my return. Not surprisingly, being a *Sun* exclusive, the *Mirror* had me, Murdoch and *The Sun* down as the devils incarnate. The editor at the time: a certain Piers Morgan. I am sure he is the first to admit that he would have loved the story if he had had the opportunity. As it was, the *Mirror* coverage was going to be sour grapes from start to finish.

Across the world the media were door-stepping Charmian and *The Sun*'s Jamie Pyatt got her to say a few words after he presented her with some photos of me in Rio. She thought I looked like a 'walking corpse'.

At the house, Bruce, Nick and Chris all kept asking me if I was sure I wanted to return to Britain? Did I fully appreciate the likely outcome? From the coverage they had seen in the UK, and the way the government was reacting, they had no doubts I would be locked up and the key thrown away. Clemency and forgiveness were not to be on my dance card.

Under my agreement with *The Sun* I had the right to have a letter published on my return, so with the help of Bruce, Nick, Mike and Chris we pulled something together. As my contract with *The Sun* was torn up while I was on the flight back, that letter never got to be published. At the time I did not think much about its non-publication, but it came back to haunt me as one of the reasons the Justice Department gave for not granting my parole was that I had never apologised or shown remorse, which the letter was full of.

Despite seeing the clock tick down on my time in Rio, I tried to stay as upbeat as possible, although a lot of tears were spilt that day, especially when I cradled Ingrid in my arms. I realised this might be the last time I would see my granddaughter whose innocence shone through.

I spent my last night in Rio alone, except for the good company of Woody and his family. The reason was that the neighbouring property had been hired for a wedding reception. Normally I might have joined the party, but it turned out the bride was the daughter of a senior Rio police chief and many of the guests would be law enforcement officers. Not that any of them were looking for me as I had done nothing wrong in Brazil, but it would certainly have blown the cover of the safe house and might have been an embarrassing distraction.

I woke up early on Sunday and enjoyed breakfast with Woody who was supervising the clearing up. Perhaps it was a case of the condemned man eating a hearty breakfast.

As the morning ticked by we started to regroup. One of the *Sun* team turned up with my emergency passport that I had to countersign. Bruce and Nick also arrived, and looked as if they had had a good night out in Rio.

Mike checked and double-checked that all my most precious personal possessions, including my photos, favourite CDs and medications, were packed and ready to go.

I posed for a few last photos for *The Sun*, including one with the paper's entire 'Biggs Team'. I like to think that most of them had started to realise that I was actually okay, and not the mythical figure, sometimes of hate, that had been painted in some sections of the media, including their own.

As per my contract I swapped my Die Toten Hosen 'Carnival in Rio' T-shirt for a bright red *Sun* T-shirt that I had to wear on the drive to the airport and while getting on to the plane. I was also wearing a baseball hat but my ever-generous host insisted that I wore his prized cowboy hat. Some of the media made a lot out of the choice of the cowboy hat, but there was nothing more to it than wearing a present given to me by a good friend.

Around 1 pm I could tell the *Sun* team was getting itchy feet. They were still far from convinced that I would ever get on the plane. Probably not helped by the fact that Mike, Nick and I had been winding them up whenever we could. Word arrived from the airport that the waiting press pack at Terminal 2 were growing in numbers and getting restless.

At 1.30 pm it was decided it was time to hit the road. I had one last bit of theatrics up my sleeve. As we were about to board the van I whispered something in Mike's ear. He turned to Sullivan and said, 'Dad's changed his mind. He's not going.' I'm sorry we did not have a camera to catch the look on the face of team *Sun*. I broke into a grin and gave them the thumbs up and nervous smiles filled their faces.

The ride across town to the airport was fairly uneventful. A bit of good-natured banter between team Biggs and the *Sun* guys, but no sign that anyone had spotted us or was following us.

The approach road to Rio's international airport is wide and open and required us to loop back on ourselves to get to the terminal building. But we would be able to see the terminal from a good distance. Sullivan explained that the British Consul would be there and the airport had a wheelchair waiting to push me through immigration. I should not say anything to the media, he explained. While they wanted to keep the photos exclusive, they were not overly concerned given that any photo would have to feature me in the *Sun* T-shirt.

As we got closer we could see the assembled press pack now numbered in the hundreds. From our viewpoint we could see they were behind a barrier, but not penned in. It was still not clear if they realised this was the van they were waiting for, but they sure as hell would when we pulled up.

As we swung up to the terminal I was certain this was not going to end well. We had not even come to a stop and the pack had broken out and was surrounding the minibus which, just as you've seen in the movies, was being rocked from side to side. I could see the tearful face of Rosa, who had come to the airport to see me off. Snappers desperately stuck their cameras to the window to try and get a shot off, and when the door of the van was opened some even tried to get in. I stayed put but my hat got knocked sideways, so if you see the photos it often looks as if I had been on the piss.

Airport security told the driver to drive on and come back around. They pulled people off and away from the van so I could make another escape.

Nobody was sure what to do or where to go but Mike pointed out that Chris knew the airport better than most. He took us to the old terminal building on the other side of the airport, where appropriately I had first stepped foot in Rio. There we could park under trees that would hide us from the helicopters that were circling overhead.

We had a number of options, none of which included going back to Terminal 2. The sensible one was to drive on to the airfield from the old terminal and cross the airfield to the new terminal buildings. However, certain parties wanted us to walk through the airport, as it made for a better story and better pictures.

The eventual solution was boringly simple. We would go back to the airport but at the last moment go on to Terminal 1. There was a good distance between the terminals and given the athletic prowess of most journalists I have met, if we moved quickly there was little chance they could all get across to intercept us.

We composed ourselves in the van and when the word came, we set off again. The helicopters spotted us as soon as we broke cover and the TV viewers in Rio could now follow our every movement as we headed back. A few quick goodbyes were said in the van to those staying behind. There would be no time for proper goodbyes or other pleasantries once the van pulled to a halt.

Security at Terminal 2 had not been tipped off that we were

going to Terminal 1, so when they saw the van approaching, they started trying to reorganise the press pack baying for blood.

Our driver did well. As we came up the approach road to the airport he started to slow, so it looked as if we were positioning ourselves to pull into the terminal. At the last moment he floored it and we sped on around to Terminal 1. Looking back we could see the penny had dropped and the press pack was running in every direction.

We pulled up to an almost empty terminal where there were only a few bemused tourists. A wheelchair was waiting and everything went to plan B. Bags were bundled on to the trolley and Mike quickly kissed Veronica and Ingrid goodbye and John Askill pushed me at double time through the airport. The authorities just wanted to get me airside, so they had more control of the situation.

Mike quickly caught up with me, as did a couple of quick-thinking snappers, including one from *O Globo*, the main Rio paper that had the manpower to send a photographer to cover both terminals. The other was a freelance photographer who simply took his chance and swapped terminals. Those photos went around the world as *The Sun* continued to sit on its exclusive. As I was being pushed through the airport, *The Sun* was already beaming photos back to London for Monday's paper.

The chosen photo was of me being pushed through the terminal by Askill and Simon Hughes, the cowboy hat still knocked to one side. The headline was simple and to the point. 'GOT HIM'. Inside were more photos of me taken at the house over the weekend, and photos boarding the plane. For good measure there was a screen grab taken from Sky News showing the moment we were airborne.

We might have outsmarted the press pack, but now *The Sun*

had to deal with the Brazilian authorities; the point at which Slipper had become unstuck.

I have said it before and I will say it again. I have the utmost respect and admiration for the Brazilian authorities and the way I was treated throughout my time in Brazil. I had my differences on occasions, but I was never treated as a number, always as a human being. Perhaps I was just a lucky gringo.

Once we were safely airside, the senior federal police officers took Mike and me aside and put us in a separate room from the *Sun* team. The officers painstakingly made certain I was getting on the plane and going to London by choice. They questioned if I was under any form of intimidation, if any family member or friend had been kidnapped, and if this was being used to get me to Britain. One word from me and the *Sun* team would have been sent packing empty-handed.

Once I had convinced the federal police that I was genuinely happy to get on the plane and fly to London, they shook me by the hand and wished me well. They even said they hoped to see me back in Rio in the future. I had been with them for 40 minutes.

We reassembled the team and were taken to the gate where a van was waiting to take us out to the plane. At the stairs to the plane I stopped for one last photo. Then we settled ourselves in to prepare for take-off. On board were Mike, Bruce and Nick, as well as Mike Sullivan, John Askill, Simon Hughes, Harry Page and Nigel Cairns from *The Sun*.

As a world television audience can attest from images beamed live, I took to the sky at 5.18 pm Rio time, 9.18 pm in London. *The Sun* had their man, but for Scotland Yard there were still 13 hours to wait and 6,000 miles to cover.

I do not deny that tears filled my eyes as I took one last look at Rio and Brazil, a city and country that had been so hospitable and

generous to me since I had landed at the same airport 31 years and
two months previously. I shed a few more tears as I thought about
the city that had been my home for so many years, and had brought
me so many more adventures than I could ever have dreamt of.

As the plane started to climb, I decided to enjoy my last hours
of freedom as much as I could, helped by Bruce and Nick, who
kept the atmosphere buoyant, as I knew it was much harder on
Mike to see the up side. Once the seat belt sign was off there was
time to relax as we were wined and dined. I posed for a toast with
Bruce, but didn't drink.

At 2.55 am on Monday morning, we landed on Ilha do Sal on
the Cape Verde Islands to refuel. We had been flying for nearly six
hours. Everyone on board was keen to stretch their legs with the
Sun team making their way to the terminal building, leaving me
alone with Nick. There was an empty Land Rover parked nearby
and Nick joked about us driving off into the night. Disappearing
from justice one final time. But a joke was all it was.

While on the ground, Sullivan spoke with his office in London.
What he was hearing was that the other newspapers were putting
pressure on the government to investigate what the deal was that
The Sun had. They were going to have to explain themselves to
the Press Complaints Commission. *The Sun* had already changed
its posture over the week. Originally it was all about 'Ronnie asks
Sun to fly him home' but it was now how the paper was flying me
home to justice.

An hour after landing on Ilha do Sal, we were airborne on
the final stretch to London. Next stop, RAF Northolt, a secure
RAF base in Hillingdon, in north-west London. The main *Sun*
editorial on the day of my return would see *The Sun* cosying up to
the authorities, and everyone from the Metropolitan police to the
RAF were thanked.

Given the stress and strains of the previous week and the day ahead, I decided to catch a bit of shut-eye at the back of the plane while the others partied on.

In the morning I returned to my seat so I could watch Britain come into view across the English Channel, the same Channel I had escaped across 35 years earlier. I could recognise below England's green and pleasant land. My 13,087 days on the run were about to come to an end.

At RAF Northolt, last-minute preparations were under way for my arrival. Security was tight and only Kevin Crace and the legal team had been allowed in. Jane Wearing of Leftley Mallett Solicitors and my barrister, Guy Kearl, of St Paul's Chambers, would be allowed on the plane first to explain the legal procedures to Mike and me.

I later learnt that there were some heated discussions as to exactly who would be the person to board the plane to arrest me. In the end, Detective Chief Superintendent John Coles outranked the lot and got the job. The media worked out he would have been nine years old when I took flight.

We landed at 8.47 am. The images beamed around the world as the plane touched down and taxied to a secure area. What the images did not show were the sharpshooters on standby. They were part of a team of 90 police officers and 20 RAF police with dogs that had sealed off the base. The legal team were told that if I did not leave the plane when instructed, then the plane would be stormed.

Having sorted ourselves out, and made myself as presentable as possible, Jane and Guy came on to the plane. Mike explained about my medication and how I needed my food to be cut up if I was to swallow it. Mike sat next to me as he could understand best what I was trying to say or write.

At precisely 9.05 am, 18 minutes after we landed, and what must have felt like an eternity for Scotland Yard, Coles was allowed to enter the cramped cabin with Detective Terry Wilson in tow. This was their historic moment, but it was also mine. I extended the hand of friendship to greet the boss of the Flying Squad.

At first he ignored me. Pleasantries were clearly not in his script which was in a blue folder that he was nervously clutching.

'Are you Ronald Arthur Biggs?' he demanded. I nodded in reply. 'Were you born on 8 August 1929?'

I managed a barely audible: 'Yes.'

Coles then showed me his warrant card and announced: 'I am Detective Chief Superintendent John Coles from New Scotland Yard.'

It was clear everything was going to be done by the book so that my legal team would have no comeback later on for anything they might have overlooked. Perhaps they had learnt a lesson from Barbados.

I extended my hand again and managed to croak out, 'Pleased to meet you.' Mike translated.

It took a while, but to give Coles his credit he firmly grasped my hand and looked me in the eyes.

'Pleased to meet you,' he replied. 'How do you do. I have here in my possession a warrant granted at Bow Street Magistrates Court on 27 July 1990 for your arrest for being unlawfully at large from Her Majesty's Prison Wandsworth,' he continued in the arcane language of a bygone time. 'The warrant issued at Bow Street Magistrates Court addressed to each and all the constables in the Metropolitan Police, accuses Ronald Arthur Biggs, address no fixed abode, of he being a prisoner of Her Majesty's Prison Wandsworth, serving sentences of 25 and 30 years' imprisonment concurrent passed upon him at the assizes of the county of Buckingham on 16 April 1964 upon conviction of (a) conspiracy to stop mail with the intent to rob the said mail and (b) robbery with aggravation, and having escaped from the said prison in which he is required to be detained after being convicted of the said offences pursuant to section 72 of the Criminal Justice Act 1967.'

Then just as you have seen a million times in the movies I received my caution from Coles. 'You do not have to say anything but it may harm your defence if you do not mention when questioned something which you later rely on in court. Anything you do say may be given in evidence. Do you understand that?'

I nodded and at the same time was advised not to say anything else. I was back in England and well and truly nicked! The running had stopped. I was home, but not exactly free.

CHAPTER 19

JUSTICE FOR SOME: MORE PORRIDGE

As I sat on the jet that had brought me back to Britain, Detective Chief Superintendent John Coles explained that I was to be taken from RAF Northolt to a local police station, and then on to the magistrates' court.

Mike was allowed to help me off the plane, as was *The Sun*'s Mike Sullivan. I squinted in the sunlight and did a quick double-take on the number of police vehicles surrounding the aircraft. Thirteen in total. Somebody clearly did not get the memo that I was a sick and elderly man who had chosen to come back to the UK under what little steam I had left.

I was put in a police van with blacked-out windows and under heavy police escort driven to Chiswick police station. At the station they gave me a perfunctory medical and allowed me to catch my breath. Jane and Guy arrived, along with Guy's boss, Nigel Sangster QC.

As one newspaper put it, they were a legal team that any self-respecting villain would kill for. There was also the publicist, Judy Totton, whom Kevin had brought in to look after the media. With no voice of my own, I would need to borrow one.

Jane explained that Kevin was taking Mike to a hotel that had been organised by *The Sun*. They were expecting John Pickston and Gio to turn up soon from Rio. Raimunda, Mike's mother, was also on her way over from Switzerland to offer our son some morale support.

In a nice twist, *The Sun* did not want Mike to check into the hotel under his own name, so he chose one of my old aliases and was registered as Terence King.

Before midday we were on the move again. This time to the West London Courthouse in Hammersmith. As I was leaving Chiswick police station, some photographer and a TV crew managed to snap a couple of photos and footage of me in my blue sweater, yellow shirt, beige trousers and walking with a stick. They were the images the media would turn to again and again for the next nine years and whenever they ran a story of my return.

I arrived at the Hammersmith courthouse at 11.55 am in a white police van and an escort of two police cars and an unmarked Flying Squad Vauxhall. I shuffled into a packed Court No. 4 where there were a lot of people who wanted a first glimpse of the 'notorious Ronnie Biggs'. I was starting to realise that stories of my fame in Britain had not been overstated.

The clerk of the court stood and addressed me: 'Mr Biggs, I'm going to ask you to identify yourself. Is your full name Ronald Arthur Biggs?'

I got to my feet and grunted in the affirmative as best I could. I was then asked to confirm my date of birth, which I did with another grunt and a thumbs up.

'And were you the person sentenced at Buckingham Assizes on

16 April 1964 to 25 years' imprisonment for conspiracy to stop mail and to 30 years for robbery with aggravation?'

If I hadn't been so tired I might have signalled no, instead I simply grunted in the affirmative.

My day in court that the authorities had craved for 13,087 days had lasted exactly eight minutes. I was then taken across London to my new home at Belmarsh.

Built in 1991, on the site of the former Royal Arsenal in Woolwich, HMP Belmarsh was home to about 900 prisoners and considered to be one of Europe's most modern and secure. As a Category A prison, the inmates are those whose escape would be considered 'highly dangerous to the public or national security'. If I hadn't been so fuckin' tired, I would have felt flattered.

Slipper told the press that he was astonished that I was being sent to Belmarsh. 'I saw him get off the plane at Northolt and unless he's a John Gielgud, he looked as if he was finished. I hope they will give him the chance to be with his son for the last few months of his life. You know, I had a certain amount of respect for Biggs because he brought up Mike by himself. I had time to sit down with him, have a few beers with him. He was quite a likeable chap, a man's man, didn't talk about shopping or anything like that.'

On arrival at Belmarsh I was subjected like any other prisoner to a strip search for illegal substances. I was fingerprinted and filmed. My prison number was just the same as when I went over the wall at Wandsworth. I was again a number – 002731.

I swapped my clothes for a prison tracksuit and was taken to the prison's three-storey medical unit where I was allocated one of the unit's 38 beds. I would be under observation as they tried to assess my true physical and mental state.

I was keen to find out how much time I might have to serve.

It would be upsetting not to see Mike, but I expected that once the initial dust had settled and we knew how long I would have to serve, he could head back to Rio to his wife and child and try and pick up the pieces of his life. This was, after all, one of the main reasons I had come back to Britain.

That Tuesday, *The Sun* led with a photo of me stepping off the plane. The attention-grabbing headline was 'THE END: Moment justice caught up with Ronnie Biggs thanks to The Sun'. The paper now had a strip across all its spreads that read 'The Sun Puts Biggs Back in Jail'.

Considering the prisons I had experienced over the years, Belmarsh wasn't that bad, but I knew it would still be a shock for Mike. He got the okay to visit me on the Tuesday before his press conference. *The Sun* organised for a car to take him across from Tower Bridge to Belmarsh; a trip he was to make many, many times, although not always in the luxury of a chauffeur-driven car.

Mike was brought in through multiple doors and security checks to a cell in the medical centre. He found me being poked and prodded by a doctor and a couple of nurses. The doctor was glad to see Mike as he was having a problem understanding the medication and dosages that were all in Portuguese. It helped distract Mike and I wanted him to stay strong in front of the screws. I had yet to establish myself in the nick, and did not want them to see Mike or our relationship as a weakness they could target.

When the doctor left we were given some time to sit at the table and chat. Three screws remained to watch and I could see this was upsetting Mike. It was the first time I had seen Mike in a suit, which he had bought for the press conference, so to break the ice I scribbled on my pad. 'You look like a doctor from the clap clinic!' We both laughed. It was good to have tears of laughter again. I then jotted down for Mike: 'Don't break down in front of the slags. Don't give them the satisfaction.'

All too soon it was time for Mike to leave and it was explained that as I was a Category A prisoner he would only be allowed to visit me once every 15 days in Belmarsh. I tried to reassure Mike not to worry. I could not see any reason why I would be kept for long either as a Category A prisoner or within Belmarsh, which I assumed – wrongly – they would use as a staging post until I was allocated to another lower grade prison. As it turned out, Belmarsh was to be my home for the next six years and two months.

Mike returned to the hotel to hold the press conference. He admitted to being more nervous facing the British press than performing in front of 200,000 people in the Maracanã. He had also been told how much the legal fees would be to put up any sort of case for an early release. It was many times more than he had been expecting.

To make things simpler for Mike, the legal team and Judy had helped prepare a statement that he could read. He tried, but after just a few words he started shaking and broke down. Judy took over.

Mike's statement explained that I had voluntarily returned to Britain, contrary to his wishes, to end my days in England, 'a country that he (Ron) still thinks of as home'.

Mike's first major interview on my return was done with the *Sunday Times*, the sister paper of *The Sun* and also owned by Mr Murdoch. I'm not sure what he would have thought of his journalist, Margarette Driscoll, saying of my return: 'It was all in the worst possible taste, with Biggs, frail and disabled by two strokes, in a straw hat and *Sun* T-shirt.' Margarette was surprised that Mike, who told her he was a 'psychological wreck' due to lack of sleep, was 'thoughtful' and 'articulate'. At least her piece was generally sympathetic.

I now had to adapt to life in Belmarsh as Mike adapted to life in London. Don't expect many exciting stories and tales from my time behind bars as they are few and far between. In truth, the way I got through my time was to cocoon myself in sleep and sleep through as much of the day and night as possible, watching TV, when possible, or listening to my CDs. The general tedium was broken by the friends and strangers who dropped by to visit.

After the strain and uncertainty of my return, I did feel I was starting to feel stronger in the first few weeks at Belmarsh. The doctors told me my heart and lungs were in good nick. I was even starting to put on weight and was able to give up the wheelchair and take short stumbling walks.

The recuperation did not last long. On 2 June I collapsed after complaining of severe head pains. I was rushed from Belmarsh to Queen Elizabeth Hospital in Woolwich, where I was diagnosed as having had another stroke.

Not being able to reach Mike, the governor of Belmarsh managed to get hold of Kevin Crace. He was not allowed to tell Kevin what the problem was, but told him it was urgent that Mike contacted the prison.

Tracked down, Mike got through to the duty governor who told him what had happened and where I was. It cost Mike £100 to find a taxi to take him 'south of the river'. When he got to the hospital, the press were already camped outside and Kevin was waiting for him.

Mike found me with a drip attached to one hand while my other hand was cuffed to a prison officer. There were a total of six prison guards and four police officers in the small room.

Mike could sense that even the hardened prison officers were uncomfortable with the scene.

Thankfully in a hospital the doctors tend to outrank all others. It was the doctors that decided that as I was drifting in and out of consciousness I would need a CAT scan and possibly an operation.

The hospital staff and Mike had to negotiate with the guards, as the CAT scan was not going to work if I was still chained to a screw. The doctors had no problem with a guard being in the room, but not with all his bells and whistles attached. Finally they relented and the scan went ahead which confirmed I had had a stroke, although not as bad as feared.

Waiting for the results, Mike took it upon himself to go and brief the waiting press and tell them that I was being guarded by ten men and chained to the bed.

By chance, a live feed was going out on one of the news channels and surprise, surprise, in a matter of minutes a call went through to the hospital telling the guards to remove the handcuffs.

I was in hospital for a week, but was guarded around the clock by four guards. During my time in hospital, I had surgery to install a feeding tube. The doctors feared my throat muscles were now so weak that food would enter my lungs instead of my stomach.

As I was recuperating, Mike was called in by the Home Office to discuss his visa situation. At the time he thought little of it, and now had the support of Veronica who had arrived in London with little Ingrid.

At his first interview the immigration officer said there could be problems as the paperwork from Mike's arrival at RAF Northolt was wrong. Hardly Mike's problem, you would think, given the manner of my arrival.

The authorities grilled Mike and told him that it was clear to them that his wife and child were coming to settle illegally in the

UK. Whatever argument Mike put up, they swept it under the carpet. They declined his application for a visa and his only way to stay in the country was to appeal the decision and keep appealing.

In case you are confused as to why my son did not have the right to be in the UK, you would not be alone. While nobody was questioning I was British, or that my children had the right to a British passport and to live in Britain, the problem was that I had never legally married Raimunda and therefore at the time, Mike was not considered by the law to be my son and had no rights to live in Britain.

My visits to the hospital caused a bit of tension between Mike and the governor of Belmarsh. Mike would often only learn I had been taken to hospital from the media, normally TV or radio, but the governor swore to Mike that each time they did try to contact him first and if not would leave a message. What neither Mike nor the governor were to know was that somebody was intercepting the messages and wiping them from Mike's phone. Sound familiar?

*

One illustrious guest to arrive in Belmarsh was Jeffrey Archer. Following his conviction for perjury and perverting the course of justice, Archer arrived on 19 July 2001 and was gone by 9 August. He even managed to turn his 22 days and 14 hours in Belmarsh into a best-selling book, *A Prison Diary Volume 1: Belmarsh: Hell.* Little fuss was made of Archer benefitting from his prison time.

I imagine I was one of the few people in Belmarsh that his Lordship might have heard of, or recognised on sight. Because there were concerns as to how Archer might take to Belmarsh, or the inmates might take to him, they put him in the hospital wing and on suicide watch. When he saw me he came over to shake my hand. At first I pretended not to recognise him, but then I wrote down: 'Nice to meet you, Lord Archer.'

'Please don't call me Lord,' he replied. 'Call me Jeffrey.'

Jeffrey became my neighbour in the cell next door until somebody tried to torch it and he had to be moved.

I would love to say that it was Archer's friends in high places that helped him to move along so swiftly from Belmarsh, but I can't. For the sort of threat that Archer represented to society, the time he spent in Belmarsh was par for the course. You have to ask yourself then, why the authorities thought six years in Belmarsh was the correct decision for a man in my condition? The stock answer was always that Belmarsh provided the best prison medical facilities in the land. If that is the case, then God help the other sick inmates in the prison system.

One footnote to Archer's time in Belmarsh. At the end of July 2001, when I was still recovering from my stroke, Mike received a call from the *Daily Mail*. The *Mail* and its readers are traditionally not the most sympathetic or supportive of my plight for the way I put two fingers up to 'their' beloved establishment. The reporter told Mike he had something of interest to show him and needed to meet. What he had to show Mike was a picture of me in my bed in Belmarsh.

I looked terrible in the picture. My head was back and propped up against some towels. Also visible were the tubes that fed me and kept me alive. It all looked very tired and squalid. The reporter did not want to tell Mike how they got the photo, but because of privacy laws they felt they needed Mike's permission to publish it. Looking at the picture, Mike decided that making the photo public could only help with the argument that I should not still be in Belmarsh.

Given where my cell was located in the hospital wing, and the security that surrounded it, I can tell you that a visitor or another prison inmate could not have taken the photo. It had to have been taken by a guard or another member of the prison staff. My theory, given where and when it was taken, is that it was to be the big money shot of Archer in Belmarsh. I don't know if the photographer panicked or lost his nerve, or simply never got the chance to get a shot of my then neighbour, but what the *Mail* got for its money was Biggs in bed and not Archer in chokey.

The photo was published on 28 July 2001, about a week before my legal team formally submitted appeal papers to the Criminal Cases Review Committee. My QC, Nigel Sangster, was arguing that my original sentence was 'excessive'. He was also looking at a direct plea for clemency to the new Home Secretary, David Blunkett.

I had noticed since my return to prison that the set-up was not that different from when I was inside in the 1960s. Even in a maximum security prison like Belmarsh, if you wanted something brought in, it could be organised. And it is the staff and screws that bring the contraband in, not the visitors. In a place like Belmarsh the visitors are far too well screened.

Visiting Belmarsh was never easy for my friends, especially as I was classified as Category A. If you wanted to visit I had to have a Visiting Order – VO – sent to you in the post, and there was a strict limit of two VOs per month, although three adults could be on each one. You then had to call Belmarsh and book the visit 48 hours in advance. Visiting times were 2.15 to 4 pm.

Coming to visit you had to turn up early to check in at the visitors' centre, and as everyone wanted to maximise the visiting time, most visitors turned up at the same time resulting in lengthy queues. You would then get in line, show some form of picture ID plus proof of address. Fingerprints would be scanned, photos taken and ID cards issued. You then had to put everything you were carrying away in the lockers. The only items you could bring in were the VO, the locker key and £10 in cash to buy something at the coffee bar. If you had brought anything for me, that had to be handed over at the visitors' centre and it would eventually, if suitable, make its way through to me.

You would then cross from the visitors' centre to the main prison and go through a series of security checks for your identity. Men had their hand stamped with a symbol that showed up under an ultraviolet light. Sniffer dogs would check for drugs, and then you would go through more airport-type scanners.

Anyone expecting visitors were rounded up and put in the visiting hall in set locations. Mine was normally 'A1'. We would wear our normal clothes, but had to wear a fluorescent strap, like cyclists wear to be seen at night. We were not to move from our set locations. Visitors could go to the coffee bar, and there was an area with toys for the kids to play.

The visiting hall at Belmarsh was not what you may imagine from the movies. There were no glass partitions, no phones, just tables and chairs, although all firmly nailed down so nobody could start chucking them about.

Most of the inmates of Belmarsh were not thieves, rather a colourful mixture of murderers, terrorists and general undesirables. If visitors realised whom they were sharing the visiting hall with they would probably be surprised and even alarmed. I was aware that I was often pointed out, and some visitors would break the rules and come across to shake my hand and say a few kind words.

Some of my visitors attracted attention. Record producer Gus Dudgeon looked suitably rock 'n' roll when he came to visit, his big buckled belt setting off all sorts of alarms. Setting off alarms for a very different reason was a visit from Uri Geller whom I had met in Brazil. Mike got a right bollocking from the prison authorities for that, and was told he must warn them in advance of other high-profile visitors.

Uri had visited me in Rio in 1995, just after I had broken my leg. We had talked about doing a trick together that was to involve the disappearance of a train. I think in Belmarsh the screws were more worried he was going to pull off the trick with a disappearing high-profile prisoner.

A prisoner I would have been happy to see disappear was the Soham killer, Ian Huntley. I was not happy when Huntley was moved to a cell close to mine and told the screws as much. They said they were concerned for Huntley's safety and it had been decided the hospital wing was the safest place to keep him. I was ignored.

Early in his stay, Huntley approached me as I sat in my wheelchair. With nothing much else to hand, I threw my box of tissues at him, and he got the gist of my message and feelings to stay away.

There was the occasional happy day in Belmarsh, and one of the happiest was my marriage to Raimunda in 2002. She had come to my rescue once, and now she was to come to the rescue of our son.

Immigration officials were still harassing Mike, refusing his requests to stay indefinitely in the UK. Even Veronica found herself stopped at Heathrow while coming back into Britain from Brazil with baby Ingrid in her arms. She was given a red stamp in her passport to say she was *persona non grata*!

It was during this time that the legal team decided to check a hypothetical case with the Home Office of what would happen to a child's status if the mother and father do legally wed. The answer was that the child's status would be the same as any child of a couple married at the time of the birth.

Raimunda offered to come from Geneva and become my legal wife in the eyes of the British authorities, but first I had to show I was no longer married to Charmian. Mike searched high and low through my papers for the right documents. But none were to be found. The lawyers contacted Australia House, but the authorities were not inclined to help, and so in January 2002 Mike got on the phone to ask Charmian for her help. As much as it must have hurt, Charmian came up with the goods and sent over the necessary documents, even knowing that the wedding would put her and the family back in the spotlight and open old wounds.

I married Raimunda Rothen inside Belmarsh on 10 July 2002 and even got to wear a suit again. The nearest I got to consummating our marriage was a quick pinch of her bum as she stood next to me. Our courtship had lasted almost exactly 31 years from when we first met in Rio to getting her to the altar.

Sadly I was not allowed to attend my own wedding reception, but I'm told a lively time was had even without me. It was held at The Punchbowl, a pub in Mayfair, which was then owned by Freddie Foreman's son, George, who later sold it to Guy Ritchie. Two weeks after the wedding, Mike was granted his British citizenship. Once Mike got around to making an honest woman out of Veronica, so were she and Ingrid. Even Raimunda can have a British passport if she wants one, and I think she could even have a British pension. It goes to show how some of the people when trying to fuck me, just manage to shaft themselves and the country.

At this stage I should apologise to the website Death List and its followers. I had been high up on its list as one of the next to pop his clogs since I came back to Britain. I first featured in the top 50 in 2000 in a very modest 40th. By 2002 I was at number one and was solidly in the top 10 ever since and back to number one in 2009, but slipped behind the Lockerbie bomber in 2010, to be back on top again for 2011. Their only consolation was that one year they would get it right, and they did!

I tried to keep my sense of humour while I was in Belmarsh, and sometimes it would get me into trouble. One day I found that at lock-up somebody had forgotten to lock the door to my cell, so I found a Post-it note and put it on the outside of the door. It said: 'Cheers – Rio here I come!' I then went and hid in the toilet block and waited for a reaction. When I heard all the alarms go off I realised I might have overstepped the mark. Honestly, where did they think I was going and how?

Saying that, when I first arrived at Belmarsh I received an offer to get me out. There were certain people who thought it would be the ultimate two fingers to the establishment if 'Ronnie Biggs' was to disappear from Britain's most secure prison within weeks of getting there. In the end I had to get the word out that I had not come all the way back to start running again.

I can't remember the exact date when Giovanni di Stefano came into my life. It must have been in the early part of 2005, although Giovanni says he met me in Rio back in the 1970s. In 2005, any funds that Mike might have had, had all but dried up. There was no way he could afford to go on paying for a top legal team.

Mr Di Stefano, a colourful character to say the very least, rarely, if ever, took no for an answer. He also did not want any payment. A strong point for any lawyer.

Labelled the Devil's advocate, Di Stefano is an Italian who was raised in the UK but who operated out of Rome as the head of Studio Legale Internazionale. I cannot tell you what makes Giovanni tick, but some people put it down to being motivated by a sense of injustice after he had been unfairly convicted of fraud back in the 1980s. Since that time he has fought tooth and nail for the underdogs, for the undesirables, or as he himself has put it, he will 'defend the indefensible'.

In 2011, Giovanni found himself having to defend his own name and reputation after being arrested on a European arrest warrant issued by Britain. It accused him of 'fraud, theft and money laundering', the argument being that he had received money for representing people in the UK when he was not licensed to practise law. On trial in Britain in 2013, he ended up sentenced to 14 years' imprisonment after being found guilty or pleading guilty to 27 charges.

How many of his clients actually paid, I have no way of telling, but his client list makes interesting reading. It goes from Gary Glitter to Saddam Hussein, Jonathan King to the Butcher of the Balkans, from Charles Bronson to Ian Brady. He tried to buy Norwich City and Dundee football clubs, and found time to launch a political party and to record a couple of albums. He was bigger than life and enjoyed a scrap with the authorities, often embarrassing them in the process.

In 2005, Giovanni petitioned then Home Secretary, Charles Clarke, who had replaced Blunkett, to release me on compassionate grounds. It took until October to get an answer, and have it turned down, but Giovanni kept niggling away.

In early 2007, constitutional changes were made which slightly moved the legal goalposts. The post of Secretary of Justice was created and Tony Blair's mate Lord Falconer, then Lord Chancellor, was given the role. A role that gave greater power to the Ministry of Justice.

Falconer did not last long as on 27 June, Gordon Brown became prime minister. In his first cabinet he appointed Jacqui Smith to take over as Home Secretary and Jack Straw to fill the new role of Secretary of Justice as well as holding the post of Lord High Chancellor.

A week after Jacqui Smith took over I was on the move. Without warning, and without informing Mike, I was shipped bag and baggage out of Belmarsh and moved to the 'nursing home' wing of HMP Norwich, which had been specially kitted out to look after elderly patients serving life terms. The date was 4 July 2007. My 'Independence Day' from Belmarsh after six long years.

The media was told that I had been switched to the Category C prison on compassionate grounds. Mike said it was a victory for common sense.

Norwich, which I had last called home back in 1959, was a big improvement on Belmarsh, even if it did mean a longer round trip for Mike and friends to visit.

The brand new wing offered 24-hour nursing care for just 15 elderly lifers. My unit had been designed, decorated and installed with facilities with the elderly in mind. The living room was furnished with matching upholstered chairs and round tables, so that if one of us were to fall, we would not be injured by a sharp edge. The walls were painted magnolia and extra-wide doors and corridors allowed wheelchair access to the rooms and cells when needed.

The barred windows even had blinds, and my personal joy, a small garden area, had been provided to allow us a place to sit outside, weather permitting. I even had an electric bed that could be lowered to make it easier to get in and out of.

The prison regime was in theory tailored to meet the needs of the elderly and frail. What you have to take into account, and no offence is meant to the fine people that looked after me while in Norwich, but if you are at the top of your game as a doctor or nurse, why would you choose to work in the prison system?

The care, as it turned out, was not what it was cracked up to be in the brochure and I now started to wonder if I was being used as a poster boy for the 'new' Norwich Prison.

But the prison and atmosphere was more relaxed and pleasant than at Belmarsh and I was both pleased and proud to see that the prison roof that I had helped to build back in 1958 was still there and still weatherproof.

With most of the legal avenues now blocked or tried, Mike and I were reduced to making the occasional appeal for my release from Norwich on compassionate grounds. But there was simply no sign of life or compassion coming from the government.

CHAPTER 20

CLUTCHING AT STRAWS: SICKNESS AND WEALTH

The clock ticked ever more slowly in Norwich. The days dragged. Sleep my only release. In my dreams I was free and I could talk.

Di Stefano now focused his attention on making sure I got the best possible shot at parole, if and when I was eligible. He opened discussions with the Justice Department. He wanted to make sure that we were all working from the same numbers. His argument was that when the authorities calculated time served, it should not only include the time I spent in Wandsworth, but also the time I was held in prison in Brazil and Barbados at the request of the British government. As a certain supermarket likes to say, every little helps.

As the Justice Department should have learnt, you argue with Giovanni at your peril. It was amazing how his threat to go to the European Courts or some other body would get the Justice Department and stuffed suits of Westminster to rethink and refocus. What had been a definite 'no' suddenly became a 'maybe'.

At first it was the governor of Norwich, James Shanley, who vetoed my request, and this despite the clearance from his prison doctors, who said I was 'physically incapable of committing further crimes'. Even the probation services were making the right noises and were satisfied with Mike's plan to put me in a private nursing home in Barnet, close to his house.

With the governor blocking my release, Giovanni turned his attention to Jack Straw.

'It is not the role of the Prison Service to provide nursing care,' he wrote to Straw, 'but a role for the National Health Service or, as it is conceded that Mr Biggs is clearly of no risk to anyone including himself, he should be released on compassionate grounds.'

Speculation began to mount in the press as to when I might be eligible for parole, and 2010 was talked about as the worst-case scenario, but Giovanni was pushing for 2009, even Christmas 2008, and kept the issue bubbling in the papers and along the corridors of power.

By April 2008, Giovanni had shown the Ministry of Justice that I had been in custody for a total of 3,385 days. By any calculation I should be eligible for parole after 3,652 days in custody, one third of my 30-year or 10,957-day sentence. It was Giovanni's submission that I should be eligible for release on 25 December 2008.

It was not going to be a Christmas Day release, but Valentine's Day, 14 February 2009, seemed equally appropriate.

At the start of 2009 my health took another turn for the worse. In February, when I had hoped to be released, I made my first visit to Norfolk & Norwich University Hospital where I spent three days being treated for pneumonia, something that became increasingly difficult to shake off. Mike was blocked from seeing me in the hospital, the governor telling him he should wait until my return to prison.

The media again speculated as to why I was still locked up. There was a wall of silence from the Ministry of Justice, but behind the scenes a lot was going on that not even I was aware of. In February 2009, various bodies and agencies met to discuss the case and tried to tick the appropriate boxes.

In March, Giovanni filed the official request to the Parole Board for my release under the Discretionary Release Scheme. The paperwork ran into hundreds of pages of documents and forms.

As nobody at the prison or Parole Board had the time or the patience to sit with me to go through everything point by point, it was left to Giovanni to help fill in the details on the interminable forms, most of which had not been designed for a crime such as the Great Train Robbery. Sweeping generalisations were taken, so it was put down that I was carrying an offensive weapon at the robbery, an iron bar. I did not, but I was told these were minor bureaucratic details and not to worry.

The meeting of 23 April turned out to be a major anti-climax. Without an agreement between Barnet and Norwich Primary Care Trusts, nothing could move forward. The only positive factor was that for the first time I had in writing that it was agreed that my Parole Eligibility date would be early July. Even the press reported that I had been judged as being 'suitable for parole'.

On 15 June, the Parole Board came up with its report. Its version of the events surrounding the Great Train Robbery was an interesting read to anyone who knew the facts. It had me saying that what happened to Jack Mills was a 'light tap', not language I used or would use. There were a number of major errors, but I was told to ignore them, as the bottom line was that the Parole Board had recommended my release. It was, I was told, a bit like quibbling over the small print in an insurance policy. The stuff nobody ever reads.

The Parole Board sent its recommendation through to the Ministry of Justice that I should be released. It was nearly time to celebrate and 3 July was now being talked about as the date for my release, almost two years to the day that I had been moved from Belmarsh to Norwich, and eight years and two months since I had landed back in Britain.

Having learnt never to count my chickens, I remained calm on the exterior and told Mike I would only believe I was free on the day it actually happened. We were still waiting for Jack Straw to sign off on the Parole Board's decision, but Giovanni assured me it was a formality.

On 28 June, a week before my release, I had a stupid fall that resulted in me being rushed to Norfolk & Norwich 'University Hospital' with a suspected broken hip and, for good measure, a serious chest infection.

It was clear I was unlikely to be fit to go anywhere by 3 July. I would gain my freedom lying in a hospital bed. I could take that.

Wednesday 1 July 2009 is a day I would never forget.

Giovanni received a devastating fax from Jack Straw. In a covering note of just two paragraphs, Straw told Giovanni: 'I have considered very carefully the recommendation of the Parole Board Panel that Ronald Biggs, currently detained in HMP Norwich, be released early, when he becomes eligible for early release on 3 July. For the reasons given in the attached statement, I have declined the Panel's recommendation and so refuse Mr Biggs parole.'

It was a hammer blow, and nobody knew how to tell me, or Mike. There seemed no logical reason for Straw's decision and even the Parole Board were surprised, as never before had its recommendations been ignored. And why wait until just two days before my expected release date? Even my bed was made up in the care home. We were that close.

Straw's main beef was that I remained 'wholly unrepentant' for my crime or my life on the run. This was all based on the Parole Board report, rather than anything that had gone on before in my life or might have appeared in the press. Even comments on film or in my autobiography that I had made were ignored. The fact that the Parole Board had never asked me directly if I was repentant was considered not relevant. According to Straw's office I should have second-guessed them.

I was being told to reapply for parole in a year or two's time. Mr Straw had effectively passed a death sentence and the state of my health immediately caused concern at the hospital who called Mike and said he should get there immediately. They had concerns if I would make it through the night.

Even in my weakened state I was stunned. Mike, who called Straw's decision 'vindictive', was also in shock. The media, which were preparing themselves for my release, were left speechless and – trust me – that doesn't happen often.

Giovanni may have been stunned, but he was outraged and demanded an immediate judicial review, pointing out to the Justice Secretary the factual errors in the judgement, and that he appeared to have made that judgement based on 'speculation, gossip and opinions', rather than facts.

Mentally I was spent. I had no interest in staying alive and spending another year in Norwich, and my body started to shut down. It had been a good run, but it was over.

Photos reached Giovanni that showed the state I was in and these went out to the press to show what a 'dangerous man' I clearly was.

Giovanni also discovered that it was not actually clear in law if the new position of Secretary of State for Justice had the power to block the Parole Board's recommendations. The issue was even raised in the House of Commons, but the concerns were dismissed by the argument that the government could treat me under old laws relevant to the time of my crime.

After a few terse letters between Giovanni and Straw's office, it was suggested by the Ministry of Justice that 'this correspondence is now at an end'.

Bollocks to that, and Giovanni continued to explore every legal avenue still open to us, including the legality of Straw's decision. Other people close to me opened a more informal dialogue with Straw's office to try and work out how Straw and his team could get it so wrong.

The penny, it would seem, had still not dropped with the Ministry that I had not committed a crime since the Great Train Robbery in 1963, unless you count jumping over the wall at Wandsworth, entering a few countries without the proper papers and enjoying a few joints or driving without a licence. I was a risk to nobody but myself.

As my health deteriorated I do think it crossed the minds of a few people in the government that I might die on their watch. Certainly the hospital did not want me to die in their care, especially as they could not treat me in the way they wished. But Norwich Prison also did not want to be held responsible.

The judicial review was filed on 17 July, the same day that I was recalled to Norwich Prison against the wishes of some of the doctors looking after me. I slipped in to deep depression. I was not well physically or mentally.

Ten days later I was rushed back to Norfolk and Norwich University Hospital suffering again with severe pneumonia. Mike was called and told to get to the hospital as they felt it was now a question of time. They were talking hours to Mike, days at best.

Doctors told the press that I had 'little hope of recovery'.

They also came to an agreement with Mike that I would not be resuscitated if my heart stopped. Mike stayed by my side telling me to keep fighting and not to give up.

Mike, Veronica and Ingrid were the only people allowed in to see me; my hospital room being treated as an extension of the prison, with even a metal detector at the door and three guards on constant watch. MPs who wanted to come and see for themselves how ill I was were turned away, glibly being told they could visit me when I was back in Norwich.

So many calls for my release on compassionate grounds had been made that it was felt to be a futile gesture that would yet again fall on deaf ears and fallow ground, but one that should be made all the same.

There was a difference, however. In talking to the doctors, Mike had been told that I would never recover from my chest infection as the saliva would always be running down my windpipe because I could no longer control my throat muscles. Mike asked them if they would put this in writing, and they said yes. After nine years, Mike finally had the piece of paper that said I would never recover. He quickly scanned it and sent it over to Giovanni to add to the growing paperwork.

Two days later, on 30 July, the High Court granted the legal review of the decision surrounding the blocking of my parole. It would take time, and time was not what I thought I had on my side if I wanted to die a free man.

A week later, Mike received a number of calls from friendly journalists. They had been called to the Ministry of Justice where Jack Straw would issue a statement with regard to my condition, and they wanted to know if Mike knew why. There had been no warning and the feeling was that the Ministry would not call the press together unless they had something of importance to impart.

On Thursday 6 August, Justice Secretary Jack Straw issued a short statement on the 'release of Great Train Robber Ronnie Biggs':

'Mr Ronald Biggs has been informed today of my decision regarding his application for compassionate release on medical grounds.

'On 1 July I refused Mr Biggs' release on parole. These two decisions however involved different considerations. I made the decision to refuse parole principally because Mr Biggs had shown no remorse for his crimes nor respect for the punishments given to him and because the Parole Board found his propensity to breach trust a very significant factor.

'In this case, I have had to consider the medical evidence against well-established criteria – specifically whether death was likely to occur soon and whether the prisoner was bedridden or severely incapacitated. The medical evidence clearly shows that Mr Biggs is very ill and that his condition has deteriorated recently, culminating in his re-admission to hospital. His condition is not expected to improve.

'It is for that reason that I am granting Mr Biggs compassionate release on medical grounds. I have therefore been satisfied that the relevant conditions have been met, which I was not in respect of the recommendation for parole.

'Mr Biggs will be subject to the same strict licence conditions as other prisoners on release. He must live at an approved address, behave well, and cannot travel abroad without approval. If he were to breach those conditions or commit any further offence, he would be liable to immediate recall to prison.'

As I've said before, I am a great believer in fate. Although the date of the train robbery was 8 August, it had been a Thursday.

So news of my release from Mr Straw came exactly 46 years after that fateful day in 1963 when the 16 of us stopped the Glasgow to London mail train.

The actual date for my release was set for the following day, Friday 7 August. The weight of the world was being lifted from my shoulders, but I was still too ill to fully appreciate what was going on.

Neither Mike nor I had any prior warning of the decision to release me. Nothing had come out of the Ministry to suggest this decision was even on the table. Why common sense suddenly prevailed, we do not know.

Lovers of a good conspiracy believe my release was a smokescreen for the more politically and internationally sensitive release of the Lockerbie bomber, Abdelbaset al-Megrahi, on similar compassionate grounds just two weeks later.

To be honest I did not give a bollocks as to what was true and what was fiction. I was just grateful that I was a free man and could die a free man. I had never given up, and neither had my family and close friends. I had served a total of 3,875 days for my part in the Great Train Robbery out of the original sentence of 10,957 days. I had also spent 13,087 days on the run. It had been a long, challenging and tiring 46 years.

Despite slipping in and out of consciousness, I felt I was almost home and free. I slept well.

As news of my impending release broke, the press started to gather outside the hospital, as well as at Mike's house in Barnet. Giovanni explained to Mike that despite Straw's announcement there was still paperwork to take care of, including the licence for my release, and that is why my 'official' release would take place on the Friday.

Mike drove to the hospital early that day and we waited. It

was afternoon when the deputy governor of Norwich turned up with the paperwork. He explained the rules by which I was being released, and I put my weak scribble on the licence at about 1.50 pm. With that the guards packed up their stuff and bade me a fond farewell. I shook each of them by the hand and then gave them a little wave as they left the room. A room that was no longer a prison cell, but a hospital room. You can't start to imagine how good that felt after 46 years. Even in my frail state I was looking forward to celebrating my 80th birthday, and the 46th anniversary of the robbery, as a free man.

I would no longer be a guarded man, but equally I might be exposed to any nut job that decided that the only good Ronnie Biggs was a dead one. The hospital itself did a great job of keeping unwanted guests at arm's length. Even the most tenacious of the paps had not got in to see me. The hospital reassured me that they would keep me safe, even once the guards had left.

The Ministry of Justice formally told the press at 2 pm that I was a free man. Mike said he felt he owed it to the waiting press pack to go and say a few words and give them a photo opportunity. As he went to leave the room he turned back and thanked me for 'sticking around'.

Mike went out to meet the press and took a copy of my licence with him. He waved it for the cameras; he kissed it and told the press it 'smelt like freedom'.

'As a family, we are absolutely thrilled,' he told the press. 'My father is now a free man and that's all there is to say. It was very emotional when the guards left. The media made Ronnie Biggs into what he is, and the media is here when Ronnie Biggs is about to close this last chapter. He will now be retreating fully from public life. This is not going to turn into a media circus. There is absolutely no chance of my father being seen in the West End with a couple of girls around him. This is not going to turn into some sort of freak show and my father is not going to turn into some sort of Z-list celebrity. It is going to be very private from now on.' Speak for yourself, Mike!

Well-wishers inundated Mike's phone and the hospital switchboard, but given my health we decided that I should have a quiet family birthday on the Saturday with just Mike, Veronica and Ingrid in the room. But some friends could just not stay away and made the trek to Norwich.

Given the media interest, Mike allowed *The People*, which had been supportive of my cause, to come and get some exclusive photos of the birthday boy for the Sunday paper.

We owed another journalist a favour, and that was Marcos Losekann, a good friend and neighbour of Mike's in Barnet who was also the TV Globo anchor in Britain. It was nice to be able to do something that would be seen by my friends that I had left behind in Rio and whom I had not had the chance to say my proper goodbyes to.

Once I was a free man I decided the least I could do was to fight for my health and try to stay alive; if only to piss a few more people off. I did this by setting little targets. So I promised Mike that I would stick around for his birthday. I promised I would get myself well enough to make it to the care home and visit his house.

Using Mike's mobile we put in a few calls to people that mattered. The first was to Charmian in Australia and there was not a dry eye in the room. I wept and wept as I heard her voice over the speakerphone. I could not talk, but I could make a noise to let her know I was there and that I still cared, and always would. Through the tears she promised to come and see me, which set another target to aim for.

At 2.40 pm on Monday 17 August, the day after Mike's

birthday, I was covered from head to toe in a blanket and wheeled out from my room and into an ambulance for the transfer to the care home in Barnet. Barnet had had a few famous residents over the years, and it was about to get another.

*

The care home, Carlton Court, was more than I expected and I am the first to admit more than I deserved. It was modern and clean. Comfortable, and importantly for somebody who lived in Rio, warm.

The staff on the whole were saints, and needed to be to put up with me. Given the years I spent in prison I was used to institutional living, and how to survive and make it work best for me. So if that meant hiding the TV remote so I could watch the horse racing in the main lounge, then so be it. I also installed a large aquarium that somebody kindly gave me, next to my favourite seat in the lounge. It was my territory.

Not knowing how long I had, but I did not think long, I wanted to crack on and update my autobiography. It was important for me to have a truthful record of my life and in my words. There had been enough falsehoods and mistruths written about me.

Luckily Chris Pickard, my 'ghost', had already got inside my head doing the first book back in Rio, so even without speech, and by using my spelling board, devised by Chris, we quickly moved ahead. And we did not have the distraction of the boozy lunches that we had in Rio.

I asked Chris to contact Charmian and tell her if she still had any problems or a beef with the first book, now was the time to raise them, or forever hold her peace. Charm being Charm sent Chris a detailed list of what she thought was wrong, or would like cut, and other suggestions. Some I agreed with, others we haggled over until we came to a mutual understanding of the facts with Chris as the go-between Barnet and Melbourne.

The home and its residents had to adjust to having such an infamous patient in their midst, and on the whole handled it very well. I was put in a room by the nurses' station, close to a main lounge. It meant they could keep an eye on me, not so much for what I might do, but what others might want to do to me.

The home's reception also took precautions so that if visitors had not been listed and given the OK by Mike or Chris they would not be let in. In the early days, a number of people did try to drop by, and I had no idea who they were. This included one claiming to be my child.

Old friends came calling, which was a real boost and pleasure, and new friends were made. I won't embarrass them all, but Breiti from Die Toten Hosen came over to see me, as did Roy 'Pretty Boy' Shaw who became something of a welcome regular visitor. Nick Reynolds would also drop in to update me on Bruce and his mother. It was harder on Bruce who still felt responsible for my frail state and spending so much time in prison. He had nothing to be sorry about and in his autobiography he had ended it: 'When I look at his frail frame, I see my own mortality. C'est la vie!' Both of us were sure I would go first, but it was not to be and sadly I did not get to see Frances 'Angela' Reynolds, who died on 30 December 2010.

Of the old gang, Jimmy Hussey was kind enough to drop by so that we could catch up on the many lost years. We both knew we did not have many more years to lose and on 12 November 2010 Jimmy passed away. Somebody with him in the hospice called *The Sun* to say that on his deathbed Hussey had confessed to hitting Jack Mills. He had not, so I assume somebody was looking to make a quick buck. Another of the gang, the always colourful Jimmy White, died around the same time.

I was sorry I was never able to track down Mike and Jess Haynes, or Eric and Carol Flower. Sadly many from my past, like Paul Seabourne and Jack Slipper, had already passed. But for all the negatives we got a positive with the birth of Mike and Veronica's second child, Lilly, on 8 May 2010.

The ever-generous Brian Running, who used to visit me in Rio and paid for the beers at my 70th, dropped by to cheer me up, and managed to take me to the Scotland v Brazil game at the Emirates and a number of jazz lunches. Terry Dunne, who lived locally, was another good source of company. One-arm Kev Rawlings and Kerry also popped in, as did Richard Keaney, Frank Werner, Alan from Bristol, Tony Last, Aaron Smith, Jack Cook, Roy Pickard, Rene Moserman, Mike Wade, Dee Morris, Andy Jones from Littledean Jail, David Worrow, a collector of Great Train Robbery memorabilia, who got me in a spot of bother by taking me to Bridego Bridge without permission, Tony Hastings, Steve Stephens, Alan Wilson from Western Star, Gio and Dickie Finch; Dickie being Mike's neighbour at the time, and the reason we ended up calling Barnet home.

Dickie was a good friend of Lee Thompson, a man better known for his sartorial line in headgear and as saxophonist of Madness, who generously gave me a mobile scooter that the paps caught me riding a few times. Sadly the scooter got vandalised by some local youths, but the up side was I did get a letter from the Metropolitan Police that began: 'Dear Mr Biggs, We are very sorry that you have become a victim of crime . . .' They never caught the villains!

The press did not let me rest in peace. Some were chancers, mainly local photographers getting a snap if I left the home, saying I was on the way to the pub.

There were a few exceptions. A team came over from Germany

for *Bild*. Germany has always been fascinated by the robbery, and my recordings with Die Toten Hosen had kept me in the spotlight in Germany. While I tapped out answers to their questions, Chris spoke to them about Karin, the German wife of Brian Field. He had died in 1979, but she had returned to Germany shortly after the robbery and remarried. The team from *Bild* tracked her husband down, but Karin had died a few years before, taking with her the truth of the part she and Brian played in the robbery, which was a lot more than people ever imagined or credited them with.

I also received two media requests that I would not turn down. Piers Morgan was in contact and reminded me he had been to my house in Rio with the Happy Mondays. He was keen to get me on his 'Life Stories', but it appeared ITV had cold feet as it kept making excuses whatever solution Piers and I came up with. I would have enjoyed that as I would have wanted to ask about his coverage of my return. An obvious case of sour grapes from the *Mirror* for *The Sun* having the exclusive.

I was also contacted by Sir David Frost who was looking to tick off the great interviews he had not managed during his long and illustrious career. I was flattered to be on that list. We made plans and everything was shaping up until Sir David died on 31 August 2013 while cruising on the *Queen Elizabeth*. We will never know what Piers and Sir David might have made me tell them!

It was a great tonic to see my old Rio buddy, John Pickston, even if he was in the UK for some medical treatment. We may not have been fighting fit, but we were still well enough to laugh and cry, and reminisce over old times.

The star of the show was, as always, Charmian, who found herself in the UK thanks to a TV series called *Mrs Biggs*. The less said about that and the 'facts' it presented, the better. I understand you have to make changes for the sake of the drama, but they could not even get the date of the robbery right. We offered to check the facts for them, but they were far too arrogant or scared to accept the offer. But it gave Charm a nice payday and I would never begrudge her that.

Sadly with the passing of time, our two sons, Chris and Farley, now both grown men with their own families, had decided they wanted nothing more to do with me; to the extent they did not want their children to know who their grandfather was. It was sad and probably tougher on Charmian as they were almost choosing to erase their mother's early history. Charm had done a magnificent job of bringing them up, with no help from me, so I respect their views but never stopped loving them, but I still hope the grandchildren will get a vicarious thrill when one day they do discover exactly who their grandfather was and what I did during my life, which is not just what happened on 8 August 1963.

After all I put her through, Charmian remained the love of my life. I hope when I am gone, history will be kind to her and the boys (and that includes Mike), because they all deserve it for what I put them and their families through.

CHAPTER 21

THIS IS IT! END OF THE LINE

If you had told me when I returned to Britain in May 2001 that I would survive eight years in prison and still be alive over a decade later, I would have said you were taking the piss.

I do know that by the time you read these words I will be dead and buried, and possibly long forgotten by some. My story at the end stood as it began – hard up. Hard up, but happy, contented and thankful for a life well lived, those last precious years of freedom, and that I could die a free man.

For the want of a few quid sixty years ago, I had plunged into an enterprise that led me into almost 40 years 'on the run' and ten years locked up. Had I heeded the advice of the old fortune-teller back in 1963, things might have turned out very different. I might have spent the rest of my life freezing my nuts off on some bleak, boring building site somewhere in Britain.

If you want to ask me if I have any regrets about being one of the train robbers, I will answer, 'NO!' and without hesitation. I will go further: I am proud to have been one of them, and equally happy to be described as the 'tea boy' or 'the brain'. As you now know I was neither, but I was there that August night and that is what counts.

So all that is left for now is to tidy up a few loose ends.

I never kidded myself on my return to Britain that my days were not numbered, and always felt that the Death List might have had a better idea as to what was going on than my doctors. On 1 January 2013 I was back at number one on the Death List, my 13th appearance on the annual list, and due to having taken it in good humour, which I always took it to be, they made me an ambassador for the site. A dead one, but it still counts as nobody beats the Death List.

When I could, I did still try and live life as if every day might be my last, which I knew it could easily be. I spent more than my fair share going backwards and forwards between the care home and neighbouring Barnet Hospital due to my various medical ailments.

My first big public outing from Carlton Court was for the launch of my updated autobiography, *Odd Man Out: The Last Straw*, the 'last straw' being Jack Straw who had blocked my release for no good reason. The book was a weighty tome of some 464 pages, but I wanted to set the full record straight, if only to help future historians who care about facts not fiction.

The launch took place at Shoreditch House in East London on 17 November 2011. I put on my Sunday best – despite it being a Thursday – including my skull and crossbones braces, my hat, shades and an Arsenal scarf.

With Mike, Veronica and the Barnet crew, we got a little waylaid on our drive across from North London to Shoreditch, leaving Chris the short straw of trying to keep the antsy journalists and photographers happy, and as time went by some did start to think that it was all a con and I was not going to put in an appearance. Frustrating for many in the media, as this would be their first chance to meet, quiz or photograph me in the flesh.

I was a little more than fashionably late by the time I got to Shoreditch House, but once 'Elvis' was in the building the media pack started to calm down. My first duty was the TV interviews, which would not take long given I was using my spelling board, but they needed to show that their reporters had sat with me.

It was then time to hold my first ever UK press conference in person as nobody had been interested in speaking to 'Ronnie Biggs' prior to the Great Train Robbery or my escape.

Knowing there would be some hanging around we had planned some background music. It was a mix that included my own greatest hits, including 'No One Is Innocent' and 'Carnival in Rio', and some tongue-in-cheek tracks like The Clash's 'I Fought the Law' and Elvis's 'Jailhouse Rock'; and by pure chance, and with nothing planned, I entered the room to Thin Lizzy's 'Jailbreak' that was to give palpitations to certain papers that never liked me.

The snappers wanted their opportunity to get as many shots of me as they could. I knew some would want to catch me in a good light, while others would look for shots to paint me in the worst possible light. All part of the game.

Once the photographers had had a fair shout, we started taking questions. There was a mix of intelligent and stupid questions, presumably aimed at trying to wind me up, and you could tell that the ones asking those questions really did not like it if I answered them. But I had nothing to hide. A real shame I could not speak and debate the issues more. They were not seeing me in my prime.

I was always thankful that for all the strokes I suffered, most had not impacted on my mobility or mental state. The damage was done to my throat and speech, and I discovered that because I could not speak some people would assume I was either deaf or mentally impaired. I was neither.

It was a good and lively press conference after which we treated the media and friends to pizza, beer and wine. A chapter of the Hells Angels I knew, and once had a memorable night out with, had turned up to support me, and possibly kept the press and other guests on their toes. Nick Reynolds was there for support, and it was a treat to finally meet the journalist and broadcaster Fiona Phillips who had been a rare, brave voice in the media calling for my release. We did have a laugh that day.

It should surprise no one that I did feel the urge to visit Bridego Bridge, the location that had totally changed my life, but which I had only seen once, and then in the dark. So I did. One day there will be a plaque on Bridge 127 to mark it as the site of the Great Train Robbery, but I doubt it will happen while I am still around. Pathetic, but true.

In 2013, the 50th anniversary of the Great Train Robbery dawned, but the year did not start well as on 28 February, Bruce died without warning in his sleep. Thankfully Nick was with him at the flat. I had always assumed I would go before Bruce, and I am sure he felt the same way.

Nick, who told me Bruce had not been looking forward to the fuss that might surround the anniversary, organised a wonderful send-off for his father at St Bartholomew the Great in Smithfield on 20 March 2013. A worthy setting for Bruce who had called the train robbery his Sistine Chapel.

Nick performed 'Too Sick to Pray' with Alabama 3, and told the congregation that his father was 'my best friend, soulmate and older brother. He chose a lunatic path and paid the price.'

Speakers included the actors David Thewlis and Ray Stevenson;

writer Jake Arnott; and punk poet John Cooper Clarke. From the gang, Bob Welch was there. Gordon was too frail to travel, but sent a note, and the same for John Daly.

I checked with Nick if he wanted me to attend. I did not want to distract from a day that should be all about Bruce, and we knew any appearance I made tended to turn into a bit of a circus. But Nick said Bruce would want me to be there, and it would increase the media attention on Bruce and the funeral.

I arrived by van with carers from the home and close friends from Barnet. I noticed a sizeable turn out of photographers. Nick, with so many other things on his mind, generously came to escort me into the church. As the photographers called my name, I decided to give them what they wanted. A two-fingered salute.

I always appreciated that the snappers had nothing personally against me, and were just doing their job. So if I could help them, and give them a memorable image and payday, so be it.

It was a very moving service and I make no apologies for sobbing throughout. Tears not just for Bruce, but for all the other now 'absent' friends that Bruce and I had lost over 50 years.

After we had said a final goodbye to Bruce, Nick took us to a pub in Shoreditch where I met many friends, some that I had not seen for 50 years or more. It was a long and emotional day, by my standards, but also a very memorable one. A day Bruce well deserved. RIP my dear friend.

Ten days later, Bruce's brother-in-law John Daly died from multiple organ failure. He lived in Launceston, in east Cornwall, and it turned out none of his neighbours knew of his colourful past. John was the only one of us to be found not guilty at the trial. A surprise to us, and to John who very nearly pleaded guilty.

I was often asked about 'the three who got away' after the robbery, and was offered serious sums of money to name them.

I never did and won't confirm speculation of their names as I always felt it was up to them or their families to confirm or not their participation. What I will confirm is that it was one of the three that hit the driver. The novel I wrote about them, *Keep on Running,* was mainly fiction, but not all.

As I have mentioned, in 1963 I was at first delighted, if surprised, that Peter – the back-up driver – had not had his collar felt. I did not think it would be difficult for the Yard to track him down. With the passing of time I realise that Butler knew exactly who Peter was, but had made the decision that if Peter was sitting in the dock with us, and called as a witness, it might undermine the entire prosecution's case.

In hindsight we could have asked Peter to hand himself in as with his testimony and presence in court it would have been impossible to have given us 30-year sentences, but even if the sentences had been 14 years or less I doubt he would have survived inside.

So good luck to Peter and I hope he managed to enjoy the money he earned from having the guts to join us on our little adventure. Few people would have. And let me say it again, he could have driven the train if given enough time for the pressure to rebuild, which it had by the time Jack Mills replaced him in the driver's seat. But it has suited the narrative of some to suggest that I had brought an incompetent train driver along and there was something wrong in Bruce's planning. There was not.

All too soon it was Thursday 8 August 2013, the 50th anniversary of the Great Train Robbery and my 84th birthday. There had been speculation as to what I and others might do on the day. One rumour had us holding some sort of celebration or rave at the bridge. It was Nick Reynolds that came up with a much classier option. His idea was that we would bury Bruce's ashes next to Angela in Highgate Cemetery, and Nick would also unveil the sculpture he had done of Bruce's head.

Prior to the 50th we also decided to produce a book, or what I am told is a 'bookazine', that covered as many facts and details about the robbery as we could include. The bookazine was pulled together by Nick, who already had some final thoughts from Bruce, and Chris. The timeline is the closest you will ever get to what actually happened before, during and after the robbery.

The bookazine was set to be released just before the anniversary so Nick and Chris went up to Salford on 6 August to go on BBC Breakfast TV on the seventh. Following that, and for a few short hours, we were number one on the Amazon book charts.

A deal had also been done that the *Mirror* newspaper would serialise it in the week of the anniversary. Monday through Wednesday extracts were run, and then nothing. No official explanation was ever given, but behind the scenes we were told that pressure was put on the management to drop the serialisation. You could be forgiven for thinking that somebody was paranoid.

The day of the 50th anniversary was a lovely, sunny summer's day and I was driven to Highgate by Mike to meet up with Nick and other friends. We got a good turnout to mark the occasion, including the children of Roger Cordrey, Billy Boal and Jimmy White. Freddie Foreman joined us, as did my old friend from Rio, John Pickston, and Brian Running and his dad.

As we gathered around the grave, Nick's mobile phone rang. 'Hello, Dad,' he said, not missing a beat, lightening the mood of everyone who realised we were there to celebrate Bruce and the Great Train Robbery, not to mourn them.

From my wheelchair I asked Nick if I could walk up to the grave to add some of the ashes. Nick laughed and said: 'Don't

do that, Ron. They will think you are Andy from *Little Britain*!'
I stayed put.

Ceremony over, it was time to talk to the media that had turned up, including a number of TV crews among which were my old friends from Brazil's TV Globo. Always nice to know that friends in Rio would see I was still alive and kicking. If only just.

More celebrations and much reminiscing took place at the Old Crown Inn, above the cemetery, where a sign spelled out the Rules of the Inn: 'No thieves, fakirs, rogues or tinkers.' Not sure which we were.

I was glad I had survived to see and mark the 50th anniversary; most had not. Bruce had talked about 'closure' in bringing me back from Rio, and this did feel like closure to me. I also had a feeling that it might be my last hurrah; appropriate as it would be to be my final curtain.

It was, and assuming I have now gone, I give you a condemned man's final thoughts.

I hope you have enjoyed my story as much as I have telling it to you. Hopefully it might inspire you to try and live your life to the full, even if at times we do have to cut a few corners and handle a few knock-backs. And remember fate will play a part, and you can't control that.

As I am often asked, yes, it has been a life worth living, even with a few regrets, but as Mr Sinatra would say: Regrets, I've had a few. But then again, too few to mention . . . The record shows I took the blows. And did it my way . . .'

I certainly did do it my way, and some might want to criticise me for that. I will take that.

Finally, I do want to thank all of you for being a part of my life and my journey. It does not matter if you love me or hate me, if you know me or have never met me, but as clichéd as it sounds, my journey would have been nothing without having you along for the ride.

So this is it.

The end of the line.

All change please!

How it breaks my heart to leave you;
Now the carnival is gone.
High above, the dawn is waking,
And my tears are falling rain,
For the carnival is over;
We may never meet again.
Now the harbour light is calling;
This will be our last goodbye.
Though the carnival is over,
I will love you till I die.

'The Carnival is Over', The Seekers,
November 1965

LET US SAY GOODBYE, TO THE ONE AND ONLY . . . RONNIE BIGGS

Ronald Arthur Biggs's story ended in Barnet Hospital in North London in the early hours of 18 December 2013, the year of the 50th anniversary of the Great Train Robbery. He died of old age as his ravaged body finally gave up its ghost and decided to stop running.

As his 'ghost', who never gave up on him, and helped him write his two autobiographies and the novel, *Keep on Running*, Ron asked me to complete his story once he had left us stage left.

I was due to see him the week of his death, but Mike had called to say Ron was in hospital. That was not unusual and often just precautionary, usually due to some internal bleeding. Ron had even been in hospital the final time he saw Charmian. But if you had the choice it was easier to wait a few days and see him when he returned to the care home and his aquarium.

Ron had returned to Carlton Court and all seemed well, but on the night of 17 December he was moved back to hospital.

We don't know what Ron felt, but one of his carers said that as he was being pushed out in his wheelchair he ran his finger across his throat. It was as if he knew that this was his last journey.

Mike got several calls that night until in the early hours the hospital said he should get up there quickly. He and Veronica were with Ron when he died.

For a reason I will never know, I had turned off my mobile that night, so when I woke on the morning of the 18th and switched it on I discovered I had hundreds of missed calls and messages. I also turned on the television, and there was the explanation. Ron had died overnight.

I reached Mike on a number known to few. We were all in shock because as much as Ron's death was a death foretold, it was still a surprise as Ron had seemed immortal at times.

I headed for London to do the media rounds of radio and TV, as it was better for Ron to have somebody who really knew him to speak for and about him rather than a bunch of chancers who thought they knew Ron's story and that of the Great Train Robbery. The print media – and their websites – made the usual presumptions and errors about Ron, but as has been mentioned by Ron, it often suited their narrative and that of their readers.

With Ron's impeccable sense of timing, his death occurred just hours before the first broadcast of a new two-part BBC drama series *The Great Train Robbery*, and at a time when his beloved Arsenal were top of the league. Equally Ron's timing was not great, dying just a week before Christmas. Mike had his work cut out to try and organise Christmas for his daughters, the funeral of his father, as well as clearing Ron's belongings from Carlton Court, of which he had accumulated a few!

If we did not want to delay his funeral until the end of January, Mike was offered a slot at 2.30 pm at the Golders

Green Crematorium on Friday 3 January 2014. He took it and we scrambled to get everything in place with the help of Lori Mackellar of Leverton & Sons.

Ron would be adding his name to an illustrious roll of honour of those whose funerals had taken place at Golders Green, including a few other hellraisers that had led life to the full such as Peter Cook, Keith Moon, Peter O'Toole, Jack Hawkins, Sid James, Peter Sellers, Marc Bolan, Jack Bruce, Vivian Stanshall, Ian Dury, Joe Orton, Ronnie Scott, Barbara Windsor and Amy Winehouse, to name just a few.

The funeral cortege left from Mike's house in Barnet around 1.30 pm. It was a cold, crisp day, but the overnight rain stayed away. The cortege first passed and stopped at Carlton Court, so the staff and 'inmates' could say their goodbyes to one of its most colourful residents.

En route to Highgate, the cortege picked up a guard of honour from a chapter of the Hells Angels that would escort it the rest of the way.

The hearse slowed close to the crematorium and was led in by the six-piece London Dixieland Jazz Band playing songs including 'When the Saints Go Marching In', 'When You're Smiling' and entering the church, 'Just a Closer Walk with Thee'.

As expected there was a massive turnout from the media with photographers everywhere, but to avoid a circus we had invited the Press Association to be the only photographers in the actual church, and the media were just those that had had personal contact with Ron. At Ron's request we told the *Mail* that its reporters were *persona non grata*.

Not having the inside track, the *Mail's* coverage contained a number of howlers that would have made Ron very happy. They printed photos of 'Charmian' getting ready to join the cortege in

Barnet, only it was just a neighbour of Mike's. Charmian was over 10,000 miles away in Melbourne.

They compounded that by reporting on Charmian reading William Shakespeare's *Sonnet CXVI* during the ceremony. Not allowed inside, and the only video feed being just the coffin, the reporter did not realise it was a recording she had sent from Australia, not her in person.

Charmian sadly would last less than a year after Ron. She died peacefully in Melbourne on 11 December 2014, and as she would have wished it was several weeks before the media noted her passing.

Ron's coffin was covered by the Union Flag, the flag of Brazil, as well as his hat and an Arsenal scarf, not a Charlton scarf as many of the press reported. It was carried into the packed church where it was standing room only, with many left outside watching and listening on the monitors.

The service was conducted by the Rev Dave Tomlinson, who found himself under criticism for presiding over the ceremony. Tomlinson told the congregation: 'Jesus didn't hang out with hoity-toity, holier-than-thou religious people. He seemed much more at home with the sinners. At the end of the day, we are all sinners.'

Mike gave the eulogy, wearing Ron's skull and crossbones braces, followed by emotional tributes from Ron's granddaughter, Ingrid, from Nick Reynolds, Howard Marks, myself and last, but far from least, Steven Berkoff. We were concerned somebody had put pressure on Steven not to appear as he had not arrived at the church when the service began. It turned out he was simply stuck in the traffic that the funeral had caused. He spoke last, making a dramatic entrance from behind the altar.

Nick, with the help of members of Alabama 3, performed

the Seekers' 'The Carnival Is Over', an all-time favourite of Ron and Charmian. Other favourites played during the ceremony including Bunny Berigan's 'I Can't Get Started' and Luiz Bonfä's 'Manha de Carnival'. But perhaps the best was saved for last. As when the time came for the coffin to slip away, it did so to the strains of David Rose's 'The Stripper' and a standing ovation from the congregation.

The wake was held at The Refectory in Finchley Road.

The funeral made front page news in the UK, Brazil and around the world, and if anyone thought that would be the last they would hear of Ronald Arthur Biggs they were very much mistaken, as his name, image and likeness continues to pop up in the media on an almost daily basis ten years after his death. And it will do for many decades to come as Ron reminds us that in the end no one is innocent including, as we now know, the people who make the rules and laws; the very people that chased him around the world.

Like it or not, Ronald Arthur Biggs was and remains a global punk and pop icon. One of the great characters of the 20th and 21st centuries. Hero or villain? You decide. But love him or hate him, you could not ignore Ronnie Biggs. This has been his remarkable life story.

Goodbye, Ron. The world would have been a much duller place without you.

Christopher Pickard
Rio de Janeiro, Brazil / London, UK

CAST OF CHARACTERS

BIGGS ALIASES (1965–74)
Ronald King
Terence Furminger
Terence 'Terry' King
Terence 'Terry' Cook
Terence King-Cook
Arthur Robert Carson
Michael Haynes

Biggs Family – UK / Australia
Ronald Arthur Biggs
Charmian (Brent) – wife
Nicholas – son (died 1971)
Christopher – son
Farley – son (born in Australia)

Reynolds Family
Bruce Reynolds
Frances 'Angela' Reynolds – wife
Nick Reynolds – son
John Daly – brother-in-law

The Great Train Robbery: Bruce Reynolds's Firm at the Track

Bruce Richard Reynolds

Douglas Gordon Goody

Ronald 'Buster' Edwards

Charlie Wilson

Jimmy White

Roy James

John Daly

'Mr One'

'Mr Two'

Ronald Biggs

'Peter'

The Great Train Robbery: South Coast Raiders – Cordrey's Firm at the Track

Roger Cordrey

Thomas Wisbey

Robert Welch

James Hussey

'Mr Three'

Support Team

Brian Field	Lawyer
Karin Field	Brian's German wife
Leonard Field	Lawyer
John Wheater	Lawyer
'Ulsterman'	Informant
William Boal	Innocent man / friend of Cordrey
Mary Manson (Macdonald)	Friend of Reynolds

Train

Jack Mills	Driver
David Whitby	Fireman
Frank Dewhurst	HVP Carriage (in charge)
Post Office sorters x 76	

The Police

Tommy Butler ('Grey Fox')	Det. Chief Superintendent / Head of Flying Squad
Gerald McArthur	Detective Superintendent (Flying Squad)
George Hatherill	Head of CID
Brigadier John Cheney	Chief Constable Buckinghamshire Constabulary
Malcolm Fewtrell	Det. Chief Superintendent / Head of Bucks CID
Frank Williams	Detective Inspector (Flying Squad)
Basil Morris	Detective (Surrey Constabulary)
Jack Slipper	Detective Inspector (Flying Squad) / Arrested Biggs in Rio
Dr Ian Holden	Forensics (Met Police)
Maurice Ray	Fingerprints (Met Police)

Court

Lord Chief Justice Edmund Davies	Judge
George Stanley	Biggs's solicitor
Wilfred Fordham	Biggs's barrister
Michael Argyle	Biggs's barrister

HMP Wandsworth

Paul Seabourne	Prisoner – organised Biggs's escape
Eric Flower	Prisoner – escaped with Biggs
Roy 'Pretty Boy' Shaw	Prisoner – would visit Biggs in Rio
Freddie Foreman	Organised escape from UK, plastic surgery, trip to Australia
George Gibbs	Helped Ronnie escape to Paris
Henri / Barney	Helper in Paris

Australia

Mike and Jess Haynes	Good friends from UK. Biggs would use Mike's passport to leave Australia
Anne Pitcher	Ran boarding house in Adelaide
Carol Flower	Eric's wife
Jim Milner	Chief Superintendent – Victoria Police
Molly Evans	Love interest on RHMS *Ellinis*

Biggs Family – Brazil

Raimunda de Castro	Girlfriend / wife
Michael Fernand Nascimento de Castro	Son
Veronica Biggs	Mike's wife
Ingrid and Lilly	Mike's daughters

Brazil

Nadine Mitchell	First contact in Brazil
Adauto Agallo	First friend and clerk at the American Express office
Edith	Adauto's sister-in-law, Biggs's first Rio girlfriend
Werner and Joyce Blumer	Invited Biggs to stay in their apartment
Scott Johnson	Early Rio friend – American
Phyllis Huber	Early Rio friend
Bruce Henri	Friend and musician (would record *Mailbag Blues*)
Ana Paula	Biggs's love interest
Lucia Pereira Gomes	Biggs's love interest – with him at time of arrest
Constantine Benckendorff	Sets up deal with *Daily Express* for return in 1974
Colin Mackenzie	*Daily Express* reporter

Bill Lovelace	*Daily Express* photographer
Henry Neill	British Consul General at time of arrest
Inspector Carlos Alberto Garcia	Police chief or *delegado* at time of arrest
Fernand Legros	Top French forger, Mike's godfather
Dr José Paulo Sepulveda Pertence	Biggs's Brazilian lawyer
John Stanley Pickston and wife Lia	Good friends / looked after Mike when Biggs was kidnapped
Ursula (Ulla) Sopher	Biggs's long-term girlfriend in Rio
Rosa	Biggs's cook and maid
Chris Pickard	Friend and ghost
Harold Emert	Rio-based journalist, musician and friend
Tomas Muñoz	Head of CBS Records in Brazil
Mike / Simony / Toby / Jairzinho	Balão Magico
Albert Spaggiari	France's most wanted man for robbing bank in Nice in 1976
Gus Dudgeon	Friend and record producer
Uri Geller	Friend and psychic
Volkmar Wendlinger	Friend and chef at Casa Suiça
Wellington Mousinho	Biggs's Brazilian lawyer
Mauro Quintaes	*Carnavalesco* of Porto de Pedra samba school
Breiti	Friend and guitarist for Die Toten Hosen
Kevin & Lou Rawlings	Friends from UK
Brian Running	Friend from UK

Sex Pistols

Malcolm McLaren	Manager
Steve Jones	Guitarist

Paul Cook	Drummer
Julien Temple	Filmmaker
James Jeter	US actor who would play Martin Bormann

Kidnapping

John Miller / John McKillop	Head kidnapper
Fred Prime	Kidnapper – first and second attempts
Norman 'Norrie' Boyle	Kidnapper – first attempt
Armin Heim	German friend of Biggs, and a respected photographer
Patrick Richardson King	Pretended to be a journalist for second kidnapping
Anthony 'Tony' Marriage	Kidnapper – second attempt
Mark Algate	Kidnapper – second attempt
Thorfinn Maciver	Skipper of yacht
Greg Nelson	Crew
Lewis Gilbert	Film director (*Moonraker*)

Barbados

Kenrick Hutson	Chief of Immigration
Whittaker	Assistant Police Commissioner
Ezra Alleyne 'Sunshine'	Biggs's Barbadian lawyer
Frederick Smith QC	Biggs's barrister
David Neufeld	Biggs's US lawyer

Prisoner of Rio

Lech Majewski	Director
Steven Berkoff	Actor
Paul Freeman	Actor
Peter Firth	Actor

UK Return

Kevin Crace	Organised return
Graham Dudman	*The Sun*'s assistant news editor
Mike Sullivan	*The Sun*'s crime editor
Jack Straw	Home Secretary / Justice Minister
Jane Wearing	Biggs's UK lawyer for return
John Coles	Detective Chief Superintendent / Serious and Organised Crime
Giovanni di Stefano	Final lawyer to represent Biggs

Bands and Musicians

Sex Pistols
Die Toten Hosen
Pilsen
Rolling Stones
The Police
George Harrison
Happy Mondays
Exploited
Extreme
Big Audio Dynamite
Whitney Houston
Steve Tyler (Aerosmith)
The Seekers
Rick Wakeman
Rod Stewart
Ozzy Osbourne
Bruce Henri
Ritchie
Dado Villa-Lobos (ex-Legiao Urbano)
Os Intocáveis
Porto de Pedra Samba School